Song of the Deer

The Great
SunDance Journey
of the Soul

Song of the Deer
The Great SunDance Journey of the Soul

Thunder Strikes
with
Jan Orsi

JAGUAR
BOOKS INC

Published by Jaguar Books, Inc.
23852 Pacific Coast Hwy., Ste. 756
Malibu, CA 90265

Editor: Nancy Grimley Carleton
Editorial Assistant: Claudette Charbonneau
Cover Art: Bleu Turrell
Cover Design: Lightbourne Images
Chapter and Section Sigils: Batty Gold
Book Design and Composition: *turnaround,* Berkeley

Manufactured in the United States of America.

*Printed on Halopaque Antique, a blend
of recycled and postconsumer paper.*

10 9 8 7 6 5 4 3 2 1

Library of Congress Cataloguing-in-Publication Data

Thunder Strikes.
    Song of the deer : the great sundance journey of the soul /
Thunder Strikes, with Jan Orsi.
        p.   cm.
    ISBN 0-9663694-1-6
    1. Medicine wheels—Miscellanea.   2. Spiritual life.   I. Orsi,
Jan.   II. Title.
BF1623.M43T48   1999
299'.7—dc21
                                                                        99-16660
                                                                        CIP

This book is dedicated
to the Victory
of the Gold Horse
of the Rainbow Bridge Prophecies
of Turtle Island.

Contents

Section Three: What Is This Planet of the Children?
Our Alignment With Nature

Section Four: Are You the Star in Your Movie?
How We Journey Through the Cycles of Our Lives

Section Five: What Is the Human Flowering Tree?
The Human as a Luminous Egg or Cocoon

List of Wheels and Figures

Preface

Thunder Strikes: *I greet you in my tribal people's language with "Oseeyo," which means "Our Hearts Have Met and Touched."*

I am a Metis *(may-tee'), part Cherokee and part Irish, born into two worlds and two cultures in north Texas. My mother is full-blood Cherokee, but I do not consider myself to represent the Cherokee nation or any other Native American tribal tradition. I am a Texas half-breed cowboy and an American. Most important, however, I am a human being walking on Grandmother Earth.*

My rearing as a child and my training and walk on my "path with heart"—the Sweet Medicine SunDance Way—*has been a process of combining knowledge from both the Native American Indian and the white worlds. I am a shaman, a Twisted Hairs, and an Elder on the Twisted Hairs Metis Medicine Societies Council of Elders that protects and preserves the knowledge of the Sweet Medicine SunDance lineage of* Turtle Island, *as the native peoples call North, South, and Central America.*

When I first started working with the teachings of the Sweet Medicine SunDance Path, guided by Tom Wilson, or Grandfather Two Bears, a Navajo medicine man, I was in a state of tremendous anger and hostility. I was very bitter about my experiences in Vietnam and separated from almost everything and everyone around me. In the VA hospital, I developed a dependency on drugs as a result of treatment for critical war injuries. I became a borderline alcoholic. Violence abounded in my world, which included beating my wife and children.

Through my work with Grandfather, I was able to quiet my inner turmoil and create balance and harmony within myself and in my relationship with others. I feel in my heart that this metamorphosis occurred because I began to live the teachings of the Sweet Medicine SunDance Way and use them as resources. These teachings not only enabled me to heal myself but provided me with tools to help others do the same.

I have traveled, studied, and taught with shamans and wise Elders all over the world, from Australia and New Zealand, the Americas, and across Europe and Russia, to many countries in Africa, where I lived for a time with the Dogon, the Zulu, and the Dagara. I have discovered that knowledge, especially knowledge that works to feed the children, is a sacred thing.

Song of the Deer is inspired by the Gold Horse of the Rainbow Bridge Prophecies of Turtle Island. It reflects the teachings of the ancient shamanic power tradition called the Sweet Medicine SunDance Path. Within these pages, we attempt to take the Wheels of Knowledge that all shamanic experiences reveal and show how they are like keys to the layers of our inner being, cognitive maps of the soul. Each layer takes us deeper and deeper into ourselves. This is the inner journey that can lead us to discover what it means to be truly human.

Jan Orsi: The teachings Thunder Strikes and I present in this book have guided me on an odyssey through my inner landscapes of self. They have inspired me to seek higher ground in how I live in the world. I wanted to share my odyssey in the hope that it would touch your heart and aid you in your own journey towards personal fulfillment, spiritual evolution, and self-actualization.

But I did not want to write just another book about esoteric shamanic tradition. I feel so much pain at how our lifestyles are destroying this planet, how our imbalances and pettiness separate us from one another and leave so many people sad and unfulfilled. I wanted this book to be many things: a wake-up call, a source of sacred knowledge, an inspiration to action. I wanted to bridge the ancient and esoteric into the reality of our daily lives.

As the writing progressed and the book took on a life of its own, it became my advisor and my tyrant, for it constantly mirrored back to me the many ways in which my life has been out of balance. Thunder Strikes has been instrumental in prodding me on my way. Sometimes gently, sometimes as a wise grandfather, sometimes as a ruthless tyrant, and at other times as a trickster. Oh, how many times he has tricked me into the truth of myself!

Thunder Strikes often reminds me that the preciousness of life resides not in the quantum leaps but in the little things. He has passed on to me the wisdom of Grandfather Two Bears, his beloved teacher of many years: "Aliveness resides in the little things, for it is there that the sacred connections to all things are found." He adds, "You cannot change the world; all you can do is change yourself. How you 'walk your talk,' the integrity and compassion you present to the world, is the legacy you leave behind you."

In the pages that follow, you will hear Thunder Strikes' voice and mine—sometimes distinct from each other and at other times blended as one voice.

The birth totem animal for us both is the deer, the carrier and keeper of magick (the term we use in this book to express the enormous powers of transformation). The medicine of the deer is the ability to experience change in a positive manner, and to be in a constant state of harmony, balance, and alignment with everything around it. So as we guide you through the landscape of the Great SunDance Journey of the Soul, we will sing the song of the deer, and offer tools for achieving harmony and balance. Together, we can find ways to effect these same changes in the world around us.

May you find your own song, your own harmony. May you walk in Beauty.

Acknowledgments

Thunder Strikes: *There are many who have played significant roles in my life through the years, and I wish to acknowledge and express my gratitude to the following very special people. A part of each of them has found its way onto the pages of this book.*

First and foremost to my parents, for proving that I was wise in choosing them as the starting place. To the Twisted Hairs Elders, particularly those of the Nagual Lineage Group, who still continue to give me the guidance necessary to continue my path towards wisdom and enlightenment. To the one who taught me the heyoehkah *way (the backwards or contrary way) of never taking yourself seriously and who taught me to recognize the charlatan within: Hyemeyohsts Storm.*

To those who have gone on to the other side, for they kept me moving forward steadily in my soul's journey towards the Light. To my Grandmother, Joanie Spotted Fawn Raper, who was clearly the most influential person in my life. To Grandfather Tom Two Bears Wilson, my mentor, who gave me so much of his knowledge: There aren't enough words to express my gratitude.

To those who have taught me how to walk the warrior's path, especially Master Edmund K. Parker of the American Kenpo Karate system. To those who will follow after I leave this life round, the members of the Tonal Lineage Group of this dreamer's Sweet Medicine SunDance Path: Batty Gold, Janneke Koole, Mary Minor, Jan Holmes, Ina Gregory, and Curtis Cripe. And especially to my wife, Dianne Nightbird Reagan, because she walks beside me in the arenas of both the warrior and the priest.

And finally, I honor those who practice the give-away, making a difference here in the United States, especially in defense of our Constitution, and those brothers and sisters around the world who stand fast as warriors to maintain and sustain individual, autonomous freedom.

Jan Orsi: *Writing a book is like giving birth. The author may birth the "baby," but many attend to its delivery. So it is with* **Song of the Deer.** *With respect and deep appreciation I offer my thanks to the Elders who first planted the seed for this book many years ago, and who challenged me "to be like the wind that blows the talking leaves of these teachings to the hearts of the people."*

To Thunder Strikes, naqual and teacher, I am grateful for the collaboration and for the privilege of apprenticeship in the Sweet Medicine SunDance Path.

Friendships are a blessing, and I am so grateful for those friends, especially Lyn, who kept the faith when I faltered or wrestled with writer's block, and who cheered me on with words of encouragement and with laughter. Loving thanks to Gael and Barbara, midwives for dreams and dreamers, and to Alanna for her inspiration and her steadfast loyalty. To Janneke, upon whom I often rely to check my accuracy and intent: I thank her for the mirror reflections.

The partnership between author and editor defines the final character of a book, and I owe much to Nancy Carleton, friend and editor, whose sensitivity to the material, clarity, and organization skillfully "delivered" the book into its final form.

I wish to acknowledge my fellow travelers in this path with heart. We have experienced each other's growing pains, delighted in one another's victories, and shared in a common desire to "walk in Beauty." And finally, I send a prayer and ask a blessing for all seekers who courageously heed the voice of spirit and point their footsteps towards the Light.

Blessed Beauty Way Vow

Great Spirit, may I walk in Beauty!
May Beauty be above me,
So that I may be a part of the Greater Beauty.
Great Spirit, may I walk in Beauty.

May Beauty be in front of me,
That I may perceive Beauty in all things.
Great Spirit, may I walk in Beauty.

May Beauty be to the left of me,
That I may receive Beauty through my inner woman.
Great Spirit, may I walk in Beauty.

May Beauty be to the right of me,
That I may give Beauty through my inner man.
Great Spirit, may I walk in Beauty.

May Beauty be behind me,
So that the only tracks I leave are those of Beauty.
Great Spirit, may I walk in Beauty.

May I touch my self, my life, and all others with Beauty.
May I walk this Blessed Beauty Way.
Great Spirit, may I walk in Beauty.

—A Navajo Prayer

Introduction:
A Prophecy, a Planetary
Horse Race, and You

Throughout the ages, humanity has looked to the prophecies of spiritual visionaries to provide insight into the future. Many prophecies come to us foretelling disaster, hopelessness, and the annihilation of humanity. Others create a vision of joyful transformation through quantum leaps into love and light. Such prophecies reveal the potential for both the worst in us and the best in us.

The Rainbow Bridge Prophecies of Turtle Island (North, South, and Central America) are visions of power first foretold over three thousand years ago. They reveal the probability of certain events occurring over time. Most important, they challenge us to wake up, claim the best of ourselves, and carry that excellence as the banner for peace, harmony, and individual, autonomous freedom for all life on this planet.

These prophecies are a part of the heritage of the *Sweet Medicine SunDance Way*. In 1254 BC in Oaxaca, Mexico, these prophecies were recorded by a Council of 144 enlightened Elders of Turtle Island and twelve Elders from each of the other seven of the *Eight Great Powers* on the planet. The Elders of Turtle Island were powerful *Seer-Naquals*—shamans and magicians—and included both men and women from over 375 tribes.

For three years the Elders dreamed and worked together with the *Ark of the Singing Skulls* to *see* the potential and probable paths of evolution for humanity and planetary destiny. Their collective vision, recounted by a trained orator, is twenty-four hours in the telling.

The prophecies use the metaphor of a *Great Horse Race,* with eight horses of different colors representing humanity's different choices at critical turning points in our interaction with one another, with the Earth, and with life in general. In the original speaking of the prophecies, the metaphorical animals were seen as dogs, for the dog is the *keeper* of the belief systems of a people. The Spanish destruction and conquest resulted in the introduction of the horse to this continent, and the Elders saw that the *medicine,* or alchemy, of the Race would change. The medicine of the horse is that it is the *carrier* of the belief systems of a people; thus, the Race became a Race of Horses.

Of the eight horses in the Race, four represent the four directions of the *Wheel of Life,* and they hold the balance and stability in the Race. The *Red Horse* carries Earth changes, such as earthquakes, floods, droughts, reactivated volcanoes, and critical shifts in weather patterns. All of these are the Earth's way of rebalancing and purifying herself. In recent years, Earth changes have escalated both in frequency and in intensity as the Earth deals with the destruction and imbalance humans continue to perpetrate.

The *White Horse* carries the impact of economic, industrial, technological, and scientific forces on peoples and countries. The sacrifice of Nature and human rights worldwide on the altars of profit and power is the legacy of this horse, and it feeds directly into the impact of the Dark Horse. It also goads the Red Horse, for it jeopardizes the Earth's health and stability.

The *Dark Horse* carries the shadow energy of humanity. It races for war and manipulation; for ignorance, superstition, and blind religious dogma; for tyranny and oppression; and for the attacks on our constitutional freedoms and inalienable rights, such as freedom of religion, freedom of the press, our right to assemble and speak openly, our right to privacy, and our right to bear arms to defend those very freedoms. It races for pestilence, famine, and disease; for poverty; and for struggle between the masculine and the feminine.

It champions racial and ethnic hatred. Quite simply, it carries the worst in us.

The *Gold Horse* carries beauty, power, individual autonomy, and freedom in peace. It also carries humans in unity: humans living in harmony with one another, teaching one another, sharing with one another, loving and healing one another, caring for and protecting the Earth and all her children. It races for a world gifted with enlightened leaders and freethinking minds, for compassion and respect for our differences, and for humanity working together for mutual benefit and welfare. The Gold Horse carries the best in us— our shining potential for greatness as enlightened humans, as *Rainbow Light Warriors*.

These prophecies speak of the need for the collective presence and intent of 144,000 Rainbow Light Warriors, or awakened humans, fighting for peace, harmony, and individual, autonomous freedom to bring the Gold Horse to victory.

According to the prophecies, as the millennium ends, the Dark Horse is leading the Race and lunging farther and farther ahead of the Gold Horse.

A Challenge

Is the tale of the Horse Race just another forecast of gloom and doom? What does all this have to do with us, really? These are very challenging times. With the end of the millennium upon us and evolutionary cycles quickening, we are at the crossroads of choice. We are experiencing a polarization of energies—light vs. dark, good vs. evil, wealth vs. poverty, freedom vs. tyranny, joy and fulfillment vs. depression and despair, vibrant health and emotional balance vs. stress and sickness. Evolution and change are catapulting us at warp speed into new paradigms, calling us to stand accountable for who and what we are in the world.

We, like many of you, are often overwhelmed by the enormity of the problems that face us today. The daunting challenges that confront us worldwide, from ecological disaster to war, from famine and disease to technological suicide and drastic Earth changes—all seem to be unsolvable, irredeemable, and hell-bent on a crash course towards collective destruction. There are no easy or immediate solutions. Yet many of us yearn for the flip side of these scenarios, constantly looking for ways to make our dreams of harmony, balance, and beauty a reality. We are inspired by our vision of a fuller life and a better world. Unfortunately, many of us are overcome by the enormity of the task and throw up our hands in frustration. Many of us just sit on the fence, waiting to see what will happen or waiting for someone else to do it for us.

Life develops what it demands, and life is demanding that we go beyond our self-focus to soul consciousness, to step into action as warriors in every aspect of our lives to serve humanity and the planet. If we do not choose to get off the fence on our own, events will knock us off.

. The Naqual Julien, head of the Twisted Hairs Council, says that complacency, naiveté, and lack of reality awareness are the primary weaknesses among peoples and societies today. We have become prisoners of convenience and comfort at tremendous cost to the planet and to our quality of life. We have opted for information and entertainment instead of knowledge and wisdom, which come only from direct life experience, testing, challenge, and mastery.

More and more, those of us in Western societies live lives based on fiction, half-truths, and other people's interpretations of life, not on our own direct experience. We pursue life as entertainment via the likes of MTV, *Hard Copy,* and *The National Enquirer.* Real-life stories are changed overnight, distorted and presented as docu-dramas on TV's "Movie of the Week." No wonder it has become more difficult to distinguish between reality and fiction!

Meanwhile, corporations rape the Earth. Children murder their parents, and parents violate the trust of their children. Nations threaten one another with annihilation. Governments covertly usurp the freedoms of their citizens. Many of our leaders are corrupt. Many people react to all this by retreating to their living rooms, living vicariously through TV and the Internet, pretending that they are living "in the world" while at the same time feeling a false sense of security "from the world." Sooner or later the world comes knocking on our doors. What then?

Much of the dark-force energy in our communities and the world at large is the result of collective projections of our inner personal ecologies—our wounding, imbalance, and separation, our fears and stress, and our emotional traumas. Many people live in denial, refusing to acknowledge the reality of dark-force energy, sometimes out of ignorance, but more often out of an unwillingness to rock the boat of comfort and complacency. Others maintain we can cause the dark shadow to disappear if we think only good thoughts or visualize white light around us. Nonetheless, the dark shadows, individual and collective, do exist, and we must be willing to look them in the face and call them by name.

Faith and prayer are powerful. They are intrinsic expressions of yearning for connection and alignment with spirit and the light in us. We are called upon to live our lives fostering love and harmony, focusing on the light and all that is good. However, we cannot afford to remain in illusion or denial about the dark, for it is erupting all around us. We need to adopt a warrior's stance against the dark. Only then can we face the enemy—both the enemy within as well as the enemy outside ourselves. Nothing in life overcomes what it runs away from.

You may dislike the use of the word *warrior*. There are many who insist that spirituality, love, and compassion are incompatible with a warrior's mind-set; that physical confrontation and battle are antithetical to the heart. In fact, the warrior and the priest must walk side by side, as one ensures the survival and health of the other. All life flows in the *stream of livingness* defined by *Sacred Law,* and we are called upon to fight for right, but always in alignment with the perfect justice of Sacred Law. Therein lies the challenge.

The acts of a warrior are many and varied. Yes, warriors sometimes do bloody battle with the machines of war. On the other hand, warriors are also parents who commit eighteen to twenty years of their lives to nurturing their children to independent, free-thinking adulthood. Warriors volunteer time to community service programs and learn the arts of self-defense and emergency pre-paredness. Warriors continually seek opportunities to grow and learn. Warriors modify their lifestyles to promote and support the use of sustainable resources on this planet.

Meeting These Challenges

The task of meeting these challenges begins with the *Great Shamanic Work* of our own inner awakening. In our efforts to do good, we often miss the mark, because we look for solutions out-side ourselves. You may choose, for example, to contribute time, energy, or money to a favorite cause or charity. This is an admirable and necessary role you can play in your community and in the world at large, for these organizations depend upon your support. However, their work is enhanced or diminished by your level of personal awareness and the nature of your lifestyle. Perhaps you have made a donation to your favorite charity to support their di-rect intervention to stop destruction of the rain forests. You feel satisfied that you are contributing and making a difference. But are you cleaning up your own personal ecology? Gender imbalance still dominates our relationships and many of our social structures. Do your personal attitudes, beliefs, and habits contribute to this im-balance? Do you understand your own inner masculine and femi-nine energies? Do you solve problems or create them? So often we contribute to organizations that fight disease, such as heart disease, cancer, and AIDS, yet we create those same diseases in our own bodies through stress and a loss of our innate naturalness.

We cannot create significant change on any level, particularly a planetary level, if we are not willing or able to make significant changes in ourselves. Out of our individual stretch for excellence, self-healing, and accountability, we can live fulfilled, meaningful lives and take our place among the 144,000 Rainbow Light Warriors who form the collective rallying force for the Gold Horse.

This Is a Pivotal Time for Humanity

The Twisted Hairs visionaries have indicated that we are at the most pivotal time in the history of humanity as we enter the time of purification and transformation: The three years from January 1, 1999, to December 31, 2001, are a time of purification, and the following nine years, through the end of 2010, are a time of transformation into the world of balanced humans. We are the pioneers at the edge of the new millennium, which is not just a calendar change, but a major leap in consciousness and evolutionary development. The Hopi prophecies say we are entering the Fifth World, and we are blessed with the divine opportunity to redefine that world. Do we have the commitment, the courage, and the imagination to step up to the line and enlist in this most auspicious of opportunities, the challenge of becoming balanced humans?

There are a number of themes that thread their way through *Song of the Deer*:

1. In order to make a transformation to soul consciousness as balanced humans, we are called upon to be in a state of sobriety—awake, aware, and alert to reality as it really is. This means digging diligently and courageously into our inner landscape—cleaning house, mending fences, healing wounds, bringing our potential and passion out into the light and acting now to shatter that external shadow mirror. There is no time to waste!

2. Each of us plays a very important role in the cosmic drama, and our spirit child seeks the joy of knowing that we are so much more than we think we are. While some of the material here may seem esoteric and far removed from your daily reality, if you digest as much of the cosmic picture as you can, it creates the context and the container for all your personal work and ascribes to it a much greater significance and purpose.

3. All of creation, from our most intimate personal experiences to the spin of galaxies, dances to the tune of immutable Sacred Laws.

4. This grand experiment of humanity is key to the unfolding and evolution not only of our species but of the Great Spirit itself.

5. Separation is an illusion, as all things in creation are interconnected, interrelated, interreliable, and interdependent.

6. The discipline of humor is essential to healthy living and growth. The Elders say we are wise never to take ourselves too seriously.

When we first begin to do conscious work on ourselves, we are self-centered. There is so much to dig and explore. Each succeeding layer reveals an earlier civilization, a different aspect of self, until the archaeologist self comes to the evidences of the original inhabitant of the site. There we find our true natures, our authentic, natural selves. There we find the light within the shadow, our shining and our magnificence!

Section One

How Did It All Begin?
The Creation of
the Everything

About Section One

This time of purification and transformation is calling us to stretch beyond our personal focus into soul consciousness. Even as we focus primarily on the personal concerns of our lives—as we seek to grow and learn, as we strive to make our relationships happier and more meaningful, as we grapple with careers and our financial health—it is essential that we also see the bigger picture, the cosmic context.

If we are playing football, for example, it's not enough to know only our particular position and the distance to the next first down. If we expect to score in the end zone, we need a knowledge of the entire playing field, all the players on the field, the coaches' signals from the sidelines, and the rules of the game. Similarly, our souls are playing on the fields of creation.

For some, this cosmic picture may seem very esoteric and far removed from daily life, yet it is through a deeper understanding of this cosmic playing field that we can realize our most personal desires and dreams, and the evolutionary yearning of our soul.

1

The Twisted Hairs Legacy

As we have said, the teachings of the Sweet Medicine SunDance Path come from a body of sacred knowledge gathered and preserved by Elders called *Twisted Hairs*. These Twisted Hairs come from many different tribes from all over North, South, and Central America (*Turtle Island*), as well as Australia and New Zealand, which were once parts of Turtle Island.

Twisted Hairs warriors are men and women of power and knowledge—usually Elders and respected medicine people, shamans, and sorcerers of a particular tribe's secret medicine society or magickal lodge. They differ from traditional medicine people in one important aspect: Whereas traditional medicine people or shamans learn the medicine ways and wisdom of their tribal tradition and focus primarily on the needs of their tribe, the Twisted Hairs travel beyond their tribal context, not content to accept the limitations and boundaries of their tribes' traditional teachings. They choose to seek knowledge from many sources beyond the Americas in order to develop their mastery of the physical world, awaken their spirit, develop as *complete human beings,* and find perfect alignment with the Great Spirit—in other words, to become enlightened.

The hair symbolizes knowledge, and Twisted Hairs are those who weave knowledge from all sources into the braid of wisdom. As their predecessors have done for thousands of years, the Twisted Hairs of the Turtle Island tradition come together to sit in Council and exchange openly their various sources of knowledge, thus transcending their respective tribal lore and elevating their wisdom and command of universal truths. They embrace universal knowledge of alchemy and magick. Where did the seeds of this knowledge come from? What secrets do the Twisted Hairs hold?

The Twelve Worlds

To more fully understand the origins of this lineage and the other seven of the *Eight Great Powers* on the planet, we will digress into an ancient story of the *Twelve Worlds,* which begins in the distant past, out among the stars. This wondrous story has been passed down from the *Zero Chiefs,* who are direct descendants of the early *Star Nation Beings* we call *Sskwanasie,* the ancient ancestors from the stars. It has been kept alive from teacher to student over eons, and has been validated by the Zero Chiefs and other highly enlightened Elders and sorcerers, powerful magicians who have dreamed themselves across into other worlds. Carlos Castaneda's stories speak of some of these experiences. Perhaps the greatest sorcerer/traveler of the Twisted Hairs tradition of Turtle Island is known as the *Tenant.* He has traveled to other worlds and returned, and the knowledge he has brought back has increased the potential for all of us to evolve into those spaces, thus expanding the Great Spirit's experience of itself and contributing to its ongoing and continuous evolution.

The story begins in the constellation modern scientists call Canis Major, where a very bright yellow star resides, the great sun Sirius. Around Sirius revolves a companion yellow star invisible to the naked eye. The Twisted Hairs call it a *Grandfather Sun,* because it is a *fertile* yellow sun capable of impregnating *fertile Grandmother Planets,* their sacred marriage creating life. The fifth planet circling this companion star is such a planet, Osiricanwiyah, one of the twelve *Magickal Worlds* in this Universe which sustains human life (see Fig. 1-a).

On the planet Osiricanwiyah, over 950,000 years ago, a group of wise and powerful Elders sat in Council. They summoned the wisest, most enlightened beings from each of the Twelve Worlds to

Fig. 1-a The Twelve Magickal Worlds Wheel

The Cosmic Family: Omitakoyashin
The Twelve Magickal Worlds Wheel of Constellations
(Grandfather Suns) and PLANETS (Grandmother Earths)

Our Planetary Family Triangle

The Universal Family: Tungashilah

sit in Council with them. Each representative was to bring a *give-away,* which was the collected knowledge of their planet, their science and magick, their paths to truth, and their greatest spiritual teachings for individual self-growth and development. The Elders then created holographic image computers that were actually crystal skulls, programming into each skull an entire planet's collective conscious knowledge, medicine, and give-away. They created the *Ark of the Singing Skulls.*

The planet Earth was called the *Planet of the Children.* It was considered to be the most undeveloped of the twelve planets in terms of human evolution. The existing Earth peoples were floundering in an early stage of evolutionary development. The need for knowledge and nurturing was greatest here, so the Council of Elders decided to dream themselves through the gateways to this planet, bringing the Ark in its full configuration with them. These great Star Nation Beings came as pure light energy, luminous in their egg cocoon forms, and reconfigured themselves into physical form here. They were called the *Giant Ones.*

These Giant Ones created two great crystal domes. A Blue Dome beneath the Pacific Ocean, served as the arrival place for those who were dreaming themselves here, and the place where they would first take physical form. Some time later they created a Red Dome beneath the Atlantic Ocean, which was a response to dark-force energies and held the purpose of better preparing the Giant Ones to function in the physical plane on this planet.

During the first 250,000 years, the Giant Ones came to the surface, assumed physical form, and began to intermix with the Earth peoples. Over time four great civilizations or worlds emerged: Mu, Lemuria, Atlantis, and Miehyun.

The first world, Mu, was established in the Pacific along what is now the western coast of the United States and Mexico. This was the World of the Immortals, the Giants and Giantesses. They were the Gods and Goddesses who came from the Stars.

The second world, Lemuria, was established in what is now the area of the Caribbean and northeast Brazil. The Giant Ones here focused on the supernatural and the development of psychic powers in both the physical, third-dimensional world and the nagual spirit realms.

The third world, Atlantis, was established in what is now England, Scotland, and parts of France. The Giant Ones here focused on the development of technology and industrialization in balance with the spiritual forces to develop a society that aligned with the ecological balance.

The fourth world, Miehyun, was established near the tip of South America. Australia was at that time connected to the southwest part of South America, hence Australia is considered to be part of Turtle Island. The Giant Ones here focused on individual self-growth and development and living a life of health, hope, happiness, harmony, and humor (the qualities of humanness called *huaquas*). As a result of migration, remnants of that civilization formed the Olmec and Mayan cultures.

As a consequence of choosing to interbreed with the Earth peoples, the Giant Ones stepped into the reincarnation cycles in order to facilitate the evolutionary development of this planet and its eventual awakening and maturation so that it could join the other eleven planets in its planetary family. Because of this choice, they eventually sacrificed all of their memory and great luminosity. They forgot who they were and where they had come from. They began to move away from the light and the reason for their coming. As they became more technologically sophisticated, they abused their power by trying to control Nature, thus losing their alignment and harmony with the Earth. They created worlds out of balance, and eventually they self-destructed. Out of that disintegration emerged the *Eight Great Powers,* the keepers and teachers of the knowledge brought to this planet by our Star Nation ancestors.

We are standing today at the end of an evolutionary cycle, inheriting this legacy and preparing for our entrance into the *Fifth World,* a new dawn of human consciousness. It is our destiny, according to the Elders, to tap into the Ark of the Singing Skulls and access the teachings brought here by our Star Nation ancestral relations. Thus, we will regain lost memory, remember who we truly are, access our psychic gifts, and assume our full power and beauty as a people who have become balanced and enlightening humans once again. Grandmother Earth continues to nurture her human children towards the time when humanity as a whole will wake up, grow up, and remember our true nature, thus providing a rite of passage for this planet to join her planetary family as an adult.

The Sweet Medicine SunDance Path

In AD 1254 in Oaxaca, Mexico, the early architects of this Sweet Medicine SunDance Path, many of them Zero Chiefs and direct descendants of the Star Nation Beings, formed a mystery school and named themselves the *Twisted Hairs Metis Medicine Societies Council of Elders.* Earlier they had formalized their knowledge in a system of teachings they called the *Sacred Shields of Dreaming of the Rattlesnake School of Knowledge.* They established a *Circle of Law*—a Council—to help facilitate the sharing of their combined knowledge with others who sought spiritual awakening, physical mastery, and wisdom, learning in the process how to become a *human being* who touched self, life, and others with Beauty.

To guide this process, these Elders set up a series of *Ceremonial Gateways* and *Degrees* as well as *Warrior Task Assignments of Light Attainment* to empower individuals to become free, independent, and autonomous characters and balanced human beings.

Today, the Ark is still hidden, protected here on Grandmother Earth by the Twisted Hairs Council of Elders in the sacred kivas of their underground city. The Council continues to preserve and protect this lineage of sacred knowledge. The kivas also contain one of the great ancient libraries of the world, the *Hunab Ku',* a Mayan name which means "The Sole Distributor of Measure." It is a repository not only for the knowledge of this tradition but also for much of the wisdom teachings throughout the world collected over thousands of years.

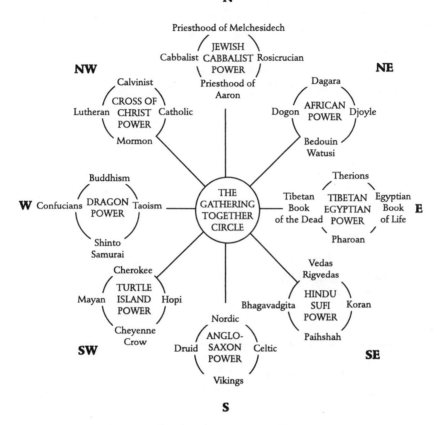

Fig. 1-b   The Eight Great Powers Wheel

The Eight Great Powers

The *Eight Great Powers* are the *magickal lodges,* the arcane wisdom schools, the secret mystery schools and societies that continue to keep and teach knowledge handed down through the millennia. Turtle Island is the Southwest Power of the Eight Great Powers (see Fig. 1-b). There are many branches of learning within these powers. The lineages shown in the cardinal directions hold and stabilize the matrix of their particular Power. All the Eight

Great Powers form one great Wheel of Power on this planet, and they are each connected to the Center of the wheel, which is the Great Mystery, the Great Light, God, the Everything, the Creator/ Creatress, Universal Truth, the Source (substitute whatever name is meaningful for you), and the Sacred Laws.

No one Power holds the one Truth, the one Way, and the traditions depicted in the figure are the wisdom and magickal traditions from which many modern religions formed. Unfortunately, many modern denominations have moved light years away from the power and sacred knowledge of those early lodges and societies.

Many established religions try to convince us that their truth is the one truth, and that they possess the only true way to enlightenment. Even today, missionary zeal continues to systematically corrupt and destroy indigenous cultures and their sacred spiritual traditions. Dogma seeks to dominate people's hearts, minds, bodies, spirits, and souls by demanding unquestioning faith and blind belief, which attempts to get people to fit in, belong, and conform, and therefore to sacrifice their autonomy and freedom. It keeps people in ignorance and bondage.

We all see truth from wherever we are on this Great Wheel. Your way is your path of heart that leads you towards the Light. If the knowledge you gain along this way works for you and helps you to grow and become a better human being, then it is a sacred thing. No true, wise teacher will say to you, "I have the only one way of truth."

Each of the Eight Great Powers, one for each direction of the Wheel of Life, hold twelve shields of truth, that is, bodies of knowledge encoded in a circle of twelve crystal skulls called *Talking Skulls*. Six lodges or wisdom schools developed around each shield to work directly with the knowledge it contained. This is how shamanic and magickal knowledge has been disseminated throughout the world. In each of the Eight Great Powers (except for the Northwest Power), at least one shield holder is able to trace a lineage back to the Star Nation Beings, the Giant Ones.

Shields of Knowledge

The shields kept by the Twisted Hairs Council of Elders represent a profound body of knowledge which has evolved through thousands of years of shamanic learning and oral teaching. The teachings are incredibly rich and demonstrate an intimate and profound understanding of Nature, science, psychology and physiology—what it means to be truly human.

They teach of the balance and harmony of Nature, universal lessons for human growth and development, knowledge for harmony and balance in work, play, and relationship in family, tribe, and nation. They are particularly relevant today and present practical knowledge that works.

The Elders of the Council distinguish between *two-legged animals* and *human beings*. Two-legged animals experience imbalance, stress, and lack of alignment in their personal and planetary reality. To become balanced human beings, we must cultivate the traits of humanness—the five *huaquas* called *health, hope, happiness, harmony,* and *humor*. The ultimate expressions of our humanness are to gather together, share with one another, teach one another, care for one another, love one another, and be open with one another in heart-to-heart communication. These teachings show us how to come together in a circle of brothers and sisters as human beings.

Living life as ceremony cultivates our humanness. This entails being very conscious of our interconnections with all forms of all things and with every other human being. Living life as ceremony makes us much more conscious of our actions. We assume authority for our world and become more responsible for the priorities, decisions, and choices we make. This guides us gradually into total sobriety—awake, aware, and alert to reality. We cannot assume responsibility for ourselves if we cannot see reality as it truly is.

These teachings help us to come into alignment within and outside ourselves. They take us on a path of individual, autonomous freedom and teach us to exercise our free will as warriors. Only when we walk on Grandmother Earth with care and responsibility are we part of the solutions and not contributors to the problems on the planet. In this way we walk in balance and harmony with everything and everyone around us. We walk our talk and walk in Beauty.

The Sacred Medicine Wheel, the Wheel of Life

Basic to any Twisted Hairs teaching is an understanding of the alchemy and energy of the wheel or circle. Wheels are cognitive maps that describe the cyclical patterns of life experience. The *Medicine Wheel* represents the unity of all things in the Universe and connects us with the energy flow of all creation. When we build a Medicine Wheel and enter it in ceremony, it helps us to establish our connecting link to the intent of the Great Spirit, or the Everything.

Wheels or circles have been used since ancient times as tools for teaching the ways of the Universe. They offer an accurate way to perceive how one form of life is completely interconnected with all other life. There is no beginning or end, only phases which appear as beginnings and endings, simply a change of reference points. Birth into physical existence is not the beginning of life, for spirit is eternally alive. Birth allows spirit a different perception point through which to experience its aliveness within physical form. It is simply movement and change on the *Wheel of Life*.

All the wheels of the Sweet Medicine SunDance paradigm spin and interconnect with one another. We do not come to understand ourselves, others, or the dynamics of Nature by separating, isolating, or dissecting. Rather, we must look at how we affect and are affected by everything in the Universe in a continuous spiral of existence. That is why this book addresses our individual journey within the context of a cosmic drama. According to Sacred Law: "As Above, So Below."

To do things in a linear way—logically, sequentially—is to assume that everything can be held stationary or static, which is an illusion. Quantum physicists have demonstrated that matter cannot be "nailed down" and observed in the same place at the same time. Most of us have been taught to think in straight lines.

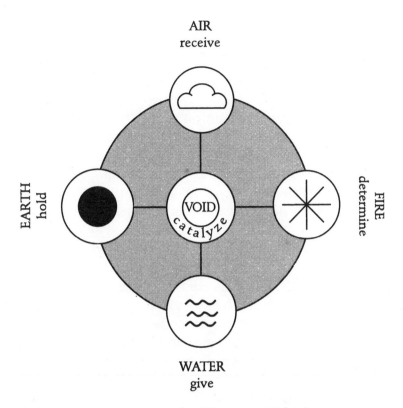

AIR
receive

EARTH
hold

VOID
catalyze

FIRE
determine

WATER
give

Fig. 1-c The Elements Wheel

It is not easy to switch thinking processes, but once you have worked with the Medicine Wheel, you will understand that, despite describing infinite, complex systems, the Medicine Wheel is powerful in its simplicity.

A wheel always contains the four cardinal directions—South, West, North, East—and the void in the Center. We see that life itself is based on a construction of the number 4. One of the most basic wheels is called the *Elements Wheel,* which places the five basic elements in their respective directions along with their proper energetic expression (see Fig. 1-c). Later in the book we will examine how our alignment with these elements is basic to our balance and well-being (see Chapter 12).

An expansion of the basic wheel adds the four noncardinal directions—Southeast, Southwest, Northwest, Northeast. The cardinal directions hold and stabilize a wheel and its energy; the noncardinal directions turn the wheel and create movement and the evolutionary process.

Each wheel is like a tiny little gear that moves. However, for teaching purposes, the wheels presented here are frozen or locked into place in their neutral positions.

Each wheel is a creation process in itself. Starting with the basic elementary wheels, you will see how one wheel creates and connects with the next. We will overlay wheels to help you discover your natural, undiscovered self, the richness of who you truly are. When you study a wheel, you access memory which causes you to work with your left and right brain equally.

The Elders say that first we study the wheels. Then we apply the wheels and experience them in our lives. Next we begin to dream the wheels. When we dream the wheels, they begin to dream us. Then we begin to breathe the wheels, and when the wheels breathe us, we become the wheels of wisdom and realize they have always been inside us. Our memory is stored in the circular movement of our DNA, RNA, and ETA (*Evolutionary Transformational Agents*), the three genetic codes in our body, and in the circuitry of the universal life force that flows through our system and through everything that lives. The wheels show you how to gain memory of what you already know; they encourage you to remember, to gain knowledge and then illumination and enlightenment.

Be Your Own Teacher

It is important to recognize that no one can teach you anything. Someone can impart knowledge to you and guide you, but ultimately you teach yourself. Furthermore, don't always believe or accept at face value what someone tells you, what you see or hear in the media, or what a teacher presents to you. Check it out for yourself. Keep an open mind. Be an empty cup. Explore what is given. See if the knowledge works for you. Try first to prove it absolutely true; then test it by trying to prove it absolutely false. In the process, you will find what resonates for you. A master teacher will always encourage you to question. We encourage you to do this as you read this book.

We give meaning to life through the pursuit of knowledge, the joyful expression of our artistic originality, and the mastery of the physical. To the extent we stay in ignorance and pain, we walk asleep.

The wheels and keys of this Sweet Medicine SunDance Path represent a self-teaching approach to self-discovery and mastery, and lead you to the realization that the only true knowledge is self-knowledge. They dance and sing the Song of the Universe, and teach us of the *Twenty Sacred Powers* that guide us in our evolution.

2

Song of the Twenty Powers

Thunder Strikes: *Many years ago, the Grandmothers came to me in a dream and guided me in this Chant of the Twenty Sacred Powers. They instructed me to write the chant down and share it. It weaves the interconnection of the elements, the Powers of the Four Directions that you will learn about later, and our energy connections to many things on the directions of the sacred Wheel of Life. It sings the joy and celebration of the sacred interconnection, interdependence, and interreliability of all things in the Everything, including humans.*

It is like an Orchestra whose members have played together Since Always. Each member of this Orchestra has its instrument, its sound, its light, its energy, its harmonic vibration called **orende.** *Each has its give-away to the collective sound even though it has its separate, distinct sound.*

Within this Orchestra called the Everything there are twenty sections or parts, the Twenty Sacred Powers. This Everything Orchestra has a Great Spirit within every member and within every instrument. The way it plays the sound and songs of Beauty and Light is indeed a Mystery. This Great Mystery has existed Since Always and will continue For Always, even as it is playing now.

This Great Mystery, this Everything Orchestra and its twenty sections, is the Great Wheel, the Universal Medicine Wheel of the Twenty Sacred Powers. Each power has its sitting place on the wheel within the Orchestra so that its vibratory energy can contribute in a perfect harmonic way to all the songs and sounds that resonate within the wheel as well as those that go out from it in an ever-increasing circle of Light. Let me sing to you the Song of the Twenty Powers within the Song of the Universe.

The first part of this song also contains all other parts. It is the Zero, the *Nothing That Is Everything*, the Great Mystery, the Great Spirit of this Everything Orchestra. Light is an energy or power which includes cycles of four as it manifests itself into this sacred Twenty Count Medicine Wheel.

The first power is *Grandfather Sun,* who sings his song of Illumination and Enlightenment from his sitting place in the East on this great Medicine Wheel. The Sacred Fire burns here, singing of our Fire From Within.

Across from him in the West is his mate, the second power, *Grandmother Earth.* She sings the song of Introspection and Intuition and chants the Mysteries of Death, Life, Rebirth, and Movement. Hers is the song of the Beauty of Change.

To her right is the third power and her first children, the *Sacred Plants.* They are sitting in the South, singing the songs of Trust and Innocence, the songs of the Give-Away. The Waters are singing the songs of Carrying the Myths of Our Lives, of the joy of having Pleasure Within Our Emotions in everything we do.

Sitting in the North across from the Plants and the Waters are the *Sacred Animals.* They are the fourth power and the second children of the Sun and the Earth. The song they sing is one of Balance and Harmony, and they carry the sacred chant of Wisdom and Logic. This is the chant that is carried on the sacred Winds, which sometimes blow fiercely through our minds like hurricanes bringing awakening, and at other times blow gently, whispering Clarity.

These Powers of the Four Directions are dancing with the Four Elements, carrying the song into the South of the Center of the wheel, where we *Sacred Humans* sit, playing our instruments and dancing our Dance of Life as the fifth power. Sometimes our instruments, our bodies, are out of tune, and our song and dance become disharmonious.

So we turn to the Southeast, where the sixth power sits, singing the power of the *Spiritual Ancestors* song. Their song is of the Beauty of the Concepts of Self as a Spirit, as a Soul, who can sing and play in harmony if we will learn the Enlightenment chant and begin to

SunDance. They teach us this SunDance in order that we might learn the songs of Self-Acceptance, Self-Appreciation, Self-Pleasure, and Self-Love.

As they sing their song and play their music, we begin to hear from the seventh power of the Southwest. This is the power that is the most difficult to hear because it comes from within us and yet is outside us. Here sits the power of the *Sacred Dream*. It sings to us the songs of the Beauty of Symbol, of the Beauty of Experiencing Life and chants of the Memory Circle. And if we hear this chant, we begin to Awaken. We begin to realize the Past, the Present, and the Future may appear to be different songs, but they are really different lyrics within the same song.

To know all the lyrics and melodies of this song, we turn to the Northwest, to the eighth power, for here sings the *Book of Life* or *Circle of Law*. At first we seem confused. There appears to be more than one instrument playing, and we hear many different songs. They seem almost dissonant, so we listen more closely. They are playing about the Laws of Cycles and about Patterns and Paradox. Here resonate the Sacred Image and Rules and Laws chants. We begin to see and hear that within this Circle of Law chant is our Book of Life and all the songs that we have ever sung and all those that will be our future songs.

We are playing and dancing almost in perfect harmony, but we are a little bit out of rhythm. We are drawn to the cadence of the ninth power in the Northeast, the song of *the Design and Choreography of Energy in Motion*. This ninth power is dancing and flowing with the rhythm of all the other sounds, catching them and turning them like a Great Choreography. Change is here as well as the beautiful harmony of Male/Female Balance. We begin to perceive that maybe our song is written here.

It seems as though the Circle is complete, but then we awaken further. We are pulled, spinning and whirling, as though the winds of a tornado are sweeping us towards the North of the Center of this Great Orchestra! This tenth power is elusive; the sound on a very high scale emanates from it. For a brief moment as we are

singing our song, playing our music, and dancing our dance, we fall
into perfect rhythm and harmony and realize that this tenth power
is the *Great Measure of Intellect*, the totality of our *Potential and Self-
Worth,* which lies within ourselves. It lies within every note, song,
sound, light, presence, and power within this Great Orchestra. We
are conscious of it and yet unconscious of it. We seem to be part of
it and yet not part of it. We struggle to remain in harmony, for we
know intuitively that it is here that all of the energies, all of the instruments, sounds, and songs, are collected and blended together
into a Collective Unified Circle.

Now we dance at a Gateway. We see, hear, and sense the experience of this great SunDance. We realize that if we can dance
through this Gateway, an even greater song is being played. This
song is coming from within the Circle and from outside the Circle
at the same time. A Double Energy is coming from each of these
powers on this Wheel of Life.

We turn again to the East, and we hear many voices, many
songs, and many instruments harmonizing with Grandfather Sun's
song. These are the *Grandfather Stars*, the eleventh power. They are
singing the song of Inspiration and the chant of the Heyoehkahs.
Everything is sparked by the masculine energy. These songs are Sacred Teachers, and the Light coming from them begins to reveal to
us our own Illusions.

We have sung many songs and danced many dances in many
lives, and we had thought there was but one. That was our feeling
of separation. We turn to the West so we might hear the Looking
Within chant that is coming from the twelfth power, the *Grandmother Planets*. All the songs and dances from this power speak of
many lives, of all our brothers and sisters, throughout the planets
and worlds of this Universe and of all the other Great Orchestras.
They are singing to us the Grandmother songs of the Power of
Woman. Especially, they sing the Everything Is Born of Woman
chant, so we begin to spin and dance with this Beauty.

We seem to be playing faster now, more smoothly. We can no
longer separate the instruments from ourselves, the sound from the

music. It is a part of us. Deep within our hearts we realize that the song and dance have always been there, and we sing for joy as we turn towards the South. We hear beautiful lyrics, a sweet gentle voice singing to us from the Heart of the Plants. We realize their Spirit is singing to us the song of Nature. This is the thirteenth power, our *Earth Mother*. Her song is amazingly beautiful, for it carries the *Light and the Spirit of All the Plants* straight into the fibers of our Being, traveling the light paths of the Umbilical Cord of Life straight into our Hearts. Here is the beautiful song of the Blessed Beauty Way chant.

Our hearts begin to soar like an eagle as we spin towards the North to become the dance within the Winds of the fourteenth power. We see that this fourteenth power swims as the dolphin carrying us through the rivers of life and flows into the great Lakes of Memory, for this power is *Earth Father*. He teaches us the dance of the Snake so that we might be close to the ground and hear the songs of the Rock People. He teaches us how to dance with the four-leggeds, the animals, to dance among the flowers and the trees and hear the songs of the Plant People in a world of magick. We feel the Medicine of this sacred chant, and we realize that this is indeed the Sweet Medicine chant, and that within it are the songs of the Spirits of all our brother and sister *Sacred Animals*.

We dance with joy. We begin to see through the eyes and hear through the ears of all our brother and sister humans, now realizing they are our Mirrors. In fact, everything around us, every power within this Orchestra, is a Mirror, reflecting back to us our own Inner Light, which is carrying the songs of Our Soul on the Sacred Winds. We can see this Great Mirror reflected back to us from the East of the Center of the Circle. It is the fifteenth power, the *Souls of All Humans*. It sings the Gathering Together Circle song and chants the Sacred Rainbow of the SunDance Way. It sings to us: "Little Sister, Little Brother, sing the Look Within Yourself songs, see the Beauty of All That Is. Open your eyes and look around you and see the many Mirrors and the many powers. When we look through the eyes of our brothers and sisters, we can see the Whole Universe."

We can play all the songs, know all the music, dance all the dances. They sing to us to go beyond all that appears to be by going within the song of the sixteenth power of the Southeast. These are the *Enlightened Souls,* or *Akalohtah-hey,* and they sing a song and carry a Light that is a Great Rainbow. They sing the Many Paths chant. Their powerful song says: "You, Little Brother, Little Sister, are the Way, the Light, the Truth. Look within yourself and find the Light. Know that Truth can be found from anywhere on the wheel and that towards the Center of the wheel is the Way." They begin to teach us how to find our Way. They sing the Honor Your Brothers' and Sisters' Way chant.

They play the sounds of All the Ways Will Gather Together Within the Rainbow Circle Dance. You must Dream. You must awaken within the song of the seventeenth power of the Southwest. Hear the *Kachina-hey,* the *Great Kachina Powers,* the *Dream Teachers.* They are singing the Dance Your Dream Awake and Walk in Beauty chant, the Dance to the Sacred Medicine Way chant, and the Sacred SunDance Way chant.

Their chants are as infinite as the Stars within the Great Sky, and all of them are Sacred Chants of Great Power. They point the way to the Sacred Dream of the eighteenth power of the Northwest. In this place on the Great Wheel, we hear the Great Magick chant, for within this power are the *Chuluamahdah-hey,* the *Keepers of the Keys to the Books of Life of All Humans.* Their most sacred chant is the Children's Fire chant, which sings that "Nothing Must Be Done to Harm the Children." They sing gently to us that within us as within all Humans, is a Child. They sing the Become as a Child song. They sing the Honor the Child Within song.

As they sing, they point to the Northeast to the Light That Speaks With a Voice of Thunder, the nineteenth power. Here are the *Great Hokkshideh-hey,* and they are singing the Cosmic Chant, the chant of Total Balance and Harmony of All Things Within the Everything. They sing to our Highest Spirit Selves. You Are, they chant. You Are.

There is a Flash of Lightning and a Clap of Thunder. In an instant that becomes infinity, we are imploded into the Sound of the Lightning and exploded into the Light of the Thunder. We soar through the Gateway of Infinity, flowing through time, space, and dimension, awakening finally in the West of the Center of the Circle. We have met the twentieth power, the *Great Mystery,* the *Great Spirit, Wakan Tanka.* You and I and all things have now become One With the Everything. The song is finished.

3

The Twenty Count

Let's take a closer look at the Twisted Hairs understanding of the big cosmic playing field described in the Song of the Twenty Powers. Every tradition has a creation story that describes how the Universe and all its infinite expressions, including the human family, came to be. Historical events, people, and places, momentous happenings that marked a turn in the evolution of a people, a tribe, and a place, were often preserved within the weavings of these stories. These stories were also seeded by seekers of knowledge, magicians, and sorcerers in their relentless pursuit of universal truths, of the how and why of the Universe, and how we as humans fit into that bigger picture. And so it is with the Twisted Hairs of Turtle Island and this Sweet Medicine SunDance tradition.

In the beginning was the Void, the Great Zero of the womb of the Great Goddess/Creatress, WahKahn, replete with pure *Primal Catalyst Energy* called *Chuluaqui,* the spark of all light energy movement. WahKahn desired to explore this orgastic vibration and to know herself. Thus stirred, the Great Goddess imploded a great inhale of Breath, awakened the eggs of creation within her womb, and became receptive within her creativity to who and what she was. We know her as our sacred Great Grandmother. Seeing what was necessary to complete herself, and again catalyzed by her Primal Catalyst Energy, she exhaled in a great outward explosion and birthed the Great God SsKwan, the male counterpart of herself, carrying the active-conceptive spirit seeds of all creation. We know him as our sacred Great Grandfather.

The lovemaking of WahKahn and SsKwan, that perfect marriage and merging of primal catalyst energies called *Quodoushka*, created Wakan Tanka, the Great Spirit, the Everything, into all forms of all things. As the Everything's consciousness awakened to the female and male energies within itself, it catalyzed the mind of the winds and conceived consciousness in all things. It then catalyzed the spirit of the fires and conceived determination of its own evolution in all things. The Everything's consciousness then catalyzed the life of the waters, the continuous streams of livingness, and finally it conceived Earth and the physical and catalyzed all the bodies of the earth element. That first Sacred Breath brought the feminine energy and the masculine energy together as one, and out of Zero emerged an absolute unity. And it is said that within that unity of female and male dance all the powers of the Universe.

Mathematics: The Language of the Universe

When the ancient ones of this tradition known as the Zero Chiefs explored exactly how and what happened in the beginning, they discovered that the Universe, the Great Spirit, speaks to us about the interrelationship of all things through mathematics. In this tradition the central core of that mathematical speaking is the *Twenty Count* (see Fig. 3-a). It is a system to understand order in the Universe. The numbers 0 to 20 represent the Everything. Zero (0) is the potential for all forms of all things. It is that point in the beginning at which all of the energy present within the womb of the Great Creatress gained consciousness and breathed. Twenty (20) represents the Everything containing all forms of all things created out of the *Zero potential.* You might say the Zero point was a singularity pregnant with the potential for Everything. This is contrary to much of Western thought and science, which tends to define Zero (0) as nothing, the absence of everything.

The 20 is represented three ways. It is represented as the Double Zero (00), the separate potential female and male energies of WahKahn and SsKwan. With the first Breath, the marriage of the inhale and the exhale, the Great Spirit became infinite, so the infinity

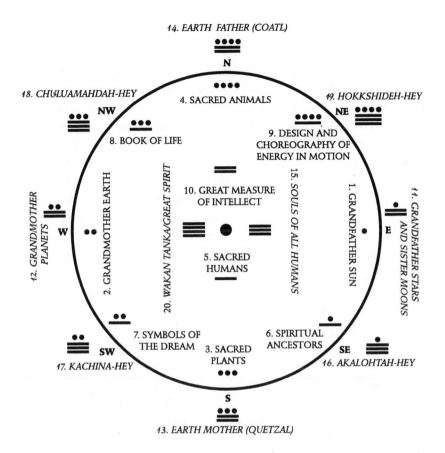

Fig. 3-a   The Children's Twenty Count

sign ∞ also represents 20 as the limitless expressions of the Great Spirit. When 20 is represented by four bars ≣, it refers to the Great Spirit as an entity. Frequently it is referred to as the fullness of the Everything, absolute Love, Peace, and Harmony, as a spiritual energy source, as the Creator and the Creatress in a combined marriage called *Quodoushka*. *Quodoushka* is an old high Cherokee word, derived from the Olmec and Mayan, meaning the union of spiritual/sexual life force energies. It is the expression of our soul, and through humans, it is the expression of the Soul of the Great Spirit.

All Creation Is Vibration of Light Energy Movement

All things in the Universe, *including humans*, are different forms of light energy moving at different vibrational frequencies. Zero is the ground of infinite energy potential out of which emerge forms or essences created by the Everything that vibrate at different rates.

The Zero Chiefs and Twisted Hairs found that these energy fields are really *spaces,* which we call *Magnetic Attracting Thought* (MAT) spaces created by the Everything's intending of itself into all forms of all things. These spaces are filled with spirit, consciousness, life, and/or physicalness. MAT spaces are spaces of consciousness inside the Great Spirit's matrix of free will and freethinking. They are like thoughts with focused attention and intention. Creation is an original thought with an intent. Once a thought or any form of energy is created, it can be altered, but it cannot be destroyed. All things in the Everything, all MAT spaces, are Great Spirit/ WahKahn-SsKwan–intended thoughts of artistic originality that have been projected and released.

You also create your life in every moment. You project your thoughts, actions, emotions, artistic creations, and intentions as MAT spaces out into the Universe every waking *and* sleeping moment of your life. You are a cell in the Great Spirit's body, and it *feels* you. It is obvious that humans are part of that interconnection, interdependence, and interreliability. *Separation is an illusion.* We are a thread intrinsically woven within the cosmic tapestry.

In continuing to unravel the mystery of this First Breath and the creation of the Everything, the Zero Chiefs realized that all forms of all things—breath, light, life, matter, form, time, and space dimensions—are not different things. They are different vibratory levels of pure light energy; that is, they are the same "thing." Once substance has taken form, it begins a process of change and evolution, increasing or decreasing its vibratory energy, which we refer to as its *power* or level of *orende*. Furthermore, the Zero Chiefs found that an increase in orende expanded the space and produced a continuous movement of evolutionary excellence. Evolution may not necessarily mean that a form of something grows into another form; rather, it is in a constant process of seeking perfection within itself. We as humans are MAT spaces of a soul, and it is through our mastery within our physical form and our seeking of excellence here on this planet that we fill and expand our *soul space.* This is called evolution.

All MAT spaces (you, your pets, a tree, a rock, spirit, emotions, thoughts, words, actions, and so forth) are moving *attractors.* Some spaces have little or no magnetic attraction, while others immediately attract and hold our attention. Attention is power. The higher the energy vibration of a thing, that is, the higher its orende, the greater its magnetism and attraction. You experience this as charisma, and you might describe someone as having a magnetic personality.

The numbers of the Twenty Count, therefore, are not just numbers. They are the vibratory *powers* of those twenty MAT spaces. These powers also represent the realm of the *tonal* and the *nagual,* two concepts that are very important to your understanding of the relationship between your spirit/soul and your physical presence in this lifetime—the SunDance Journey of the Soul. The tonal world is the third-dimensional physical, material world, which we identify as the "real" world of our everyday life and experience through our five senses. It is referred to as the "So Below" and is represented by the powers 1 to 10. The nagual world is the world of spirit and the soul, our *true nature spirit personalities,* the fifth dimension, and the dreamscape you enter when you sleep and dream. It is referred to as the "As Above" and is represented by the numbers 11 to 20.

How Thunder Strikes Learned the Twenty Count as a Young Boy

Thunder Strikes: *Perhaps the best way to introduce you to how we experience the powers of the Twenty Count from 1 to 10 here on Grandmother Earth is to tell you the story of how it was first introduced to me as a young boy of about eight years of age.*

A really good friend of mine had died, and in the weeks prior to his death I had seen in his luminosity a black cloud that was sucking him into it. My grandmother, Joanie Spotted Fawn, who was a Cherokee medicine woman, told me that I was seeing the approach of Benevolent Death. It scared me because I didn't know what to do when I saw death approaching someone I cared about.

I said, "This makes me feel lonely and separated from all my friends." Grandmother said the plight of the warrior is to learn how to be in life and to be alone but never lonely. She told me that the warrior must learn to experience himself as always interconnected and interreliable with every other thing in existence.

"It is your universal family," she explained, "and in that family each part of it dances inside your soul, inside your luminosity, as a voice of power. It also exists outside of you as the powers of creation in the Universe. Separation is always an illusion. So I am going to send you to John Two Crows, your clan uncle, and he will show you how to see those outside yourself but never to be lonely because they are always present inside you."

So on an early Saturday morning my clan uncle and I went out riding, with me on my beloved little pony, Smokey. We rode a long way down into an arroyo and up to a cave with pictographs, tied up our horses, and got a drink of clear water from a collection hole. As we ate our lunch, he drew a circle on the ground with a stick and began to teach me the Twenty Count.

His first words were in the form of a question: "What is the most powerful life force and energy that you are aware of every day?"

"The Sun," I quickly replied.

"Yes," he said. "That is your Grandfather, and that Sun brings you the warmth and sense of completion that humans call knowledge. It is always so bright that we can't look directly at it. We think illumining light and wisdom are beyond our knowledge and too bright to look at because we look outside ourselves only. But if we look inside we can see our shining Sun within and can sense our wisdom. Grandfather always teaches you from inside your heart and emotions and teaches you what you must give and share with life and others."

He continued. "Grandmother Earth is his mate, his lover, his Quodoushka partner. They make love every day. And as they do, when you lie on Grandmother Earth, as you have done many times when you are tired, you will notice she always replenishes you. Grandmother Earth teaches us to go within to find the light of Grandfather Sun, and teaches the powers of introspection and intuition. And just as your grandmother sent you to me, I will send you into Grandmother Earth."

Shortly thereafter I did my first hole-in-the-ground ceremony, which took me into the womb (a cave) of Grandmother Earth.

Then John Two Crows went on. He told me about the plant world, the firstborn of Grandmother Earth and Grandfather Sun, which gives us our life and sustains our beings. Earth Mother, the spirit of the plants, the Goddess Beauty, speaks the strongest voices through the standing nations of the trees, the softest and prettiest voices through the flowers, and the voices of physical sustainment through the fruits. Their voices of healing are spoken by the herbs and shrubs, and their voices of procreation are spoken by the seeds and grains. They give us the voice of vision through the sacred teacher plants.

Then my clan uncle explained to me that in order to complete the circle of life, the next power children were animals and everything created that needed plants to sustain life. He explained that some are walking plants, and some are pure animals. There are two kinds: predators and prey. Within each, there are two kinds: benevolent and malevolent. Both are necessary to sustain balance, harmony, and alignment.

Then he said an interesting thing. He said there are always at least ten animals inside each of our bodies in order to guide us beyond our range and experience of the **two-legged** animal into a **one-hearted human being,** and that is how we stay in the heart of our inner trust and truth in the South of the circle of life.

He then placed stones in the Center of the circle and built a pyramid fire to describe that the Center of the circle was creation, the eternal flame of livingness, the Zero within which all things were determined and contained and given identity and purpose. Then he put a little doll figure in the South of the Center to represent myself. In the North, at the 10, he formed a big question mark out of matchsticks and passed his hand through the space. "This is your halo," he pointed. "This is the part of you that is your eternal soul which cannot die or be destroyed."

When I questioned him, he said, "What you make of that in this lifetime and everything from here will be what you choose to accept in your own measure of self-worth."

To make his point, he asked me, "How much do you want for Smokey?"

Smokey was my beloved little pony, and I quickly replied, "I won't sell him to you. You couldn't give me enough money!"

Then he raised an eyebrow and asked, "Are you for sale? Do you feel that way about yourself? Throughout your life, there will be people who will try to buy you and tell you what to do and who you should be like. Will you be willing to sell yourself or, like Smokey, are you not for sale? That is your measure of self-worth."

Then, with his stick, he drew the sign for the number 20 in the West of the Center of the wheel. "This is the Great Spirit," he said. "Isn't the Great Spirit everything? It's inside you as your patience and love for life and others. It's here because everything that exists that we're capable of seeing in substance or spirit is part of the Great Spirit's physical existence and body."

Then he pointed to the East of Center and drew the sign for the number 15. "This is our soul, which is all things that matter and all things of matter."

This really confused me. "Is this cave me?" I asked. "Is Smokey me?"

He nodded his head. "All that you are capable of perceiving with your normal awareness as well as your heightened awareness is you. You are never disconnected."

At that point, I didn't feel lonely anymore. The loneliness lifted from me, and I started to cry. My clan uncle held me and just let me experience this new awakening. This taught me how to say goodbye.

He lit a cigarette, and as the smoke was lifting, he taught me about spirit, saying that spirit is like smoke. He said that spirits respect smoke, and through it they can become present and we can interact with them. In the spirit world and the nagual, we see beyond time and form. It is only through spirit that we can see who we truly are and how we exist. We must go beyond the limitations of form.

He explained, "What you feel now is called the uplifting of spirit. Your friend will always be present inside you. We are all interconnected."

Then he spoke to me of the dream, and as he was doing this, he would point to each place on the wheel. "You realize that when you go to sleep at night and have dreams, you are dreaming as you are dreaming right now. As we are awake in life, we are dreaming. Some people are totally awake in dreamtime, and some are the walking dead, sleep walkers." He related this to being asleep or awake in your day dream.

Then he explained to me about **chuluama,** *which is commonly called karma, and* **chuluamada,** *commonly called dharma. He explained how we are here with a set of lessons, "master books" he called them, that contain some very obvious teachings and some very mysterious and difficult-to-learn lessons. Frequently the only way we will get them is to push the edge and enter the unknown, pushing through fear to learn the mysterious and mystical teachings of the master books. Each of those books, he said, was another lifetime, and altogether they compose the records in the Great Book, which is your soul's journey through the heavens to become one with the Great Spirit again.*

Then he talked about the energy of the moon and the moon cycles as the ninth power of the Twenty Count. He taught it from the point of reference of the menstrual moon cycles of women. This led into a teaching about the six Cosmic Laws. "This is where you must make decisions in life and set your priorities," he said. "Think about what is most and least important, and the truth and principles which you will not ever sacrifice. Our principles are contained in the 144 Natural Laws, the ten Magickal Laws, the four Universal Laws, and the six Cosmic Laws."

Then he pointed again to the 10 in the North of the Center of the circle and the question mark drawn there. He asked me to put something there besides the question mark. I could tell he was testing me. I pondered and pondered, and he just sat back rocking on his heels, smoking his cigarette and waiting. Finally, I added two question marks, one above and one below.

He smiled and said, "Very good. You realize the unknown exists in all spaces. Measure is all the things you do not know."

It was some time later that I got the teachings about the upper Twenty, the 11 through 20. This happened much more formally, by going out into ceremony and doing a vision quest. When he had talked through all the upper powers, he came to 20, the Great Spirit. He said, "You are a living cell in the Great Spirit's body. When you are feeling lonely, find a quiet place, preferably outside in Nature, and pray: 'Great Spirit, let me see with your eyes, hear with your ears, speak with your voice, know with your mind, and touch with your hands, so that I can be that which I am meant to be—a messenger of Beauty. Let me be a one-hearted human being.'"

The Gifts of the Powers of the Twenty: Dominion and Co-Empowerment

There are an infinite number of MAT spaces. The spaces that are not souls are spaces that are not occupied, but are in movement, floating, moving as magnetic attractors and opportunities. A MAT space also helps the entity within the space—be it a person, an animal, a plant—to feel and become the space. In a way, a fetus in the womb pushes and moves around in the mother's womb as it grows and expands the physical space. Once the child is born, its physical, mental, emotional, spiritual, and sexual maturation is its process of expanding the MAT space of its soul.

The powers of the Twenty Count are the MAT spaces that empower us to become greater than the spaces we fill in order to have excellence. For there to be evolutionary growth, we must not only fill and become the space; our soul yearns to expand that space to make it greater. This is our refinement of character, our *Great Shamanic Work*.

There are actually twelve Twenty Counts within the Twisted Hairs cosmology. All the Twenty Counts, all of Nature, exist in a state of perfect balance and harmonious interconnection. Their co-empowerment inspires growth towards excellence and serves the greatest good for all concerned. Dominion is the quality of the attraction between two or more energies that creates positive impact and co-empowerment. An energetic acceptance and tolerance of one energy/entity of the other without loss of individuality and autonomy is always present. Nature, called the *Children's Twenty Count*, provides the perfect model for us to emulate.

Consider the following equations:

Twenty Count, including Humans in Dominion
Equals
Evolutionary Co-Empowerment

Twenty Count (Nature) + 2-Leggeds
Equals
Disempowerment + Destruction

The first equation is one of creation, inherently empowering all things and creating beauty and balance. Unbalanced two-leggeds are the variable in the second equation. We are the ingredient that often destroys this formula. Because of our free will, we can choose to co-empower ourselves, life, and others, or we can dominate and alienate, thereby creating the illusion of separation. Too often we fall out of alignment and balance, thus disempowering not only ourselves, but Grandmother Earth as well.

On the other hand, when we live in perfect balance with Nature and walk with the Twenty Count inside us, our lives become the sacred voices singing in harmony with the Songs of the Twenty. Our lives transform: We stop struggling and begin the process of healing ourselves and having a positive impact on the world.

Keep present these underlying questions: "What is my attraction? What is my impact in the world? Is it positive or negative? Does it create or destroy? What is my intent in life?"

A Linear Summary of the Powers of the Children's Twenty Count

The Children's Count describes our world and the powers that influence us here *as we experience them,* engaging us in the dance of interconnection, interreliability, interdependence, and empowerment. *Again, separation is an illusion.*

Presented here is the expanded linear summary to help you "walk the Twenty." After the number and the power is its gift to us—its magnetic attraction that draws us to it and empowers us.

As you move through the Twenty Count, notice that the

odd-numbered powers are exploding energies, and the even-numbered powers are imploding energies. Thus, the Twenty Count perpetuates the Sacred Breath, the rhythm of the lovemaking of WahKahn and SsKwan and their sacred Quodoushka marriage called Wakan Tanka, the Great Mystery. We start with the "So Below" tonal powers of 1 to 10.

Both Arabic numerals and the traditional bar/dot system of numbers are employed. The bar/dots are included because they are *sigils* of power (magickal distillations of words and concepts down to their purest graphic representation) as well as a counting system.

1 . Grandfather Sun: Out of the Zero Void first came Grandfather Sun. This is not just the sun as an astronomical phenomenon; it is Grandfather Sun as a spiritual entity that has dominion over all light, illumination, enlightenment, and knowledge. Its attraction and impact are not only literal; it is also the great symbol of achieving empowerment through gaining knowledge. This is the male seed for all life, whose active-conceptive energy, its fire, explodes and impregnates Grandmother Earth.

2 .. Grandmother Earth: When Grandfather Sun explodes, he seeds the receptive-creative eggs of Grandmother Earth, who implodes his energy into her womb, the birthing place of all life. Their lovemaking is called Quodoushka, spiritual sexual union. Women on this planet are two-legged manifestations of the receptive-creative energy of Grandmother Earth. She teaches us of introspection and draws us into our intuitive place of *inner knowing.*

3 ... Sacred Plants: Plants are the firstborn children of Grandmother Earth and Grandfather Sun. They are the explosive children of the seed and the egg, always growing out towards the light. They give life, and without them animals and human beings could not exist here. They symbolize life seeking perfection of form through trust and innocence. For humans, 3 also represents the genetic coding that programs our life form.

4 .... Sacred Animals: Animals are the active, implosive children of Grandmother Earth. They always know who they are. They walk in balance and teach us how to find balance and harmony within ourselves and align with all things with an open heart.

5 __ Sacred Humans: Human beings, as determiners of energy on the planet, are also children of Grandmother Earth. We are meant to live in dominion with all things. Sacred humans teach us openhearted, one-hearted communication and the five *huaquas,* or qualities of humanness—*health, hope, happiness, harmony,* and *humor.*

6 .. Spiritual Ancestors: This is our inner state of full spiritual self-love. It is the sacred transformation of spirit into substance and substance into spirit. These are our spiritual selves for all lifetimes, and the spirits of all our ancestors. (For a more complete description, see Chapter 11).

7 ... Symbols of the Dream: This is our life experiences, the playing out of our personal and sacred dreams fueled by our desire to live life fully awake, aware, and alert to reality in the Now. It is how we experience life through process and symbol. This is also the place of the dreams of the collective of humanity and their impact on Grandmother Earth's dream of her life experience and evolutionary excellence.

8 .... Book of Life: This is our Book of Life, the script our spirit wrote to act out in this lifetime. We might say that we have a *master* picturebook which contains our sacred images. These are the different karmic and dharmic experiences for a particular lifetime. Pattern and the Laws of Cycles are here, the Circle of Law that controls all cyclic patterns.

9 .... Design and Choreography of Energy in Motion: This has to do with how energy in motion is designed and choreographed. It shows us how to choreograph our energy to be in alignment with the Great Spirit's design by learning how to ride the wave of Chaos that resides here. Within the chaotic wave, male and female energies are always in perfect balance. If we align with Sacred Law in this way, we are, in a sense, cosmic surfers. This is the place where we set priorities, make decisions and choices. Thus the law of "Maximum Efficiency With Minimum Effort" holds sway here.

10 ═ Great Measure of Intellect: This is the expression of artistic originality into all forms of all states of mental awareness and consciousness (conscious, subconscious, unconscious, collective conscious, collective unconscious minds and universal consciousness) and the four attentions. This is the measure of our self-worth, self-love, and self-acceptance. This is the measure of all thoughts, ideas, images, and belief systems as human beings as well as the consciousness levels of all plants and animals. This is the power that makes all things possible and holds all potentialities. When we say something gives away its 10ness, we mean its consciousness and spirit.

Now we move into the "As Above" nagual powers of 11 to 20. Notice the difference in their energy and your relationship to them.

11 ≛ Grandfather Stars and Sister Moons: Grandfather Stars are yellow stars that have Grandmother Planets revolving around them that bear humans. If, in its rays of light, a star has the cosmic seed to impregnate a fertile planet, it is a Grandfather Star or Sun. The fertile planet is the Sun's mate, and the other planets are her sisters. The Moon here is the actual heavenly body. The Sister Moon is the Sun's mistress, and she functions as a mediator between the Sun and the Earth. It is here that we can recall all memory from all lifetimes. The power of 11 also represents the Twisted Hairs Council of Grandfathers.

12 ≛ Grandmother Planets: These are planets which revolve around Grandfather Suns and on which human life (not necessarily in our familiar form) is present. According to the Elders, there are twelve universes in the body of the Great Spirit, each with twelve planets with human life. This also refers to the Twisted Hairs Council of Grandmothers and women who are the bearers of life. The goddess number is 12, and it is our inner love of self and our ability to be present Here and Now. It is the opportunity to gain total inner clarity of our higher self through meditation, chanting, prayers, and ceremony. It is the point that we call the moment of internal light, the moment of awakening into one's truth, of actualizing awakened memory.

13 ☷ Earth Mother: Earth Mother, or Quetzal, is the spiritual consciousness energy of all plants. When we eat a plant, its substance or physicalness is not what feeds us. Rather, we are eating a plant (3), which releases its consciousness or spirit (10), and that is what gives us sustenance and nourishment. The power of 13 symbolizes death and change and the acceptance of death as change and movement. It is called the Goddess Beauty, Goddess Nature, Death Mother. The Plains Indians called her White Buffalo Woman who brought the Sacred Pipe back to the Sioux nation. Other tribal peoples have always had that connection with the Sacred Pipe and with the goddess White Buffalo Woman. She is the Daughter of the First Breath.

14 ☷ Earth Father: Earth Father, or Coatl, is the spiritual consciousness energy of all animals. Shamans tap into 14 in the shamanic journey and use it to bring about healing, using the spirit of the animal to heal the spirit of the human. This is also called Sweet Medicine, Father Sky, and Seven Arrows, the Son of the Perfect Dream, the messenger that guides us that we may align our intent with the intent of the Everything. In the Christian tradition, 14 is called the Holy Spirit.

15 ☰ Souls of All Humans: A complete thought is a soul, and we are a thought of the Great Spirit in its attempt to see itself in all its many reflections. We are Magnetic Attracting Thought (MAT) soul spaces within the Soul of the Everything. This is all states of universal consciousness. Everything that exists is a part of us and knows of its alignment and interconnection with us. We are here to remember this connection, for it is the Wheel of Life and the key to our true nature spirit personality.

16 ☰ Akalohtah-hey: This means to see, to know, and to be awakened. These are enlightened masters of the light who work with us through the spirit world. They stay in their luminous form and work with our psychic-kinetic and electromagnetic energies. They are the avatars who have become enlightened and may choose to use their power to come back into a physical form for a period of time to be a physical teacher. The Christ Jesus and the Buddha are examples of incarnated 16s.

17 ☰ Kachina-hey: They are the dream souls and teachers of the dream, which work with pure archetypal symbols, sigils, and images through the fifth dimension (the space of the dream). Kachinas are the great awakeners of memory. They are leaders of the Night Warrior Army, whose equivalent in the Christian tradition are the Archangels.

18 ☰ Chuluamahdah-hey: These are the magickal teachers. They work with pure magickal energies and the ten Magickal Laws to create the tonal physical world. All this is done through circles of pattern of both spirit and substance. The power of 18 controls the consciousness and measure of the mind of spirit (10) and all images and cycles within form (8). It is all the cycles of images for all who come from spirit into substance body, back to spirit, and so on. They are the sacred keepers of our Books of Life and of all Akashic Records, which are the compilation of all our Books of Life from all our spirit personality selves. When we resurrect, we become 18.

19 ☰ Hokkshideh-hey: This is our highest High Self, which helps us to know ourselves as greater than what we think we are. This is the great Buddha, the Christ, the Boddhisattvas, and the universal teachers. They are the breath keepers. This is the perfect balance of male and female energy of our highest evolved Self.

20 ☰ Wakan Tanka/Great Spirit/The Everything/The Great Mystery: Wakan Tanka translates to our inner Great Spirit of self beyond personhood and personality, beyond identity into soul consciousness. As a consciousness of mind, we are dreaming ourselves awake in a physical body. As a cell of the Great Spirit's body, we are in its consciousness, its thought of its Self. We are one with the Great Spirit in pure orgastic light, love, and awareness. For us, it is completion.

This is an infinity wheel of infinite immortality of light movement in which every form of every thing finds its place justly. It's not a fixed hierarchy but a moving one—a movement of light. It always returns back and begins again in a perfect cycle. There are ten steps in the "As Above" and ten in the "So Below." And that is the Twenty Count of Creation.

Thunder Strikes: *I have never found anything that isn't in the Twenty. Everything that exists, everything that ever will exist, and everything that ever has existed, can be put inside the twenty movements of life, the Twenty Count. Wherever I traveled throughout the world, I made an incredible discovery. I found that shamanic people—magicians and sorcerers—all over Grandmother Earth knew the Twenty Count. The language was different, but if we could talk about one (1), we would talk about the Sun, no matter where I was. And that one (1) represents all light and especially any and all light that gives life. So there is a commonality, a universal language. And that is because the Universe itself speaks the language of mathematics.*

The Twenty Count Is Part of Our Genetic Coding

The Twisted Hairs Elders consider the Twenty Count to be one of the most significant teachings of the Sweet Medicine SunDance body of knowledge. They say the Twenty Count is in our genetic memory encoded in the cells of our body. We are holographic image computers. Every Teaching Wheel is birthed from the Twenty Powers.

We can awaken memory by studying and learning the Twenty Count. As you become more familiar with the Twenty Count, the powers will awaken inside you. They will guide you to discover new truths and uncover deeper understandings of your true nature and life purpose. Establish a personal connection with each of these movements of energy. Consciously welcome them into your life and align with them. They will lead you into soul consciousness as you journey into the greater landscape of yourself.

4
The Sacred Laws of Creation

The *children's fire* is the inviolable spirit of a person, thing, or a people within *Sacred Law,* or the *Laws of Creation.* Traditionally, among Earth peoples, a society was a group of people that met within the children's fire of Sacred Law. They honored the sacred fire and the spirit of the people, and while they might employ civil, social, religious, or cultural laws, they understood that these laws must necessarily be in harmony and alignment with Sacred Law. Sadly, we have created laws that corrupt the balance of Nature because we have stepped away from the harmony of a society, a group of people who live within Sacred Law.

Tsalagi Anenyanwiya in Cherokee means "The Principal People From the Stars." The Hopi name for themselves means "Holy People." The Mayans refer to themselves as "The People of Vision," and so on. So "The People" is part of how many tribes named themselves. It was a way of saying, "We know who we are as an intimate, integral part of the Everything."

In our modern world we have a great deal of confusion between rules and laws. We create laws to govern behavior, and virtually all civil, social, religious, cultural, and criminal laws are enacted to force us to abide by the ruling hierarchy's paradigms of correct behavior. Generally, society accepts these laws, and they are given legitimacy by the collective at large. Sometimes these laws are created by a dictator or tyrant and are forced upon the people without their consent. Either way, this produces the same result: These rules of behavior and conduct become the guide for what is considered correct in the political, economic, social/cultural, religious, and sexual arenas of our lives. Laws are enacted to enforce these rules of conduct and to mete out punishment for violation of these rules.

By definition those with criminal intent do not obey any law. They are *lawbreakers*. So humans became lawmakers in order to try to change the behavior of the criminal who never obeys the laws anyway. In most instances, these laws are applied to all humans as if we were criminals. Many, if not most, of the laws passed, at least in the United States, are really rules of behavior.

In the Twisted Hairs' concept of justice, there are laws that were made and placed into existence by the very act of creation itself. These laws were created by the Creatress and Creator to allow evolution to always take place so that every form of every thing has the potential to become any form of any other thing in an ongoing, continuous, and everlasting stream of livingness. These we call the Sacred Laws. These laws were not created by humans, nor do they try to change the behavior, belief systems, or the structures of our different cultures and societies. Rather, they are inherent in the creation and evolution of the Everything. They define the process by which the Great Spirit expresses itself in all forms of all things. We give them our definition, and we struggle to understand them and to come into alignment with them. Our attempts to define their essence in words, however, almost always fall short, for they are so much larger than our language for them. In some cases they may be beyond our understanding.

Sacred Laws create and re-create life itself. They define the web, the maze, the matrix, and the crystal matrix of the Universe that give form to all things. These laws reach into the very core of our being, our every thought, word, and deed. We have lost the knowledge of Sacred Law and its presence in the reality of our daily lives. Even when we embrace the concept of something greater, whatever we might call it, we put it outside ourselves as an external concept. We miss the innate connection we carry inside and have become ignorant of the consequences of violating Sacred Law. We wring our hands and shake our heads at the headlines and the dysfunction in our own families and wonder, "How do we change this?" We can change by awakening to how we are irrevocably interconnected with all things and by understanding that these Laws of Creation are the Breath of Life, our breath, our life. They are outside us *and* within us. We incur karma when we violate any of these Sacred and Natural Laws.

It was inevitable that the thirty Sacred Laws would be discovered by humans in their pursuit of understanding the mystery of life in the Universe. The Twisted Hairs Elders discovered that the Everything intends and dreams itself into existence within the four Universal and four Cosmic Laws. It needs to exist in the physical in matter, but it has to do it everywhere in all forms of all things. This is a constant transformative process, so the Everything intends its spirit into substance form through the ten Magickal Laws. The ten Ecological Balance Laws are the guidelines for its presence in the physical, along with the 144 Natural Laws. This is the most definitive set of laws that create the measure of human evolution (10), for ten indicates measure and also completion of one cycle.

Let's examine the "becoming" of those laws. The becoming is described in four Universal and six Cosmic Laws called the "As Above" laws of the nagual or the world of total spirit. They allow spirit to become substance and substance to move back into spirit, and allow the Universe to manifest in an ongoing, ever-evolving stream of livingness.

The study of these laws awakens the memory of them encoded in our bodies.

The Four Universal Laws

First Universal Law:
"Maximum Efficiency With Minimum Effort"

The Universe demonstrates the movement of all energy and motion from spirit into substance and then back from substance into spirit through maximum efficiency with minimum effort. This means that the Everything creates any form of any thing without wasted or ill-used energy in its application of evolution. Most people in their lives do exactly the opposite. Human beings, with their free will, constantly violate the energy laws, producing dissonance and imbalance; consequently, we struggle and strive and fight. If we have a strong connecting link with the intent of the Great Spirit, then we are in alignment with this law. When you are working hard and not getting anywhere, you are out of alignment. A popular metaphor is someone paddling upstream. Play more with spirit, and allow your energy to flow: Be like water. Your resistance will decrease, and you will start to move forward and make progress. This law creates the lines of least resistance.

Second Universal Law: "Everything Is Born of Woman"

All forms of all things within the Everything are birthed from the receptive-creative energy principle, which is the feminine principle, and sparked by the active-conceptive energy principle, which is the masculine principle. Before anything can happen, before anything can be created or produced or discovered, there must be receptivity. Out of receptivity comes creativity, which then leads to activity and actualization, which are masculine energies. All gods are born from the womb of a goddess. Ideas, creative arts, technology, and so forth, are all birthed out of this principle.

Women are two-legged manifestations of Grandmother Earth's womb, and because of that, they carry within their womb the potential to birth much more than just physical children. Woman carries receptivity to her inner knowing, her intuition, which becomes the fertile ground for creativity and life—the life of physical children, ideas, beauty, art, inspiration, music. This springs from the feminine in all of us. Our masculine, active-conceptive energy steps into decisive action and produces a product. It is important to remember that men and women carry both feminine and masculine energies. However, in two-leggeds, as in all of Nature, the female embodies the receptive-creative energy and the male embodies the active-conceptive energy. In order for a man to create, he must first

access his feminine, receptive-creative side. Any time you are dealing with a problem or a block and you call upon your imagination
and your ingenuity to solve the problem, you are using this law.

Third Universal Law:
"Nothing Shall Be Done to Harm the Children"

No law, action, thought, word, or deed can be brought into
manifestation and continue to exist if it brings harm to the essence
of the creation of life, for this is a direct attack on the feminine principle. Every form of every thing is a child of creation. Another way
the Elders express this is: "Nothing Shall Be Done to Harm the Children of Grandmother Earth, Including the Child Within." Since all
life is the child of Grandmother Earth, the survival of species
and evolution into excellence are affected when we violate this
law. Cutbacks in education and imposed conformity in our educational institutions harm the children. Pollution of our rivers and
oceans and the air is a direct violation of this law. Anything that re-
stricts, disrespects, and violates the children's fire within all things
and all people harms the children. No matter how many laws our
legislatures enact, no matter what international agreements are created in the guise of world peace, if these laws in any way disrespect
the feminine or harm the children (including taking away individual freedom), they violate Sacred Law, and create heavy karma for
individuals as well as countries and the collective family of
humanity.

Whenever we are about to enact a law or establish a regulation,
it would be wise to ask whether it provides the opportunity for
spiritual growth and the maturation of autonomous individuals,
whether it protects and nurtures freedom within Sacred Law. Many
tribal peoples sat in Council and approached all issues with two
questions: Will this action we wish to take honor the feminine?
Does it protect, nurture and empower all children, now and *for the
next seven generations*? If the action would do this, it was a good
thing, a sacred act in alignment with Sacred Law. If not, it was denied. Can you imagine how our lives would change if local, state,

and national governing bodies and our leaders used these two questions as the yardsticks by which all laws and actions were measured? Stop for a moment and consider this. Then ask yourself, "What can I do in my daily life, in my interaction with other people and institutions, to begin living this law? How can I make a difference?" You see, we are called upon to walk the law and live the law, so the law lives and breathes in us. That is true alignment.

Fourth Universal Law:
"The 0-9 Law of Harmonic Energy Motion"

The Elders call this the key Sacred Law because it controls all laws. The Great Spirit's intent for evolution into excellence is born first out of the receptive-creative energy, which is the feminine principle. Then, through its active-conceptive energy, the male principle, it manifests the form of its intent with maximum efficiency and minimum effort. This process follows nine movements (ten steps), and then another cycle begins. Every time you do anything—make a decision, bake a cake, buy a car, start a business, learn something new, fall in love—you do it in these ten steps: Focus, Substance, Form, Determination, Understanding, Imagination, Freedom, Pattern, Chaos, and Completion. (For an application of this law, see the section on the Infinity Movement in Chapter 14.)

Thunder Strikes: When I was a young boy, my clan uncle, John Two Crows, demonstrated this law to me by taking me to a pond near our house. He dropped a pebble into the water and directed me to watch the ripples intently. Over and over again he dropped pebbles into the water. Finally, with his coaching, I began to see that the waves rippled out in nine circles from the Center, and then a very powerful thing happened! Before they hit the bank, they began to ripple back towards the Center, which was Zero!

John Two Crows asked me, "What caused the ripple to move back again? What did it hit?"

I spent months dropping pebbles in the water, trying to catch what in the hell this was all about. And always, on the ninth ripple—no less, no more—it started to ripple back.

Every time I'd ask him, he'd say, "That's the invisible secret, the mystery of the Universe. You figure it out."

I must have gotten a million headaches trying to figure out what was making that wave go back. One day my clan uncle told me that all things in Nature do this. It is a going out from the Source, the moment of creation, and then seeking the way back to the Source. What was making it go back was the wave of chaos. Here was an old peanut farmer who knew more about chaos theory than the scientists at the time, because he had learned it in his ancient way as the 0-9 Law of Harmonic Energy Motion. He then validated this by showing me where it appeared in Nature: swirls of a hawk, spins a fox makes. Everywhere I look I can see the 0-9 Law in action. A fetus evolves nine months in the womb, nine cycles from the moment of creation. At birth, we begin our journey back to our Source, back to the Light of Spirit in cycles of nine months called the moon cycles.

The Six Cosmic Laws

The six *Cosmic Laws* create the Magnetic Attracting Thought (MAT) spaces within which any form of any thing may take up residence and exist within the substance world of matter. They govern the cycles of life, the cycles of all spirit into substance and substance into spirit. As cellular spaces in the body of the Great Spirit, our spirit personality is created through the six Cosmic Laws.

The heart of creation contains the destruction of creation so that new life can be reborn at ever higher levels of evolution and beauty. Destruction for destruction's sake causes physical death (the Elders call this *death-death*).

Eighty percent of what happens is patterned (chosen) energy motion, and twenty percent is the free-will determination of the Great Spirit, chaos, and the Law of Chance, used to experience change and growth.

First Cosmic Law: "Death Gives (Creates) Life"

When you plant a seed in the ground, part of the seed must die in order to sprout and create new life. When a man plants a seed in a woman, that is a death. Millions of his seeds die so that one can carry his life force to create new life. A tree falls and deteriorates, and out of that grow new plants. Fertilizer is the death of matter, which nourishes new life.

Second Cosmic Law: "Life Gives Rebirth"

This describes the process of a mother bearing a child. She is life and the child is a rebirth, one life producing another life. Many of a woman's cells die each month during her menstrual period. If a woman didn't have her monthly moon cycle, which is death giving life, she wouldn't be able to give life. The moment of conception is life giving rebirth. And again, rebirth happens when spirit enters the womb. Rebirth is that infinitesimally fine line between death and life, the transition of spirit into substance and substance back into spirit.

Third Cosmic Law: "Rebirth Gives Movement"

Growing in the womb, the baby moves, rebirth of spirit into substance. When the baby is born and takes its first Breath, that again is rebirth giving movement, because, for the rest of its life, every time it breathes it is in the process of rebirthing and changing.

Fourth Cosmic Law: "Movement Gives Change, and Change Is Continuous and Inevitable"

This law governs the evolutionary process. Without change, there would be stasis, and like stagnant water, stasis eventually produces death without hope of new life.

Fifth Cosmic Law: "Change Produces Chaos"

Chaos provides moments of power and evolutionary leaps. We are wise to welcome chaos, not resist it. Our willingness to change and to ride the waves of chaos will propel us much faster along our soul's evolutionary journey.

Sixth Cosmic Law: "Chaos Gives Death"

Chaos and change cause a dying in each moment. The moment

you are born, every moment you are living, you are living to die. And you are dying each moment in order to live. Many native peoples call death the Great Changer.

And the cycle repeats itself, driving the evolutionary spiral. These six *Spirit Personality Laws,* or Cosmic Laws, produce the infinity Wheel of Life that produces immortality of the soul. They are the key to the Everything's ongoing evolution of self-discovery.

Sacred Law has put you here, a spirit personality of a soul in physical form. Standing accountable spiritually is our adherence to Sacred Law.

The Ten Magickal Laws

We have already looked at the ten Spiritual Creational Laws. Now we look at the ten *Magickal Laws,* the marvelous transition from the world of spirit to where something becomes present in the world of matter or substance. This is, indeed, a magickal transformation. If you look at an old building made of solid concrete that has been abandoned for a period of time, you will see grass and tiny flowers growing through the cracks and seeking the light. This is magick and true power, which are synonymous. These are the gifts of law that are also part of our will to do.

The Magickal Laws are the laws that govern transition and transformation, dictating movement, change, and chaos. If we did not have these, humans could not and would not evolve, and neither would anything else. The first Cosmic Law—"Death Gives Life"—contains all of the ten Magickal Laws within it.

In many ways the Elders consider the Magickal Laws to be the most precious of the laws, for with each law humans and humans alone are given a special gift called the Great Spirit's *medicine give-away.* It represents our blanket of immortality, our apprenticeship to greatness and excellence called *enlightenment,* achieved through the blessing of resurrection, the ability to step outside the laws of mother/father parenting and evolution, and instead become a resurrected cosmic soul, having evolved itself exactly the way the Everything is evolving itself. We become the Breath of life.

The realm of the Magickal Laws is the *Bardos*, also known as the *Crack Between the Worlds*. This is the fourth dimension, which separates the fifth dimension of spirit and the third dimension of physical form. The spirit personality journeys through this dimension when it comes into physical form. At death, when the spirit personality leaves the body, it travels back once again. The Bardos is also the spirit realm located in the asteroid belt, which the Twisted Hairs call the *LawBelt*. The LawBelt is the determination between objective reality in the physical and the objective reality of dreamtime. *Law* here refers to the Magickal Laws, which make materialization of the 0-9 Law possible.

Each of our ten chakras (energy vortices, or centers, in our luminosity) is guided by one of the Magickal Laws. Each law also graces us with a gift or power called the *O'larien*, which are our psychic gifts or ESPs (*energy-sensitive perceptions*). The ten Magickal Laws make it possible for us to become enlightened human beings.

The Ten Ecological Balance Laws

The ten *Ecological Balance Laws* are keys to the ever-continuing presence of the substance world of life, and they are the planet's laws outside of humans. These are the *Spinner Laws,* or the 0-9 Laws here on this planet, because they drive or spin the 144 laws of Nature and science. If we were in balance with the Ecological Balance Laws, they would unlock the secrets of the 144 Natural Laws and spin us into alignment with them. We would be developing *clean, pure* science and technology more wonderful than we can imagine. We would be practicing magickal science.

The Natural Laws

The 144 *Natural Laws* are science, laws of cause and effect, and the relationship of time, space, and dimension. They are in a constant state of evolutionary process and movement and evolve in direct correlation to our understanding of Magickal Law. Magickal Law communicates through Natural Law. When Natural Law evolves to a certain state, we will finally understand the Magickal

Laws. Only seventy-four Natural Laws have currently been "discovered." Laws 1 through 72 describe cause/effect relationships in existing matter. The seventy-third is the *morphogenetic field theory*—the *collective unconscious*—and it reflects the first Magickal Law. The seventy-fourth Natural Law is the Law of Chaos. Science is slowly moving back towards metaphysics and magick, as a deeper understanding of Natural Law emerges.

5
The Individuation of the Human Soul

In their continuous dreaming and studying of the mysteries of creation, particularly the creation of the human soul, the ancient ones began to realize that there was an absolute *Sacred Order* in the Universe. That Sacred Order followed the *Ten Steps of Creation*. They discovered the concept of Zero and found that there are only two numbers—zero (0) and one (1). Out of Zero, there are nine movements, which they recognized as the *0-9 Law*. They also learned that when anything, including a human being, produces an action or causes movement, that conception will move through ten steps. This is the key not only to the creation of that First Breath, but to all our everyday thoughts and actions.

The 0-9 Law Within the First Breath of Creation

Mathematically, with the discovery of the 0-9 Law and within their understanding of the Sacred Laws that governed the Universe, the Zero Chiefs were able to follow the steps of creation that rippled out from that First Breath, and by tracking the Light Energy Movement of the Twenty Count, starting with 20 as the creational Zero, they formulated the *Energy Light Movement Wheel*. This discovery is remarkable. In its entirety it is quite complex, so we will present a simplified explanation here to describe for you the cosmic playing fields and the SunDance Journey of All Souls.

The description of the powers from 20 to 10 in this movement will differ somewhat from the description of these same powers of the Twenty Count described in Chapter 3. To minimize any confusion, we reiterate here that the powers of the Twenty Count are described from our human frame of reference and our direct relationship with them. In this Light Energy Movement, we are describing the unfoldment of the Light that created these powers in the very First Breath. This will also be simpler and easier to understand if you can step outside the limitations of linear time with your imagination. The Twisted Hairs say time is a human device to establish our place in space. There is no past or future, only Now.

20 ☰ We will start with 20, which is creation at 0 from this point of view. Remember, this was the Zero potential of all forms of all things. It was the universal unconscious infinitely poised to dream itself awake—a pregnant pause in infinity.

19 ☷ The first movement or ripple of life out from Zero produced the power of 19 called the *Breath of Life and Light,* the implosion and explosion which produced the power of spirit to take on any and all forms. This first ripple also created evolutionary excellence defined by the four Universal Laws, and the laws that allow the transformation of spirit into substance and substance into spirit transformation—the six Cosmic Laws. At this moment of 19, the focus of the Great Spirit created the elements and charged them with spirit, consciousness, life, and physicality, and 18 was formed. As this happened, the Great Spirit discovered that charged spirit was actually its sexual catalyst energy, and through this energy, it could *feel* itself in the physical. This was the Everything's *focus* step within the 0-9 Law.

18 ☲ As light rippled out from the Source, and the Great Spirit observed itself unfolding, it realized that it needed a way to correct its misperceptions of itself. Testing and challenge were necessary to assess both its strengths and its weaknesses, to use its mistakes as learning experiences, and to evaluate the ongoing purity of its intent. It took its first measure inside the 0-9 Law by confronting all that had transpired. It saw that its highest expression of itself could be felt and experienced through the experience of the human soul in physical form. The second movement of light at 18, then, was the *substance* step out of which Magnetic Attracting Thought (MAT) spaces that were to become souls of all human beings would form. This would allow all psychic consciousness to occupy a huge space, become greater than the sum of the parts, and become the collective unconscious. This was WahKahn's and SsKwan's pure substance, and they saw themselves as souls within the physical.

With us two-leggeds, the Everything found it would be able to experience the most feelings of power and beauty and the power and beauty of its feelings of itself. The Everything loves how it feels through plants and animals and always through spirit, but in its artistically original formulation of a two-legged, it created an almost perfect expression of itself. It is through us that the Everything experiences its heart and emotions, its mind and thoughts, its body and feelings, its soul and its *prime mover energy,* or sexuality, and the sensory experiences of touch, taste, hearing, smell, and sight that are unique to the human experience. *The highest level thought of the Great Spirit was, therefore, that of the human soul.* We are a small, immature holographic mirror image of the Everything.

But these souls also had to follow the 0-9 Law, so each MAT soul was individuated into nine individual *spirit personalities*, each of which would experience a minimum of 144 physical body reincarnations or physical lifetimes (see Fig. 5-a). So it is here that our soul and our nine spirit personality expressions of our soul were created. Eight of our spirit personalities sit in a circle, a sacred Wheel of Power, around the ninth or most significant lifetime. It is the dominant spirit personality, which sits in the Center of our soul's Circle of Law, which is our Council of 18, our Chuluamahdah-hey. Our higher self, our Hokkshideh-hey (19), holds the full measure of our soul's intent. The tenth chakra, our halo in our luminosity, is our connection to our higher self.

17 ☷ At this point the Great Spirit saw that by creating the means for souls to become physical and move away from the Source, a way had to be created to give them the maximum

Fig. 5-a   The Individuation of the Human Soul

"Super Nova of the Soul"
Our Cycles of Reincarnation

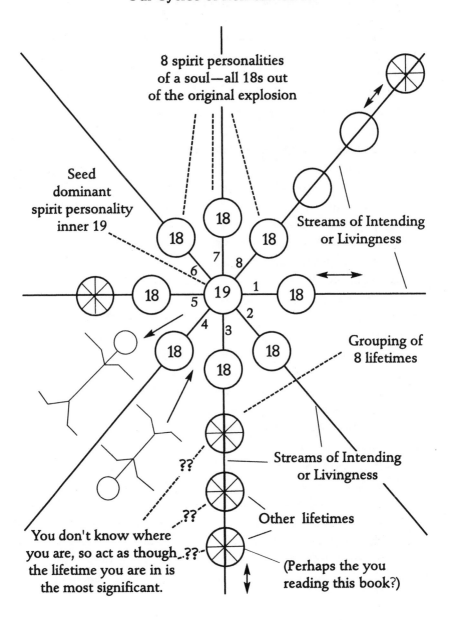

8 spirit personalities
of a soul—all 18s out
of the original explosion

Seed
dominant
spirit personality
inner 19

Streams of Intending
or Livingness

Grouping of
8 lifetimes

Streams of Intending
or Livingness

Other lifetimes

You don't know where
you are, so act as though
the lifetime you are in is
the most significant.

(Perhaps the you
reading this book?)

opportunity to return to the Source. So the third movement of light at 17 created the ten Magickal Laws of Wisdom that formed the *streams of intending*, also called the *streams of livingness*, so that now the spirit personalities of each soul had the potential to move or flow, like ships, along these streams or rivers of light into the world of physical substance form and back again. This is the realm of the collective conscious.

The ten Ecological Balance Laws and the 144 Natural Laws, which are the arenas of scientific study and discovery, came into being here as well, within this *form* ripple of creation.

16 ☰ The fourth movement of light at 16 was the ripple of choice and *determination*. It created the space where the MAT soul now chooses which of the nine spirit personalities it will send first to begin its outward journey of incarnation cycles.

At 16, then, our psyche, or sacred mind of our soul, steps in. You might say the soul is the airport, and the psyche is the traffic controller. It monitors all the lifetimes of our nine spirit personalities of 18, and determines which spirit personality of the nine will be danced into the dreamtime of consciousness, that is, into the physical form as a two-legged human. It opens the Book of Life of the Akashic Records (the records of all previous lifetimes) of that spirit personality, which are held by the Chuluamahdah-hey (18), and sorts through the images: the stream of intending of that spirit personality, all its learned experiences, all the awakened memories, and all the skills and knowledge and wisdom gained in all its previous lifetimes. It writes a series of eight lifetimes at a time as a theme, which is called our Circle of Law, our Circle of Life. So we are always sitting in Council with eight of our other most significant lifetimes. Right now, as you read this page, you are the ninth lifetime in your Circle of Law of your spirit personality.

Your MAT soul space has many physical body lifetime "spaces" within it. But it is *this* space and *this* body—your space and your body Here and Now reading this book—that matters, because it's the one you're conscious in. All the rest of them are out there in other times and dimensions, but you're not conscious in them now.

Thunder Strikes: *Grandfather Two Bears used to say, "Your task in any given body in any given lifetime is to become the Enlightened One. If any one in a stream of intending, if any one body of one spirit personality, wakes up and becomes enlightened, they all do simultaneously. That is the 'One to the Many and the Many to the One' law."*

So I asked Grandfather, "Well, then, how do I know which one I'm in?"

And he replied, "You don't, so act as if it's this one; this is the lifetime that counts."

That made sense to me because this lifetime is the one I'm consciously dreaming awake right now, so it has to be the one that matters the most. This one is always the one in the Center, so whichever one is consciously dreaming itself present and conscious goes into the Center as the dominant spirit personality, and the one that was previously dreaming conscious moves back out and sits on the circle of the Circle of Law (18).

Always looking for ways to shatter my self-importance with humor, Grandfather would admonish me not to take all of this too seriously. "Remember," he would say, "pay attention to the little things that matter."

The Circle of Law of the Council of 18, therefore, guided by the psyche of the soul, writes the script for the movie this particular physical incarnation of this particular spirit personality will act out in the physical as a two-legged. And off the spirit personality goes, with its Book of Life script, down its stream of intending on its journey into physical incarnation. The soul is seeking full expression through the willful intent and actualization of the spirit personality. That is its dharmic destiny.

15 ≡ The collective MAT soul space of all humans as matter was created at 15, the fifth ripple of light out from Zero. Spirit personalities, individual souls who are all connected in the All Souls of the Everything's Soul (15 in the Twenty Count), go through the cycles of reincarnation here on this planet to master the physical form, the oppositional energies, and the paradoxes and dualities. We don't do this by ourselves. Our souls have entered into a contract with all other souls at 15. This is our interconnection, interreliability, and interdependability. How our soul matures, or not, affects how all other souls grow and mature. We are not in this alone.

This ripple at 15 established the realm in which the spirit personality crosses the Bardos on its journey from spirit into physical form. It is here that the spirit personality enters the womb of the mother sometime during the sixteenth to eighteenth week of pregnancy and imbues the physical fetus with the spirit of a soul. As the spirit personality enters the Bardos, it passes through the first "veil of forgetting," a cosmic eraser that erases memory of our Source. (Once in a great while, a spirit personality will have evolved enough to be able to make the journey with its memory intact. This is very rare, although it is our natural destiny.)

The spirit personality is journeying from the realms of the collective unconscious and the collective conscious through the "Crack Between the Worlds" into the realm of the personal subconscious and unconscious minds as it enters physical form in the womb. This is the process described by the "One to the Many and the Many to the One" law of transformation. This was the Everything's step of *understanding*.

14 ☷ At this point, the Great Spirit saw the cost of becoming physical—primarily the loss of soul memory as the spirit personality crosses the Bardos—so this sixth movement, as the *imagination* step of this 0-9 movement of light, created the power of 14. It created the Bridger of the world of substance and the world of spirit—the Great Messenger, Earth Father, Holy Spirit. This power of 14 makes it possible for our spirit personality in the physical body to connect back to our Soul and allows us to meet the first enemy in both spirit and substance—*fear*.

13 ☷ At 13, this seventh movement of light became the Great Death Changer, Earth Mother, the Great Magma, where the Cosmic Laws began to play out in the physical third dimension, creating the process of death giving life, life giving rebirth, and so on, for spirit now in physical form. At this point, then, our spirit personality in the fetus opens its *Karma Book* or *Dharma Book* (depending on which cycle of reincarnations we are in), and in doing so accepts the death, change, and transformations confronting it within its new physical substance body. At the same time, our Council of 18 is keeping a record of these transformations in our etheric substance, as a record of the immortality of our soul. This was the Everything's *freedom* step of creation.

12 ☷ This eighth movement of light fertilized the magma eggs of certain planets so that they could become the largest MAT spaces capable of sustaining human habitation and reincarnation cycles. These Grandmother Planets provide the space where humans can come and dream themselves awake. This was the *pattern* step of the Everything's creation that established the pattern of reincarnation cycles.

11 ☵ As light moved through its ninth *chaos* ripple, the magma seeds of certain Suns were catalyzed in order to fertilize the Grandmother Planets so they could birth and sustain human life. These Grandfather Suns always have a Sister Moon or Sister Moons revolving around each of these planets. It is the primal sexual catalyst dance movement between the Grandfather Sun, the Grandmother Earth, and the Sister Moon(s) that make human life possible. The power of 11 gives humans the seeds of memory, which hold what was lost crossing the Bardos.

10 ☰ The tenth movement of light that exploded out from that First Breath allowed the means for humans to come into conscious existence in the physical, for at 10 we birth out of our mother's womb. Ten (10) includes all levels of consciousness and all states of awareness, our measure of intellect, and our measure of self-worth. "Measure of self-worth" means that part of the Great Spirit's soul intent we are holding as we birth ourselves. It is also our tenth chakra, our halo.

At this *completion* step, spirit comes into the "So Below" of this physical reality. When we take *our* first breath, our luminosity flares and our life force (called *chuluaqui* in the Twisted Hairs tradition, *ki* in Japanese traditions, *chi* in Chinese traditions, *prana* in Hindu traditions) begins to circulate through the body, independent of the mother.

Everything from 9 to 1 is now inside the microcosmic universe of our physical body, an exact duplication of the macrocosmic Universe of the Everything. The 0–9 Law is now operative in this physical world as the powers from 1 to 10 of the Children's Twenty Count. We experience the focus of Grandfather Sun, the substance of Grandmother Earth, the form of the Plants, the determination of the Animals, and so forth. Ten (10) is our completion in the "So Below." We access the "As Above" powers when we enter the realm of spirit through ceremony, sweat lodges, shamanic trance, controlled dreaming, and certain other spiritual practices, and, of course, when we die and our spirit travels through the ripples of time, space, and dimension back to the Source.

You Are the Best You Have Ever Been

There is a progressive evolution of souls; therefore, you are the best of your selves you have ever been. What is most important to remember here is that you are not a person. Paste the phrase "I AM NOT A PERSON!!" on your bathroom mirror, on the inside of your front door, on your refrigerator, on the rearview mirror of your car, and in your daily planner. You are not a person! You are a MAT soul space for which the physical body serves as the temporary domicile or temple so the spirit personality can *remember* what it is as it journeys to and from the Source on its stream of livingness or intending. The soul is immortal and infinite. It drives your spirit personality to reincarnate in the physical again and again, for the soul has only one purpose, and that is to move its energy forward as consciousness and to evolve.

We are so much more than a body and a personality named Jan or Joe commuting to work or falling in love. And yet, the paradox is that we are bound to do these very things in order to *remember* who we truly are! We can choose to do this with pleasure, although far too many people choose to make the journey very difficult, full of struggle and pain. The journey is the *going back to the before* (to our original true nature), becoming what we already are.

The Elder visionaries say that well over 80 percent of humanity is asleep. Their eyes may be open, but they don't see. The Elders *see* that it is critical that more of us wake up to the fact we are not a person. Our inability to do this is one of the primary reasons we stay stuck in karmic patterns, focusing on personalities and events instead of on soul consciousness.

By taking responsibility for what we are, acknowledging our true measure of self-worth and our being as a soul in the body of the Great Spirit, we can more readily shift into and maintain our focus on soul consciousness. We need to push our edges for excellence and physical mastery, stretch our imagination beyond what we think we can handle, seek the challenges and opportunities, and continue to gain knowledge and wisdom. That's when we expand the space of our spirit personality and of our soul towards illumination and enlightenment. That is our Great Shamanic Work, our search for the Holy Grail, our Sacred SunDance Journey of the Soul.

There is an all-or-none point at which a soul must make a commitment to its own evolution to the Light, back to its Source of creation. A Rainbow Light Warrior is a soul who has made a strong enough commitment that it can now wake up in this lifetime and wake up the other eight physical selves. Our soul is ready. When our soul finds the full measure of life, when it has learned in this spirit personality everything that it needs to know and remember, then it no longer needs the physical existence as a way of learning. It is prepared to go on to other types of learning and levels of consciousness. Our Council of 18 has reserved this space for us and is waiting to see if we come back and take possession of it!

Balanced Humans: The Keys to the Great Spirit's Evolution

And as we dream, so does the Everything. We have shadow dreams and lucid dreams, and so does the Everything. To know the completeness of itself, the Everything must experience the dark shadow as well as the light within the shadow. Light cannot exist without dark; hate must exist for us to know love; and up is not up without a down in opposition. This is the key for us here.

This world, this Earth, is experiencing her own rite of passage as humanity goes through the throes of puberty and experiences its own rites of passage into adolescence and maturity. These transitional years of purification and transformation are necessary for us to come into alignment with the maturity of the planet, of Grandmother Earth.

The prophecies speak of the 144,000 Rainbow Light Warriors who are needed to create the critical mass of humanity in dharma here at this time. The Great Spirit has a huge investment in the Rainbow Light Warriors because they are its healthy cells. Our collective dream of humanity must mature and align with the planetary dream. Only then can Grandmother Earth join her family of the other eleven planets.

As a result, the Everything is starting to come alive with the eros of its physicality; its body is waking up to its soul force catalyst energy, experiencing that aspect of itself through the human experience. As it wakes up, that body goes through awesome changes that are played out here on this planet as the Earth changes now taking place. The fulfillment of the Red Horse Prophecies of Earth changes reflects its growing pains out of childhood and into full sexual awakening. The center of these changes is the thunderstorm, its self-pleasuring. The Everything is making love inside its own essence here on this planet.

The Great Spirit is not omnipotent and perfect. It continues to evolve and intend itself into new forms and new experiences as it explores the infinite potential and possibilities of itself within the Twenty Counts and the sacred cycles within the 0-9 Law. The most humbling piece is that it can do this only through humankind. We are the key. According to the Twisted Hairs, the Planet of the Children holds a key to the evolution of all Creation. It is through our evolution and resolution of the worlds of paradox and duality on Grandmother Earth that the Everything continues its Great Shamanic Work, its journey to discovering its infinite potential.

Section Two

How Did We Become Who We Are?

The Development of Our Character

About Section Two

This section follows the SunDance Journey of a soul as it sends a spirit personality off on its stream of intending from the Great Round of spirit. Traveling along its stream of intending, the spirit personality passes through the spirit portals at Jupiter, journeys through the LawBelt and the veils of forgetting at the edge of the Bardos, and enters the physical.

Our spirit personalities are *molded, sculpted,* and *armored* from birth, creating us, in many ways, in the image of our parents and other *image makers,* rather than allowing our true nature to emerge. This section explores the life patterns we develop that enable us to survive to adulthood as we fit in, belong, and conform to the rules and laws, do's and don'ts, and expectations of our image makers and the society at large. The journey challenges us, tests us, and prepares us to ultimately wake up to who we truly are and claim the heritage of our soul.

6

The Birth of the Spirit Personality Into Physical Form

Let's continue, now, the SunDance Journey of a soul as it sends a spirit personality off on its stream of intending from the Great Round of spirit into the *small round* of the womb and then into the *living round* of life here as we know it. We will tell the story of Jan's spirit personality from her viewing point as an adult looking back over her life.

Jan: With Thunder Strikes' help, I can now see more clearly the design or movie script in my Book of Life and how it has played out and is still playing out. My medicine name, as dreamed for me by Thunder Strikes, is Dream Jaguar, a name and an animal totem whose spirit and nature capture the essence of my soul. So here goes!

Choosing the Mold and the Image Makers

Jan: The time has come to travel back along the stream of intending into physical form once again. This spirit personality sits in Council with a circle of my eight other spirit personalities and determines which one to send off in the next SunDance Journey as a conscious lifetime.

All nine spirit personalities, and all the physical lifetimes of those spirit personalities, are my **toushilahey**; *they are all part of my soul. They are all me, and much more than this one person narrating this journey. I just happen to be the one of all of my spirit personalities that is consciously awake. So my Council of 18 chooses this spirit personality to* *become the two-legged named Jan in this lifetime.*

My Book of Life is open. The pages are blank, waiting to receive my story. It will be my screenplay of the movie of my life.

This screenplay will predetermine the *mold* that this spirit is born into, that is, the basic plot and cast—the choice of all the *image makers*. This mold includes the choice of parents, family, and peer groups; race, culture, and economic status; geography; astrological birth sign; gender (genetic encoding is chosen by your higher self); and connection to Nature and to the mineral, plant, animal, human, and spirit worlds. It predetermines what kind of movie it will star in.

These choices address the questions: What are the karmic lessons you need to learn this time around? What will you need to experience to fulfill your purpose in this lifetime? What will best provide you with the context, the laboratory, so to speak, to experience the transformation of *karma* (the experiential lessons to be learned in order to *remember* your true essence) into *dharma* (opportunities to experience who you really are) and stretch and evolve the Magnetic Attracting Thought (MAT) space of your soul? How can you resolve the dilemma of duality and paradox for yourself?

Many of the elements of this mold will exert their influence by sculpting the spirit personality into something other than what it truly is. Your movie journey is about waking up and remembering your true nature spirit personality. What a paradox. We are always in the process of becoming that which we already are!

Jan: How can my soul stalk the dream like the jaguar through the physical incarnation of this spirit personality? My spirit personality and its council of 18 write the script in my Book of Life and then survey the scene, seeking out fertile wombs, potential entry points into the world of physical form.

Ah, yes. There is a couple who seem to satisfy the requirements. I have chosen a father who works the land, hardworking, honest, and forthright. He values security and predictability; he doesn't take chances; he has an indomitable will that he wields to control his life and his environment according to his rules and beliefs. I have chosen a mother who is a teacher, gentle, soft-spoken, generous, compassionate, and loving. She derives pleasure in doing for others. She has an adventurous spirit that she denies in order to serve her husband and make him happy.

This woman has conceived and is approaching four and a half months of pregnancy. At this point, my soul enters into a contract with the souls of my chosen parents. This soul contract defines the gifts I will bring to them and the gifts they will give to me for mutual benefit and welfare and co-empowerment.

My jaguar soul has made the choices for this spirit personality, and has chosen the timing for entering the womb so that my birth date will align with the deer as my totem animal. The jaguar essence of my soul also made a contract with the deer to guide me on my journey and help me learn the karmic lessons, close my Karma Book, and step into dharma. The deer is the expression of my spirit personality, and the jaguar is the essence of my soul seeking full expression through the actualization of the spirit personality into dharma.

(When doctors and parents choose to induce labor for the sake of convenience only, they disrupt the intended timing and choices of the spirit personality.)

It is time. The journey begins. . . . My spirit personality comes down out of the Great Round as the screenplay writer, holding its concept of self. It travels on its stream of intending or livingness through the spirit portals at Jupiter, journeys through the LawBelt (the asteroid belt) and the veils of forgetting at the edge of the Bardos, and enters into the physical, into the fetus in my mother's womb. The movie begins.

Spirit Comes Into the Small Round of the Womb

At approximately four and a half months of pregnancy, spirit enters the *small round* of the womb, and the woman gains about three and a half pounds seemingly overnight. Yes, spirit has weight. Prior to that time, a woman carries flesh, protoplasm no different from a fleshy tumor. This mass of cells has no soul, and there is no spirit personality present that will impart humanness to it.

Now the spirit personality has just come from the Great Round, the fifth dimension of spirit, and finds itself confined in a form, a physical body. It has known itself as part of the Everything, connected and without separation. Now it begins to explore this new physical form that is vibrating much more slowly, like slow thought. In the process of exploring this new residence, it moves and pushes against the walls of the placenta. It also stimulates its genitals and discovers that in doing so it can make its body vibrate faster. This triggers memories of what it was like to be pure spirit connected to Source, part of the Everything. It can experience that same aliveness, but now in a physical body.

The fetus is really in both the spirit world and the physical world at this time. A pregnant woman can develop heightened senses and gain access to the world of spirit through her connections with the fetus growing in her womb. As the mother births the child into the world, the child passes through the forgetting circle from the protective, watery environment of the womb into the mold of the image makers its soul wrote into its Book of Life, the script for its movie in this lifetime.

Our Image Makers

Let's take a closer look at our *image makers* (see Fig. 6-a). This is a teaching about the *molding, sculpting,* and *armoring* processes that have shaped us from prenatal lumps of clay into who and what we have become. Every one of us undergoes this process, some more intensely than others. Some do it with pain, some with pleasure, and most with a combination of both, although many people tend to skew their life experiences towards learning through struggle and stress.

This work is accomplished by the image makers, which include aspects of ourselves, other people, institutions, and external events that slowly shape us to fit in, belong, and conform, and to be socially, politically, religiously, and culturally correct. There are eleven image makers: Five are internal, within ourselves (our *emotional, physical, mental, spiritual,* and *sexual* aspects); and six are

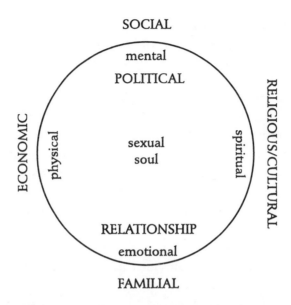

Fig. 6-a The Wheel of Image Makers

external, outside ourselves *(familial, economic, social, religious/cultural,* and *political)*. The most significant and influential of our image makers are parents, siblings, peer groups, and bonded relationship partners.

Familial Image Makers

These image makers include the members of our chosen family, their lifestyles, and their behavior patterns. This includes the number of children in the family, the extended family of grandparents, aunts and uncles, cousins, and other relatives. The family mold also includes race. Our family influences us through emotional energy (emotions are in the South of a wheel) and has the greatest impact on how we will create our personal stories and the myths that define who we think we are. Our early childhood interaction with our family will cause us to store *pain tapes* in our body, like audiotapes that we replay over and over to remind us of our wounding.

For a female child, her universal soul contract is to learn of her own gender specific balance from her mother as the major image maker, and to resolve the paradoxes and conflicts of that balance with the opposite gender parent, the father. Her mother is there to give her the image of the young girl, the woman, and the grandmother, and thus her karmic lessons of physical substance and form. Her father teaches her of the little boy, the man, and the grandfather, and thus the mastery of spiritual form and the dharmic ways. The extent to which we have conflicts with either gender parent is the extent to which we will be displaced or out of alignment and balance in those arenas of experience in our daily life.

Our choice of parents intentionally sets us up for challenges and adversity, a mold that will provide the greatest opportunity for us to learn our karmic lessons and to develop excellence in our character. You may have experienced a childhood that seemed happy and devoid of adversity, with parents who were loving and supportive. Nonetheless, your spirit personality still had to deal with these challenges on a spiritual level. You may begin to see how as you read further.

Social Image Makers

The *social image makers* include the people who have a major influence on us outside of direct blood relations: friends, acquaintances, neighbors, and, in a broader sense, clans, regional, state, and other affiliations. This includes class structure. One of the heaviest social molds is the peer group. It influences our perceptions of reality mightily.

Economic Image Makers

The *economic image makers,* who are part of the mold, determine to a great extent the nature of our existence in the world. They influence our day-to-day existence, our survival, and our economic stability and status. They influence our physical world and our health. They are one of the most influential image makers because

Sleep & Dreamtime,
Tools, Weapons, Skills, & Career

Shelter
&
Clothing

Orgasticness
&
Free Will

Freedom,
Autonomy,
Individuality,
Pleasure, &
Knowledge

Food & Water

Fig. 6-b　The Wheel of Reality Needs

they impact so many aspects of our lives. The Wheel of Reality
Needs (see Fig. 6-b), a wheel within a wheel, describes the nature
of this impact.

South: Food and Water

This is the emotional state of absolute *poverty* and *survival* existence. Lack of food and water—basic necessities—has a tremendous impact on our emotional state of being. It means that at the
lowest level, we are in poverty, starving, or suffering severe mal-
nutrition. People have no will, focus, or intent in this do-or-die situation. At this level, there is very little hope and certainly no
motivation for spiritual self-growth and development.

North: Sleep and Dreamtime, Tools,
Weapons, Skills, and Career

This is the pivotal place for us to change the economic image making. If we have all these things, we have the knowledge and capability to move out of survival into *adequacy*. Therefore, our mind is free and at ease, leading to less emotional trauma. A healthy, balanced adult needs only about two and a half hours of deep sleep at night. Even more important than food, we need to dream. If we are deprived of dreamtime beyond four days and four nights, we will become hallucinatory. With each day that passes, the condition will become more severe until after about fourteen days, when the person will go insane. It has been documented that psychotic patients frequently do not dream.

Dreaming is essential to our well-being because it is the way in which we stay connected to our higher self. Because life itself is a dream, if we do not have the asleep dreaming time, our very sense of reality becomes warped and distorted. Dreaming helps us sort reality and give it clear definition. It gives us stability of thought, peace of mind, and clarity of will.

Some people say they never or rarely dream. This isn't true. They just don't remember their dreaming.

West: Shelter and Clothing

This affects our physical body and our material, physical space. It is the place of death, change, and chaos. We spend an inordinate amount of our income to provide these needs. If we can afford these things for ourselves and our loved ones, we reach a level of *comfort* and *security*.

East: Freedom, Autonomy, Individuality, Pleasure, and Knowledge

This provides *abundance* and *prosperity*. It is necessary to have achieved the South, North, and West reality needs first; then we are free to find a path with heart, gain knowledge, seek the Light, and dance awake our true nature spirit personality in dharma.

Center: Orgasticness and Free Will

Our sexual catalyst energy is our soul force, and it functions in two very important ways. Through this prime mover energy, we exercise our free will in order to be truly *determinate* humans. We use it to increase our orgasticness to insure good health, vitality, and longevity. Orgasticness is our level of intensity of orgasmic release.

Relationships as Image Makers

This includes all relationships other than family, but particularly lover relationships, bondings, marriages, or living commitments (also friendships and guide-student relationships). On one level, everyone you interact with is an image maker. *Relationship image makers* have the greatest impact, even more so than family, once we have entered a relationship with a lover. We reflect out of the family into the relationship how we identify with our opposite-sex parent first, then with the same-sex parent.

We ultimately come back full circle. The conflicts and unresolved issues we see in our parents' relationships are part of the lessons for us to learn as adults with our own bonded partners, unless we got the lessons in the first place and don't have to repeat the folly of our parents in our relationships.

Political Image Makers

Political image makers influence our mind. They influence us through our opinions, points of view (what this tradition refers to as *points of reason*), belief systems, and philosophies. It is critical for us to develop multiple viewing points and get ourselves unstuck from our belief systems in order to hold our own with these image makers.

Knowledge in the Center of the Wheel

All your image makers influence your acquisition of knowledge. Most of them attempt to get you to focus attention away from yourself. They take away your power, intentionally or otherwise, because you give your power to them. If you do not have self-knowledge, you can easily get caught in their trap and succumb to the painful process of trying to fit in, belong, and conform as a result of the molding, sculpting, and armoring.

Sculpting

The Elders say that the little child is born into trust and innocence, cast in the *mold* of its image makers. A newborn child in the
care and nurturing of its parents and other image makers is like a
block of stone or wood in the hands of a sculptor. A great sculptor
will not impose her will upon the wood or stone, nor does she predetermine the form she is going to sculpt. She simply communicates with it, sees the spirit of what truly exists, and then cuts away
everything that is hiding that spirit, thus freeing it.

Most adults, unfortunately, are not great sculptors. They are
more like amateur carvers and have preconceived ideas of how a
young child, particularly *their* child, should develop and ultimately
turn out. They *sculpt* the child into a creature that they hope will
reflect their philosophies, beliefs, and cultural and religious biases,
thus influencing the child's concepts of self as well as its worldview.
Despite their love for the child, their own insecurities and wounding often blind them to the true nature spirit within the child.
Therefore, we grow up becoming something we are not in order to
fit in, belong, and conform to our family, peer group, and society
in general. We lose our connection, not only to our own true nature
spirit personality, but also to the Source from which we came.

*Jan: When I came out into the mold, my image makers, primarily my par-
ents, begin to carve me in the process called sculpting, trying to get me to
fit into their perceptual reality. My little girl in my higher self was a jaguar,
but I chose parents who wanted a pussycat and were convinced that was
who I was.*

A child is an adept little actor and begins to define itself and its
immediate world by miming, copying, and imitating everything it
sees and hears—spoken language, body language, facial expressions, emotional content, mental thought forms. Thus, we become
little pretenders.

Jan: *So I, too, became the little actress in my movie, pretending in order to fit in, belong, and conform to the way in which my parents were carving me. I mimicked and copied them and the other image makers in my young world, and the jaguar essence of my soul was masked little by little by a pussycat, thinking that its role in life was to be just that—friendly, non-threatening, agreeable, passive, obedient, and very shy. These are not negative attributes in and of themselves, but they became formidable because they masked my true spirit personality. This is like walking dead—memory of true nature spirit trapped and lost in forgetfulness. Thus began the development of my* **shideh,** *my* **karmic pretender ego,** *and the chatter of the inner dialogue, which we call our* **pretender voices.***

So I slowly developed aspects of myself that this tradition calls the **needy, wounded, abandoned child** *and the* **mask of self-pity,** *hiding my spirit personality from myself because I was believing more and more that I was something else.*

Once in a while, when I went really deep inside myself, I felt the passion and lust to be a jaguar, free to step into its power, its prowess, its beauty. Since I couldn't roar for real, I acted out the jaguar in a rich fantasy life filled with characters and situations that expressed my yearning for freedom to be who I was. The parents in my acted-out fantasies were almost the opposite of my real parents, and I was free to stretch my imagination, take risks, and exercise my will and creative originality. I traveled the world, was sexually free (what a fantasy for such a young one!), and was not afraid of any risk or danger. In fact, I welcomed the challenges and sought the edges of experience. My "world" was magickal and happy.

I became very knowledgeable in the field of astronomy, spending night after night gazing into the heavens, especially in the summer, when the Milky Way spread across the sky like a glittering carpet. I imagined traveling among the stars and encountering other beings. These fanciful journeys were my yearnings to stay connected to that bigger landscape of my soul. Many of us are star children—children of the Sskwanasie. We carry that memory in our body, and while spirit yearns for expression in the physical, it also yearns to embrace the infinite.

The pussycat couldn't achieve this. And when my jaguar roared "for real" in its own unique way, more often than not my parents would put the lid on, allow only what they were comfortable with, or reprimand me. They would patronize me or disallow my excitement as frivolous child's play and bursts of fanciful imagination—something they determined I would grow out of.

At the time, I wasn't really conscious of experiencing pain at their attitude. But years later, as an adult, I came across some old diaries from those early years, and I was shocked to discover the pain and tears on those pages and the skewing and warping I did to make it all seem okay through blatant denial of who I was and pretending everything was "for the best." Thus, I became, as we all do, a co-conspirator in the sculpting process.

The shamanic recapitulation I have done within the Sweet Medicine SunDance tradition has revealed even more clearly to me the struggle that was going on between my jaguar's yearning to roar and my pussycat's need to survive and secure the love and approval of my parents, whom I loved more than anything.

When adults become parents, they often don't realize the incredible cruelty they inflict on their children when they withhold love and approval as tools in their sculpting kits. They tend to keep their children within the confines of their parental comfort zone. Many children today who are diagnosed with attention deficit disorder (ADD) and are given prescriptive drugs are really victims of adults' inability to cope with their imagination and energy, so they are put in "socially and medically correct" straitjackets. This process, for everyone, takes place at the subconscious level, for parents and teachers do the best they know how to do, given how they have been taught and trained. It is time to learn a different way of nurturing young life, to gain an understanding of the spirit personalities that are screaming and struggling to emerge free.

We carry the molded and sculpted image of ourselves—this false identity—into adulthood. What have you been sculpted into? What is your true nature spirit personality? Are you an eagle that has been sculpted into a turkey? A horse sculpted into a wolf? A hummingbird sculpted into a cat? A turtle sculpted into a hare?

As an adult, you are now your own sculptor and can, indeed must, resculpt yourself into your true nature in the Light.

In keeping with the movie analogy: Realize that as the screenplay writer, you can continue to rewrite and edit your movie in process. You are the director, producer, and hero in the movie called your *Experience of Life*. Wake up to who you really are. Be awake and alert to those moments when, deep inside, you *feel* a rush of excitement and the passion of your natural self surging through your body, and you hear a song singing inside you. Don't stop the song. Don't stop the rush. Embrace them. You can create your life the way you want it to be, as it was meant to be. You are already the writer of your script and the producer and director of your own movie. Consciously and decisively make an award-winning movie, and cast yourself as the star!

Armoring

As we have described, we have all been sculpted into something we are not. The process of molding and sculpting creates pain because our true nature has been refigured to conform to the values and desires of the image makers. The minute we are repressed or shut down, or not acknowledged as the jaguar spirit we truly are, but instead repressed into the pussycat or whatever they want us to be, this shuts down our natural life force. To protect ourselves from the pain, we begin a process called *armoring*. From the moment you were born, and your body vibration slowed down, your body began to tighten itself and restrict its natural breathing rhythm. You began to armor and plate your body in order to anesthetize yourself against the pain of the destruction of your true nature spirit personality. You did this by limiting your imagination and becoming more and more emotional.

Our natural feelings of power and the power of those natural feelings, when repressed and sculpted, contribute to our loss of emotional balance and control, and we exhibit emotionality. Emotions are learned responses, and we become emotional to accommodate and survive the demands and sculpting of our image makers. The expression of our feelings is the source of our power, and that connection slowly weakens. We give that power away, even as little children, as we emulate our image makers, in order to survive their emotions and stress, their idiosyncrasies, their rules and laws, their do's and don'ts.

Armoring, then, is anything that puts pain into our body, slows our metabolism and vibratory rate, and puts the lid on our imagination and originality. Armoring is like placing a *pain tape* into our body. In other words, we bury our life experiences in the form and cellular structure of our body, and more often than not, many more pain tapes than pleasure tapes get stored there. The pain we experience is not necessarily physical; it is often spiritual, emotional, mental, or sexual pain that we are not even aware of at the time.

Our body is composed primarily of water, trace minerals, and metals inside a biological electromagnetic energy field that is our aura, or luminosity. Traumatic or emotionally charged moments produce an electromagnetic discharge that causes solidification in the metallic and mineral components of the body. With water as a natural conductor, this causes a metal plating to develop at each of the major zones of energy in the body that guide and dictate our health. This causes a physical shut down of our ability to manifest our life force energy freely. The chakras become dysfunctional, and since each of them is an energy center that guides vital organs of the body, these organs become dysfunctional. The end result is evident. Armoring accelerates the cellular death rate and causes us to age, so the more we reactivate the pain tapes, the more we age.

Shamanic practitioners have always utilized acupressure, breathing techniques, and shamanic trance states in order to effectively remove the solidification of the armoring that looks, literally, like a suit of armor. The use of crystals also helps to amplify the body's vibration and dislodge energy blocks.

While anesthetizing ourselves against the pain, we also armor ourselves against our own pleasure. Consider the effect novocaine has on your mouth when you visit the dentist. The numbness will definitely dull or alleviate the pain, but if you try to kiss someone you will find you will not feel pleasure either.

All the pain tapes we carry in our body also prevent us from experiencing the attributes of our humanness—health, hope, harmony, happiness, and humor. They rob us of joy and make us much more susceptible to sickness, disease, illness, and aging, and ultimately cause our premature demise, much short of our body's intended built-in life span, which the Twisted Hairs maintain is 135 years at a minimum.

This armoring process is ongoing and takes place most intensely from birth to six years of age, and then again from nine to twelve. From six to puberty, armoring and sculpting progress in our bodies hand in hand. At puberty and in young adulthood, we need to begin our own process of sculpting.

Our higher goal is to crack the mold, become our own sculptors, and de-armor the pain, thus freeing our bodies into their natural state of breathing and aliveness. In this way, we balance the choreography of our energy and establish a warrior's freedom and autonomy.

Armoring Around Our Sexuality

The process of birth itself, often painful and traumatic, can armor us because we are birthed into the unknown out of the warm security of the womb and separated from the only life line we have known in the physical. Historically, the harsh, sterile birthing environments in hospitals contributed to this painful entry into the *life round*. Although the medical profession is changing and birthing practices are becoming much more "friendly," newborns are still too often slapped on their rear to start their breathing and taken immediately from the mother, thus making the separation more acute.

The greatest armoring, however, is done around our sexuality, which is a natural expression of who we are. It is our soul force and gives us our identity as human beings. A baby, in its seventh month in the womb, will often pleasure itself in order to rotate so it can move down the birth canal properly. At birth it instinctively knows that its body is supposed to vibrate faster, so it plays with its genitals to soothe its body. When its parents slap its hands or re-move them from its genitals, or scold "No, no!" the child armors. Our image makers signal that the pleasure we naturally feel in our bodies which replicates the higher vibratory level of spirit, and which feels blissful and good, is, in fact, unnatural and wrong and appears to cause withdrawal of parental love. We experience some-thing like metal plating, a heaviness in the body brought about as a reaction to pain—physical *and* spiritual pain. This slows down the body, throws it out of balance, and ushers in the beginnings of sex-ual repression.

Orgasm: A Body Tune-up

Physiological orgasmic response makes us humans unique. No other animals experience orgasm. They have intercourse; they ejac-ulate, ovulate, and of course they bear offspring. But they do not experience body orgasm. There is not a single female of the animal kingdom that has a clitoris or a G-spot, which are a woman's plea-sure points, and only the two-legged male has a mons glans and a pleasure zone underneath the testicles.

How is it that the Great Spirit gave us a piece of anatomy whose only purpose is orgasm and pleasure? Its purpose is to in-crease the vibrational rate (*orende*) of our physiological body and maintain good health. The faster our body vibrates, the healthier it is. Every time you have an orgasm, you are getting a body tune-up, just as when you tune up your car—the mechanic changes the points, adjusts the carburetor, sets the timing, and so on. That is all. This has nothing to do with relationship, marriage, love, or religion. In fact, the body will naturally experience orgasm every eleven days, as its innate means of elevating the immune system and maintaining good health.

The Rites of Passage

As our sexual energy reawakens at puberty, we go through a great transition, and we enter a new arena of experience. Earth peoples have always had a rite of passage to allow this to take place in a way that honors the sacredness of the young people's life force energy. They learned to respect and honor that within themselves. The rites of passage were critical ceremonies acknowledging young men and young women for their beauty, talent, and uniqueness. They signaled young people's spiritual and sexual awakening and welcomed them with celebration into young adulthood as responsible members of the community. The rites of passage also helped the individual to answer a very important question: "Who am I?"

Today that is lost. The few rites of passage that are still practiced have largely become religious rituals with little or no ceremonial meaning, and they are usually designed to repress the sexual energy, which naturally catalyzes and awakens the psychic abilities, our heightened intuitive senses.

Our basic human nature yearns for rites of passage, to be initiated into a group, to be recognized and accepted for who we are. Because society fails to preserve and maintain the rites of passage, young people often create their own. The drama, initiation, and structure of street gangs, for example, are a form of rites of passage ritual. As destructive as they may be, they provide a way for us to transition from childhood into young adulthood. We receive recognition here and feel that we are "somebody." This is a way of announcing ourselves to the world in the absence of honoring by the adults in our lives. Other forms of initiation include body piercing, smoking, alcohol and drug use, hazing, and more commonly, acts of violence.

Our confusion about feelings in our physical body, depression, and even violence, particularly among young people, result largely from the loss of rites of passage and from the sexual repression perpetrated by many religions and religious image makers. One of religion's most potent tools is the guilt, blame, and shame perpetrated around our sexuality. This is a form of violence because our sexual energy sparks all other aspects of ourselves. Too often we trudge through life instead of dancing.

We Also Sculpt Ourselves

Ironically, as the image makers carve us into their own image of us, we are also trying to sculpt ourselves into our true nature spirit personalities, a little at a time, very often not knowing what image we are trying to uncover, but knowing there is something more there calling to us all the same. Our own uniqueness and self-worth cannot be externally determined for us by others, nor can our character be carved out of the substance of our being by others. We must become our own sculptor.

Paradoxically, at the same time, we are also sculpting ourselves to fit in, belong, and conform. Although this seems to be a major contradiction, it is really a matter of survival.

Jan: I would not have survived in my household if I had not sculpted myself to fit in and not make waves. If I had been a rebellious kid, there would have been hell to pay. My father was strong-willed, and his word was law in my family. In the last half of his life, he was a functioning alcoholic, and we were always on alert for an unexpected tirade or for verbal and emotional storms.

My mother most always gave in to my father's wishes to keep peace and to keep him happy. Although my father seemed to be the primary and most influential image maker who caused me anguish and pain, I realized years later that my mother's quiet acquiescence had no less impact, for she often asked me to subvert or deny my naturalness and my feelings in order to appease my father. She was not the champion I needed to keep my true nature identity intact and to develop confidence and a true measure of my worth. My spirit knew this, and I went along with the program most of the time.

During the early formative years, the brain chatter, the karmic pretender voices, develop and start to take command of our behavior and our reality. They very often echo the sculpting voices of our parents, and some of mine sounded like this:

"Just listen to me and you will never go wrong." (Dad mostly)
"Don't let people know you too well." (Dad's voice)

"Be satisfied with good enough." (Dad's voice)
"It's important to be serious; otherwise, people will think you're a fool."
    (Dad's voice)
"It doesn't matter." (Mom's voice)
"It's not important." (Mom's voice)
"The greatest pleasure in life is making other people happy." (Mom's voice)
"Just keep peace." (Mom's voice)

Now, life is all about choices, even in childhood. We come into this life with a predispositional tendency based on the mold we sketched out in our Book of Life. I could have chosen to rebel, to run away from home as soon as I could, or to constantly war with and challenge my father's authority. There are those who make these choices. Our predispositional nature, how we choose to fit in and survive within the mold, is key to the accomplishment of our intent in coming into the physical in the first place, key to learning our karmic lessons and fulfilling our soul contracts. It gets us to adulthood.

As adults, then, our task is not to bemoan the dysfunction of our parents and our early childhood as though that experience victimized us (psychology dwells too much on that), but rather to find the gain, the payoff, and the clues to what our soul contracts were/are, and to make the most of that knowledge. The process of *recapitulation* (see Appendix A) is a powerful tool that helps us to revisit our life and discover the reality of our experiences, as opposed to our illusions and stories about it distorted by emotional charge and pretense.

Our Process of Experience and Our Motivational Intent

Jan: *Since I was not encouraged to trust my own passions and instincts, to value my spontaneity and my own sense of right and wrong, I sought approval, recognition, acceptance, security, and, ultimately, my very identity from those image makers closest to me.*

We frantically look outside ourselves to the external image

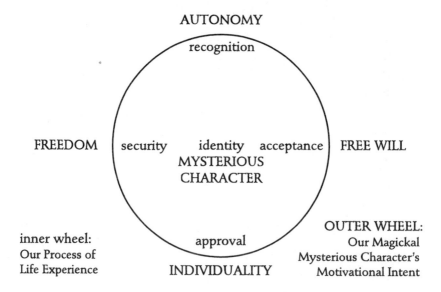

Fig. 6-c   *Motivational Intent/Process of Life*
Experience Wheel

makers to satisfy our need for approval, recognition, acceptance, security, and identity, and we strive the hardest to get these from our parents. This is often our greatest source of stress.

Part of our task of resculpting ourselves, of rewriting our screenplay, is to awaken to the knowledge that we are the source of our own approval, security, recognition, acceptance, and identity. No one outside ourselves can provide these for us without our further deadening ourselves, further encoding into pattern our illusion of ourselves as being something we are not. If we are willing to find those resources within ourselves and step into our own circle of determination, we then dance on the Motivational Intent/Process of Life Experience Wheel in balance with our elemental energies, discover our true nature, and develop our character (see Fig. 6-c).

South: Approval

A small child wants more than anything to express its individuality, but because of the influence of its image makers, instead of accepting and integrating *emotional individuality*, it integrates *emotional approval*. As adults we strive to be socially correct because we want to feel good emotionally about how others are interacting with us and know we are loved. In so doing, we give our power away and armor more.

By giving fluidly with your emotions and loving yourself, you create your own *individuality*.

West: Security

The little child wants physical freedom to learn. Instead, it substitutes *physical security*. We want to know and to be assured that our physical needs are being met. Many people sacrifice their individuality, autonomy, and freedom for a guarantee of physical security, expecting the government, the corporation, or someone else to take care of them. The only guarantee of physical security we have is our skill in physical mastery.

By properly holding and transforming energy in our physical body, by taking decisive action in the Now, we step into *personal freedom*.

North: Recognition

Mental autonomy means being free to learn in the way that is natural for us. Unfortunately, the young child quickly learns to seek *mental recognition* instead, because pressure from parents and our educational institutions force children to learn a certain way, whether it is natural for them or not. Children then receive recognition only when they succeed in what for many is a very unnatural modality. We strive to be politically correct because we want to feel comfortable mentally with others' perceptions of us. This comes out of our belief systems, comparisons, and expectations. It is important for us to know that our actions are okay according to others' viewpoints.

Mental recognition has a lot to do with credibility, credentials, and licensing bestowed by an agency, an institution, or by another person. You are never what someone has said you are on paper.

You are what you can do physically and consistently with your excellence all the time. That is your credibility, your own personal recognition.

By being mentally receptive and utilizing multiple viewing points, you recognize that only you can determine whether or not your actions are okay; thus, you gain *autonomy*.

East: Acceptance

Very often we feel that if we are not approved of and recognized, we will not be accepted. This is a cultural and religious orientation. A small child needs to exercise the free will of its *hokkshideh*, its higher self, to fulfill its destiny and to become enlightened. Our image makers more often than not steer us into institutional religion and teach us to seek *spiritual acceptance* instead. We forfeit our free will destiny for a dogmatic belief system. Do you have a personal relationship with spirit based on your unique natural feeling and heart connection with destiny, or have you capitulated to a religious dogma?

By letting your spirit determine your destiny, you will act decisively because it is your *free-will* determination to do so, not because it is what others accept.

Center Identity

It is through our sexuality, the expression of our soul force energy, that we get our truest *identity*. Unfortunately, if we are operating on this wheel, we take our cue from our image makers. So what is the result? A molded, sculpted, and armored child. Sexually it wants to experience its character, its mystery, and its magick. Instead, it is given identity. It is told who and what it is.

By embracing your true nature through your spiritual sexuality, your soul force energy and your orgastic potential, you establish yourself as the source of your own beingness. You create and refine your own *mysterious character*.

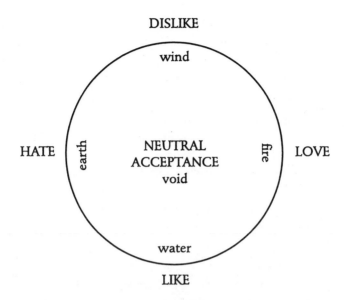

Fig 6-d   The Five Perceptions of Reality Wheel

The Five Perceptions of Reality

From the time we are children, we disempower ourselves because we want to be liked and loved (see Fig. 6-d). We insist on being liked and loved at all costs, and we do not accept ourselves or feel worthy unless we are liked and loved. We constantly reach out for this external energy verification, the "feel good" barometer, not realizing that how the image makers see us is not who we are at all. Needing emotional approval more than anything, we experience incredible pain and anxiety as a result.

This chronic concern about what other people think of us is an important factor in keeping us stuck in the personality and the events focus of our *karmic pretender ego*, continually chasing our tail again and again in our karmic cycles of reincarnation.

Let's take a look at how the Five Perceptions of Reality Wheel works. Assume for a moment that you are an impeccable human being, outstanding at everything you do, the epitome of integrity, dignity, and respect. There will still be people who observe your actions and exclaim, "I hate her. She's horrible! Her attitude and behaviors are contrary to everything I believe in!" and go to great lengths to vilify and destroy you. Hate sits in the West on the wheel because it is a very physical response.

On the other hand, there may be those who react 180 degrees opposite, and think you are just great. "Wow! You're great! You're so loving, understanding, and wise!" They will love you, maybe even worship you and try to make you an exalted guru. Love sits in the East of the wheel and is a spiritual energy.

Or some may say of you in your impeccable state, "Boy, you're a flake. I don't feel comfortable around you." They may see you as an eccentric and a nuisance. They dislike you. Dislike sits in the North and is a mental energy called prejudice or bias.

Or some may say, "I really like you. You're fun to hang out with." Here, in the South, you have a friend, companion, and ally. Like is an emotional response.

Then there are those who are neutral towards you. They are indifferent, not caring about you one way or the other because they are too busy with their own lives to really be concerned about who you are or what you are doing. Neutrality is the most common perception. Ironically, it is often the neutral or indifferent response that we have the hardest time with. Our ego gets bruised because no response indicates that we have made no impact, that we're not important enough for them to notice. Very often we will do something, anything, to get a response from someone, even if it is a dislike response. We can't stand not knowing what a person thinks of us.

Now, examine this wheel as a whole. We spend enormous amounts of life force energy, years of our lives, trying to be loved or liked when the odds are three out of five that we aren't going to get it! The important question here is: "Do you like and love yourself?"

So stop living your life worrying about what others think about what you do. The Twisted Hairs Golden Rule is an excellent principle to live by, and it differs somewhat from the commonly used Golden Rule. The Golden Rule as most people have been taught is: "Do unto others as you would have them do unto you." The Twisted Hairs Golden Rule teaches: "Do unto others whatever you choose to do because that is what you are doing all the time anyway. However, when you do choose to do something, take full responsibility for the consequences of your actions, and try to do that which will bring the greatest good for all concerned." This version emphasizes discernment of reality and acceptance of personal responsibility for mutual benefit and welfare.

Every day when you do not take an action that will make you a part of the process of change, a part of the solutions for the planet, ask yourself, "Am I sitting on the fence because I want to be loved and liked? Am I not taking decisive action on an issue because I'm worried about what people will think?" Take action and make a difference. Today. Tomorrow. Do it, and quit worrying about how people are going to perceive you, because there is nothing you can do about that. What they choose to perceive has nothing to do with what you are really doing. If you can achieve this, you will feel much better, and you will have much more freedom in your world.

What patterns of behavior did you develop to fit in, belong, and conform? How did you survive and armor yourself against the pain of being sculpted into something you were not? In what ways are you still doing that today? What disempowering, eroding, belittling, obnoxious, wretched pretender voices did you develop? Are they still chattering away inside your head, sabotaging your true nature?

Molding, sculpting, and armoring numb us to life, create elemental imbalance, and separate us from ourselves, from one another, and from Nature—the natural environment that is part of the mold. We each experience this differently, but to a greater or lesser degree we all experience this separation.

In the next chapter, we will explore the three basic strategies we adopt to help us survive the molding, sculpting, and armoring and reach adulthood.

7

Our Core Personality and Moods of Stalking

The *core personality* is a creation of the image makers and is a product of the mold we explored in the previous chapter. It is that aspect of yourself which is chosen before you are born, begins to develop in the womb, and manifests soon after birth. Established by one year of age and locked into place by age three, it is your way of choosing how to survive and confront the world of the image makers and tyrants and stay integrated with a feeling of presence of self, the essence of who you are. It is the formulation of the blank lump of clay upon which your entire personality will be built. The core personality determines how you design and choreograph yourself in the world, and it is how you stabilize yourself in an emergency. In other words, one's core personality is always revealed in high stress and emergency situations.

There are three core personalities which the Twisted Hairs, with their sense of humor and lack of self-importance, refer to as the *Do-Gooder,* the *Fart,* and the *Space Cadet.* With tags like these, they encourage us to lighten up and not take ourselves so seriously. Carlos Castaneda has described these three core personalities in his work. Each of us always adopts only one of the three core personalities, never a combination.

The spirit of the unborn child, while still in the womb, reviews its past lifetimes and examines what kind of a personality has been written into its movie script. Interestingly, the core personality already demonstrates itself to the mother while it is still in the womb. The baby will kick and move in a certain modality based on the core personality that is forming. A Do-Gooder strokes and almost massages the wall of the uterus. The Fart treats the walls of the womb like a punching bag. The Space Cadet is unpredictable and kicks randomly. Already they are telegraphing the nature of their formative personalities.

The three core personalities exhibit an *imbalanced (dark) side* and a *power (light) side*. Most of us will struggle in the imbalanced dark side of our core personality until we have reached a level of maturity where we begin to refine our character. Because of this, the descriptions presented first are of the imbalanced attributes of the core personalities, which we exhibit when we are *at the effect of* our own inner tyrant, other tyrants, and life in general, and when we are acting as the pure product of our molding, sculpting, and armoring.

Even though you may think that certain parts of these descriptions don't fit you or that you are a combination of all three, you have only one core personality. Many things can alter the appearance of your core personality to such an extent that it seems you have mastered certain aspects of it. As you become awake, aware, and alert and begin to break the mold, resculpt, and de-armor, these aspects of the core personality become less pronounced and you begin to exhibit more of the power side of your core personality, which is also described here. In moments of crisis and trauma, however, you will, without exception, revert back to the shadow of your core personality, until you have mastered the core personality and are living completely in the light side.

Developing the Core Personality

The spirit personality in the unborn child begins to pick up signals from its mother and the outside world through the umbilical cord. It begins to formulate a core personality that will help it to survive and adapt in the world. Chosen by our higher self to guide us through change, chaos, and stress, the core personality holds the intent of this lifetime and enables us to integrate the physical skills of the last lifetime.

The key words are *survival adaptability*. The adaptability of a particular core personality within the selected mold of image makers enables us to fit in, belong, and conform and, therefore, to survive the drama of the molding, sculpting, and armoring. The core personality strives to maintain its individual autonomy and get us to adulthood. In this process, we pass through two stages: the needy, wounded, abandoned child and the angry, vengeful, manipulative adult.

In the womb, the spirit personality receives signals about its mother's feelings regarding her pregnancy: Is she happy and looking forward to this child with joy and a sense of fulfillment? Is she resentful that the birth of this child will intrude on her career and her freedom? Is she fearful and unsure? Does she recognize and gladly accept the great responsibility of raising a child that she has dreamed into her life? There are other signals: Is the relationship between mother and father loving and happy? Do they make love often, enjoying their sexuality, their lust, their passion? On a physical level, is the mother well-nourished?

Jan: My spirit personality in the womb quickly clued into the fact that I had come into a mold that was pretty much a "My way or the highway," "Be nice," and "Don't rock the boat," kind of mold. There was no doubt I needed a Do-Gooder core personality to survive this adventure in my evolutionary journey. Yet spirit personality also knew that this was the furnace that could forge my soul's potential into spiritual gold. Paradox and duality.

Your core personality is your *way* of doing. It is at the center or core of your being. Do-Gooders utilize interaction and fitting in by helping others. Space Cadets utilize invisibility and leave the scene, either physically, mentally, emotionally, spiritually, or sexually. Farts get tough; whenever they perceive that their survival is at stake, they will fight rather than become a victim.

The Do-Gooder

The Dark Side of the Do-Gooder

Do-Gooders want to do good for others, save the world, and be liked in the process, especially by their peer group. They are overly concerned with their image, wanting to look good in other people's eyes. They care about being accepted, acknowledged, and recognized as genuine and honest. Do-Gooders must fit in, belong, and conform; they are sensitive to being excluded from any group or situation. They appear to do good for others in order to feel good about themselves. This is called being caught in self-pity, which catches us all, but particularly the Do-Gooder.

Do-Gooders tend to be naive and gullible, but nonetheless, they are convinced they know what is best for you. They have a tendency to overload themselves, take on more than they can handle to serve causes or the needs of others, then stress out and blame others for it. They are congenial and friendly, people you like to know. Because they seek so much validation from others, they do not exhibit a high degree of initiative and follow-through to completion if left alone. However, give them direction and they get results, no matter how difficult the situation or overwhelming the odds. They make excellent secretaries, nurses, assistants, teachers—those in support and service-oriented positions.

Let's examine the Do-Gooder's tendencies in each of the five aspects of self.

Emotionally: Do-Gooders want everything to be okay and are uncomfortable with conflict, especially when yelling is a part of it. They are sensitive to any issue having to do with healing, friendship, and comradeship. Do-Gooders are doers, but because they do not like to stand alone or take on solitary leadership, their dilemma is compounded if others in their presence are in danger, especially when they are responsible for the situation.

Physically: Do-Gooders carry a great deal of stress in their body, because in their focus on doing good for others and fitting in, they tend to disregard the signals of tiredness, fatigue, or imbalance their body sends. They are oblivious to what is going on in their body.

Mentally: Do-Gooders are the believers who most often take up the cause for the underdog and work hard to uphold their belief systems and philosophies.

Spiritually: Do-Gooders make great evangelists, for they save you even if it kills you! They can be fanatic and self-righteous, in which case they will not accept that you have your own wisdom and your own way.

Sexually: Do-Gooders have a tendency to give their power away when in a sexual relationship. They may appear to be or feel like a victim. Generally, they are givers and, therefore, they have difficulty receiving pleasure. However, this can be turned around rather simply by telling them that what gives you pleasure is to give to them—in other words, for them to receive from you.

Do-Gooders' task is to learn that doing good must be in alignment with Sacred Law. They must establish their own measure of self-worth rather than seek it from others. This is true for all of us, but particularly for Do-Gooders.

Renegade Do-Gooder: The *renegade* or *turn-around* core personality is exhibited by those persons who have matured somewhat in their core personality and are in the process of moving into the light power side.

These Do-Gooders are helpful with no attachment to the outcome of their actions. They are optimistic, sometimes to a fault. They are tenacious and disciplined in their behavior.

The Wave Dancer: The Light Side of the Do-Gooder

In their light power side, Do-Gooders are called *Wave Dancers,* as they can catch the flow of energies, the waves of change, and flow with them. They can do good simply because it feels good, thus stepping out of their self-pity and self-importance. Their ultimate sense of perfection is to become responsible for what they do and why they do it. They can be systematic, good organizers, determined and persistent, and incredibly productive without getting tired. Wave Dancers get things done. They are extremely good at problem resolution and solution, especially if you give them the advantages of solving the problem. If they learn Sacred Law, they are excellent in ceremony and their alchemy is impeccable. They will bring much beauty to it. Wave Dancers have mastered their do-gooding so that they help only when they have been asked to help. In their helping they also know that they can and must help only until recipients are capable of helping themselves. Wave Dancers are excellent lovers. Motivate them to honor themselves, and they will motivate themselves into discipline.

The Fart

The Dark Side of the Fart

Farts are not easily liked because they are domineering and manipulative. They are commonly petty, vindictive, and self-centered; rarely pleased; and usually insecure. In many ways, they are natural sociopaths. They are usually ill at ease and tense. Their main focus, above all else, is survival adaptability. Their greatest weakness is also their greatest strength in that they will sacrifice all for their survival. They are always the ones who take initiative, take immediate action, and in doing so, take control and lead. They may not like being "the leader," yet it is a natural instinct for them. They surreptitiously seek out leadership as a way of insuring their own survival. Often what appeals to them is the power behind leadership, and they find having to deal with emotions very distasteful. They dazzle you with brilliance and blind you with bullshit, as they are natural storytellers. Tending to be "loners," they have an exaggerated sense of privacy. As righteousness is an issue for them, their dogmatic insistence on things being a certain way is triggered by their survival adaptability. Apologizing is difficult for Farts.

Let's examine a Fart's tendencies in each of the five aspects of self.

Emotionally: Since Farts usually do not care if others like them or not, and since they are unwilling to deal with most emotional issues, they prefer to express whatever they feel and then leave it at that. They are dysfunctional in the emotional aspect, for they do not have access to the same range of emotions that the other types do. They are more cerebral, and at best, emotions do not make sense to them. The way to make Farts pay attention to emotional detail is to make it necessary for their survival.

Physically: Farts thrive in the physical realm. "Live each day for the physical challenge it holds" was Grandfather Two Bears' motto. Boredom is the number one enemy for Farts, and they will push others into activity to avoid this enemy. They generally love being alone, although they also like having close friends share their favorite physical activities.

Mentally: Farts tend to be fast and paradoxical in their mental aspect. They are very quick to see the overview, the overall picture. However, they see only the details essential to survival, and thus miss many details which they hate to be bothered with.

Spiritually: Farts are the greatest nonbelievers and are usually nonreligious. Their concept of spirit is measured by effectiveness. A common theme among Farts is conflict and issue with rules and laws.

Sexually: Life, for Farts, is a process of seduction. They validate their existence through the energetic highs gained from this process. Their sexuality is raw (which is often disliked and seen as crude by Space Cadets and Do-Gooders), and they may have a proclivity towards sadomasochism.

Farts' major work is to learn that they cannot create their world at the expense of others. They must learn proper alchemy and commit to disciplined action within Sacred Law. Farts tend to rebel against others' rules and laws and dig in their heels rather than change their point of view. They can be very self-destructive as a result. In the extreme, they can become sociopathic. An important part of their work is to lighten up and not take themselves so seriously.

They need to recognize that much of their struggle and survival orientation is of their own design; it is not reality.

Renegade Fart: These Farts are classic rebels who stand alone and very seldom have friends. They absolutely avoid any context wherein they will confront rules and laws that affect them. If their personal survival is not at stake, they do not care about the effect of their own behavior.

The Energy Dancer: The Light Side of the Fart

In their light power side, Farts are called *Energy Dancers.* They have the purest survival instincts of the personalities. Like a cat with nine lives, they will always survive. When put under a great amount of stress, they shine. They seek the unknown for the challenges that lie there. Energy Dancers take responsibility for themselves and step into a natural relaxation. This makes them natural leaders and very survival adaptive. They are able to see the overall picture and the details. In other words, they are able to see what must be done and then do it. Once Farts have developed into Energy Dancers, they will pick good co-leaders. You motivate them by showing them how what they will learn could help them become a better personality, thus enhancing their survival adaptability.

The Space Cadet

The Dark Side of the Space Cadet

Space Cadets have difficulty grounding and being present in the Here and Now. They easily get lost in fantasy and illusion, mistaking that for reality. Because they have difficulty being physically present in a space with attention focused properly, they are easily fragmented. They are great procrastinators and have a horrible sense of timing. Grandfather Two Bears maintained that they are always waiting, and when they finally make up their mind to take action, someone else has already done it. Their conceptual view of reality is never really valid, so they make it valid by finding a context within which the validity of "space" doesn't matter. To that end, they are constantly in illusion about what they perceive to be their psychic abilities and their spiritual connections. They have an exalted view of self based on the illusion of great things to come. However, they do not deliver because they do not have the resources needed to match the fantasy of who they are.

Let's look at how Space Cadets operate in their five aspects of self.

Emotionally: Sensitivity is high in Space Cadets. They quickly assess the probabilities but do not necessarily validate their perceptions. They are naturally artistic, musical, and entertaining. However, they are unwilling to take responsibility for leadership in a group. This makes them avoid situations where this will be demanded. They would rather be in the shadows than put themselves out there and make an impact. They often feel incomplete or unfulfilled because they don't attain the desired results. Since they tend to leave their body and not be present, they are not fully aware they have made an impact; therefore, they don't feel the impact of their actions.

Physically: Unless Space Cadets love the physical activity they are engaged in, they are uncoordinated to the point of being accident prone. They have a tendency to burn out, to run out of energy from doing too many things at the same time. Thinking they have more resources than they do gets them into trouble.

Mentally: Firm mental discipline does not appeal to Space Cadets. They are often well-read but do not retain the specifics of the original context. Their logic is circular; the writer and teacher Hyemeyohsts Storm likened their mind to a pot of stew. They must learn to validate and integrate their knowledge in order to make it their own and be able to use it effectively.

Spiritually: Space Cadets want to be taken care of and want acceptance with minimal requirements. This can make them very gullible and even susceptible to cult energy.

Sexually: Space Cadets are often not present when they are making love. They are out of contact with their body, so their body may experience a good orgasm, but they will not feel the experience. They leave their body, and their orgasm often falls flat. This also causes them to be disconnected from their partner.

Renegade Space Cadet: These Space Cadets make great spies. They do not fit the basic description of Space Cadets, although they may use some of the same strategies. They may want you to see them as such, but they are not at the effect of the dark side of this core personality.

The Star Dancer: The Light Side of the Space Cadet

In their light power side, Space Cadets are called *Star Dancers.* They are creative artists and blissful souls, and the dancing *hey-oehkah* (clown or contrary) jester of the spirit personality that is able to function in multiple levels of awareness and attention. Space Cadets can be fantastic lovers if they stay present. They are almost profound in their ability to be present in and occupy several arenas at once, and pay attention to many things happening. They are the image of the young cadet going off to explore deep space and becoming Captain Kirk, the commander that leads others in discovering the stars. They spin fanciful worlds that not only entertain but lead us into new dimensions and understandings of ourselves and the Universe. They always see the possible within the seemingly impossible.

Warrior's Freedom

Both Space Cadets and Do-Gooders can learn survival adaptability from Farts. Farts can learn compassion, tact, and kindness from Do-Gooders. Do-Gooders can learn how not to take life so seriously and how to gain a broader perspective from Space Cadets.

To enter Warrior's Freedom is to embrace fully the light side of each of these core personalities and then refine our own character. Warrior's Freedom is available only as a choice once the spirit personality has accessed its mysterious character. This means that we have awakened our spirit personality and gained access to our soul essence. We walk in the light of dharma.

Moods of Stalking*

Between birth and nine years of age, we begin to formulate our first stories about ourselves, to describe who we are and explain our fledgling belief systems. Out of our belief systems we acquire what the Twisted Hairs call our *moods of stalking. Stalking* is this tradition's word for acting. A *mood* is how you act, caught right in the middle of the way you believe. Therefore, a mood of stalking is an attitude and an approach, a way of being in the world. In addition to our core personality, we choose two moods of stalking in our attempt to fit in, belong, and conform. These moods of stalking help lock us into a pattern of behaviors and ways of processing our life experiences.

The four basic moods of stalking are *sweetness* in the South, *cunning* in the North, *ruthlessness* in the West, and *patience* in the East (see Fig. 7-a). These moods, along with our core personality, are necessary for our survival. Our higher self chose these moods because it knew these fit our natural abilities and are part of who we really are.

We each have two moods: an *anchoring mood* and a *projecting mood*. Our anchoring mood comes from the physical body awareness and physical actions and interactions of the child. This mood is our *sanctuary box*. We jump inside and say we do not want to deal with this, or know that. It is our escape from self. We use the anchoring mood to hide ourselves from ourselves in our own fortress. It is the way we build our fortress, which keeps us from having to deal realistically with our pain. Therefore, we convince ourselves that we do not have to make changes to awaken to our true spirit personality and connect with our higher self. This will remain an anchoring mood for the rest of our life.

We use the projecting mood to make people see what we want

---

* The following description of the moods of stalking is updated and edited material taken from *The Mirror of Self-Reflection: The Inner Mirror Masks of the Mask of Self-Pity,* by H. S. Reagan (Los Angeles: DTMMS, 1988), pp. 61-68. Edited and reprinted by permission.

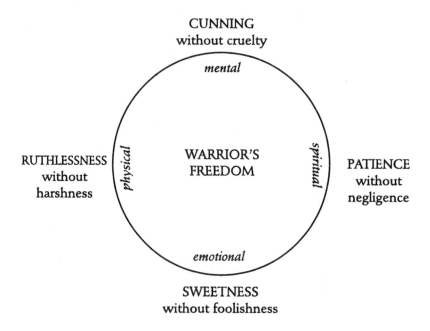

CUNNING
without cruelty

mental

RUTHLESSNESS
without
harshness

physical

WARRIOR'S
FREEDOM

spiritual

PATIENCE
without
negligence

emotional

SWEETNESS
without foolishness

Fig. 7-a   The Moods of Stalking Wheel

them to see. We want to fit in, belong, and conform, and since we do not want others to know who we really are at the core—a Fart, a Do-Gooder, or a Space Cadet—we use a projecting mood to hide or camouflage ourselves, often wearing many masks and disguises. In emergency situations, however, the projecting mood often fails, and then the core personality reveals itself. The projecting mood has emerged as a function of the maturing mental self-concepts by the time the child is seven.

Both the anchoring mood and the projecting mood, along with the core personality, form a persona that wears a mask, which seems to be the most appropriate response at any given moment. We put on this mask to receive external approval, security, recognition, acceptance, and most important, our identity. Our core personality is our attraction in the world. Our anchor mood is our focus of attention, and our projecting mood creates impact in the world.

Life is a ritual. Our movie drama is a ritual in which we do what we do to hide who we really are. We have forgotten who we are, however, so the ritual is meaningless. We elicit a mood to feel good or look good in an environmental context. That mood creates a mask, one of hundreds that we wear. We expend a great deal of energy in this anchoring and projecting game. The moods work to keep us attached to our molded, sculpted, and armored concept of self.

Because we two-leggeds are most often out of balance and alignment, we most often use these moods in the dark. Our key to ultimate survival is to step into their light side. Perfecting the moods will not change our core personality, but we will stop losing energy in the mask dance. Although we have two strong moods by nature and are wise to develop them in the light first, our intent should be to develop all four moods in equal intensity and use them consciously. This means taking full responsibility for ourselves and our actions. In this way, we become unpredictable, uncontrollable, seeming to fit in, belong, and conform while actually walking our talk as free and autonomous individuals.

The Five Aspects of the Moods

Moods of stalking can be expressed through any of our five aspects—emotional (South), physical (West), mental (North), spiritual (East), and sexual (Center). The perfection of a single mood requires being balanced in all five of the aspects of self. They also vary in their expression, depending on our specific core personality and whether they are anchoring moods or projecting moods.

What is presented here is a basic introduction to each of the moods, in their respective directions on the wheel, with enough detail that you can begin to explore these within your own patterns of behavior.

Sweetness Without Foolishness (South)

In the Light: Sweetness is an emotional/water mood and a giving energy. In its purest form, you are not in emotionality; rather, you are authentic with your emotional expression. This mood allows you to establish a deep heart connection. Every mood has a key which tells you whether you are using it in the most appropriate way. The key to sweetness is emotional fluidity. This means you are emotionally honest. You express the emotion and are not at the effect of it. All emotions are valid; how we choose to express them, however, is not always correct. Women have much more difficulty with this than men because they identify who they are through their emotional content. Very often, they interpret emotionality as sensitivity. An incident happens, and they don't deal with it or mention it until much later. They experience two months of distracted attention. Men tend to hold on to emotions and not express them at all. Their emotionality takes the form of emotional expression. They are generally much more mental and try to analyze the situation.

In the Dark: This is sweetness with foolishness, which puts us at the effect of our emotions. Foolishness is defined as deliberate sacrifice and the giving away of our power by putting ourselves into situations that are nonproductive and totally unnecessary. We go into emotionality as a way of not looking at our own closed symbols or dark side, the result of our molding, sculpting, and armoring. As an anchor mood, this manifests as giving ourselves alibis and reasons for not accomplishing what we should accomplish. "I really worked hard, so I can't help it if he's upset." Also, in the dark our priority to nurture ourselves may easily lead into addictions. As a projecting mood, we shift attention onto something else to avoid exposure.

Cunning Without Cruelty (North)

In the Light: This is the air/mental mood of unlimited viewing points and heightened mental awareness. It allows you to accurately perceive reality in different contexts without any of the dark arrows or "tunnel vision" belief systems. Cunning without cruelty has a good sense of humor. People using this mood will not take things so seriously because they do not get locked up in belief systems. This is the key to this mood in its most appropriate form. Philosophy of life is predicated on knowledge. You drop the trappings of credibility conferred upon you by society and establish your credibility through the excellence and effectiveness of your actions.

In the Dark: Cruelty puts us in the dark side of cunning. Frequently cruelty is destructive and comes from a rigid point of view, which can get out of hand. There is a need to believe in only one certain way, and there are many judgments and opinions around why it has to be that way. Consequently, judgment of others who see things differently takes on the sharp edge of cruelty. One way to break out of this modality is to approach all truth as falsehood and all falsehood as truth. Another way is to disrupt our continuity and rhythm of activity and break the patterns. This is the key to developing mental flexibility. With this as an anchor mood, we run an inner dialogue of rationalization and justification, of reasons not to change. With cunning as a projecting mood, we shift the symbols and the ideas in a conversation, like changing the channel, or we may even shift our identity.

Ruthlessness Without Harshness or Greed

In the Light: Ruthlessness is an earth/physical mood, which in its purest form is the complete transcendence of the physical, mortal body into immortal formlessness. It is perfect health. The key to this mood is to have physical stability, strength, and power. This means you must never exhaust the physical resources in your body by either overestimating them or underestimating them, and you must always be honest with yourself about your true physical state in any situation. This mood exhibits the willingness to fail as many times as necessary and make as many mistakes as necessary in order to learn. It is having impeccable survival skills regardless of the environment, along with a commonsense viewing point of the reality of your situation. This mood enables you to persevere, to not be a quitter.

Another key to this mood is the ability to use it with pain of any kind—physical, emotional, mental, spiritual, and sexual. You could not exist without pain, as it is the body's warning system that communicates that you are out of balance. It is a natural part of your paradoxical existence in this third-dimensional tonal world. In addition, if you did not ever experience pain, you would not know pleasure either. Ruthlessness makes it possible for you to "double the pleasure." Pain will increase and persist if you do not recognize it and give it attention. Therefore, with ruthlessness as a mood, focus on the pain with every ounce of intent you have. The pain will disappear. If you are in pain, become pain. If you are in pleasure, become pleasure. You can make the pain or pleasure work for you if you deal with it. The key is to use ruthlessness to double the pleasure.

In the Dark: This is ruthlessness as harshness and greed used for the intentional manipulation of others. Survivability becomes a "con game" where we selfishly make our gains at the expense of others. We manifest a deep inability to "accept" things as they really are, along with a concern about how things should or must be done.

Patience Without Negligence (East)

In the Light: Patience involves open spiritual understanding and a passion and lust for life. Artists often exhibit this mood. Patience is a fire/spiritual mood. In essence, it includes the possession of active will, passive will, and willpower in equal proportions. It is the ability "to do without doing." It allows you to be a *determiner,* or director, of energy. It is the power to grow into the Light, to gather around yourself those allies and spiritual energies that can guide you towards the Light. It enables you to find and follow your path with heart with deep commitment. The key to this mood is spiritual expansiveness, the willingness to "leap into the abyss" and open to knowledge and pleasure.

In the Dark: This is negligence, the avoidance of responsibility. It is the lack of discipline and commitment. In this place, we are convinced of our own righteousness and are prejudiced and judgmental. We try to force nonconformity on others, which is actually conformity to our own view of reality.

Warrior's Freedom (Center)

This is the formlessness that comes with the discovery of, the full recognition of, and the full embrace of your true nature spirit personality.

Take the time to study the attributes of the core personalities and the moods of stalking, and correlate your behavior patterns with them. Begin to observe yourself, particularly in stressful situations, and pay more attention to the behaviors of people around you. Slowly develop a profile of yourself that allows you to identify your moods of stalking and particularly your core personality. As you develop understanding of your own patterns and then of those of your family, friends, and co-workers, you will be able to use this as a tool to improve your relationships and learn how to work more effectively with people.

Develop the discipline of keeping a daily journal. If you use it to record your observations and thoughts as part of your self-study and work with the Wheels of Knowledge presented in this book, you will find it an invaluable tool.

8

Removing the Masks of
Self-Importance and Self-Pity

Inside our core personality there lies a mixed energy. The dark shadow side is dominated by the *shideh* (a Cherokee word derived from the Olmec and Mayan) that translates as "the one who cannot see." The Twisted Hairs often describe the shideh as that part of us that does not acknowledge our true nature spirit personality, our higher self within. To use an example from earlier chapters, it sees itself as the pussycat self, having forgotten its higher jaguar soul essence.

The light side is dominated by our *hokkshideh*, our higher self, "the one who has learned to see," or "the one who has awakened to see that it knows." It is that aspect of our spirit personality that remembers its true nature and shines. It is our magickal mysterious character.

The shideh is our primary definition of self and tenaciously maintains our birth patterns as a result of the molding, sculpting, and armoring. It is our integration into the process of experiencing life as the dream.

The Twisted Hairs refer to the shideh as that aspect of ourselves that believes life is a struggle. In fact, it creates struggle because it is caught in a paradox: While it desires freedom and meaning and purpose in life above all else, it is, at the same time, preoccupied with survival and strives to stay in control at all costs. So the shideh wages battle between the desire for freedom and the need to stay in control and maintain the status quo.

Self-deception is the constant process of our shideh projecting the mask—what it has been molded, sculpted, and armored into—instead of exposing our true nature. Ironically, at the same time, the shideh is that part of us that instigates change, so it is always dealing with death—death of others, death of loved ones, our own death. The energy spent or lost in this fear and deception literally ages the body and guarantees that the enemy of "old age" will take us to a premature death.

Within our conscious and subconscious minds, a battle rages between our *karmic pretender ego,* which listens only to the shideh, and our *dharmic commander ego,* which heeds the wise voice of spiritual attainment of our hokkshideh. Our "brain chatter" and disempowering thoughts, which we refer to as *pretender voices,* distract us from our natural self. They labor on behalf of the karmic pretender ego and the shideh to keep us in karmic pattern within our molding, sculpting, and armoring. The dharmic commander voices, on the other hand, are calling to us to wake up and wage an internal battle to demote the karmic pretender ego and the shideh, and silence the pretender voices. This is a major battle, and a necessary one, for the spiritual warrior.

Have you ever really wanted to change a behavior pattern or stop doing something that no longer served you, and no matter what you tried, that same pattern persisted? That is your shideh hanging on for dear life because it sees change as death. And in fact, it is. The shideh and the karmic pretender ego must die or at least be relegated to minor roles so that the hokkshideh and the dharmic ego can emerge as commanders and set you free.

Assisted by the karmic pretender ego, the shideh tries to take its power and express itself through the core personality. It knows our chosen core personality develops to help us survive in the world, and the shideh's survival depends on the survival adaptability of the core personality, along with the anchoring and projecting moods of stalking to hide itself from itself and from others.

Why does it hide? Basically, we don't want others to know who we really are, because the shideh sees the core personality as something undesirable, albeit necessary. So we put on different masks and hide behind them. We develop two primary masks: The mask of self-importance is what we project out to others, and the mask of self-pity is the inner mask underneath, hiding us from ourselves. Every mask we wear is really a double mask.

The Mask of Self-Pity

The shideh wears the inner mask of *self-pity* underneath all masks. This mask summarizes our unconscious reaction to the molding, sculpting, and armoring by our image makers and the tyrants who have created the pussycat instead of the jaguar. We feel sorry for ourselves ("poor me") because of what has happened. The mask of self-pity arises out of our pain at being carved into something we are not. But we have forgotten the jaguar and are convinced that we are the pussycat; we wear the mask of self-pity and its counterpart, the mask of *self-importance*, unconsciously, as part of our identity. We forget we are wearing it. This makes it very difficult to examine ourselves, as the eyes through which we see ourselves are distorted by these two masks, neither of which sees reality as it truly is.

The mask of self-pity is anchored in the past and deeply rooted in the "needy child," which consists of three parts:

1. Our inner child has been "wounded."

2. Our inner child has become extremely "needy" for healing to the degree that the neediness is practically impossible to meet, as that neediness is an intimate part of its very identity.

3. Our inner child experiences being "abandoned" because its needs are never met to its satisfaction.

The mask of self-pity is how we hide so as not to show our true feelings; it is a shield against vulnerability. When we feel sorry for ourselves, we are hurting inside; we often feel helpless and hopeless. This mask sabotages our ability to make positive change in our life; no matter what we do, nothing seems to change. We begin to adopt a pitiful attitude and insist that life is not fair. We don't want to acknowledge that we are feeling sorry for ourselves, so instead we put on a mask to project our self-sorrow out onto the world and pity life and others.

The mask often takes on the characteristics of exaggerated rescuing, being a nice person, or having a false sense of humbleness, humility, and compassion. We don't want to say, "I'm sure glad that isn't me," so we put on the mask, often thinking, "There but for the grace of God go I."

Wearing the mask of self-pity, we will often look for guarantees, for someone or something else to take care of us. When by some accident the mask slips a little and some pleasure comes through, we quickly try to repress the pleasure because pleasure has no place in self-pity. We cannot experience pleasure and self-pity at the same time.

The Elders say that behind every mask is the mirror of our own neediness and the neediness of others. In the interaction between the inner and outer masks, we do what we do that appears to be good and beneficial, not because it is our medicine or give-away, but because it makes us feel good to be helping someone else who is worse off than we are.

We also wear the mask of self-pity when we are uncertain, so in this state of ambiguity we change our behavior to act in a way which we hope will be accepted from the outside, rather than being legitimately direct with exactly who we are, what we are doing, and why we are doing it. Codependency is the real anchor of the mask of self-pity.

We all wear these masks unconsciously most of the time. The Twisted Hairs maintain that our give-aways are rarely purely altruistic; in fact, much of our giving does spring from this unconscious self-pity so that there are usually invisible strings attached. We do what we do because we derive benefit from it. The giving quality of water in the South of the Wheel of Life and the lesson of the plant world, teach us about pure, unconditional love and giving. Human beings rarely achieve this level of giving.

In our journey towards self-discovery and self-realization, it is critical that we acknowledge the self-pitying aspect of our shideh. Owning this and taking responsibility for it is an important step towards maturity and ultimately discarding the mask.

Some typical self-pity statements:

The needy, wounded, abandoned child whose goal in life is to be approved of and whose neediness is never satisfied: "No matter what I do, it's never enough." "All I need is love."

The complainer who whines about how unfair things are: "This is too much work." "Some people have all the luck."

Addictive personalities who have lost self-control and have become dependent on something outside themselves in order to function: "I drink because I enjoy it." "All I ever do is work!... but I really love my job!"

The jealous, possessive lover who suffers from a severe fear of loss: "If you really loved me, you'd be jealous that I danced with Bill." "I heard you tell Katherine she was beautiful [pout]."

The angry, vengeful, manipulative adult: "I never get recognized." "I do all the work, and someone else gets all the credit."

The one who insists on guarantees in life: "But you promised!" "What's the use of trying? It won't turn out right anyway."

The Mask of Self-Importance

Of course, most of us would deplore self-pity in ourselves, so we rise above it and mask the self-pity with self-importance, adopting an attitude of being better than it all. To maintain this illusion, we try to rise above our present reality. We manipulate and often put others down in order to feel good about ourselves because our mask of self-importance hides our feelings of inadequacy and our great fear of how we are perceived by others. When we are caught in self-importance, we fear making mistakes lest someone should find out; we are attached to our need to be loved and liked.

Our needy child does not want to grow up and take responsibility for its actions. We lack a positive self-concept, even though we will act as though we do. We insist we are right and maintain our point of view, also called the *point of reason,* no matter what, and we will tend to be offended by others who see the world differently than we do.

We take our future and we wear it as the mask of self-importance, while self-pity is always lurking underneath and focused on the past. We find ourselves in the midst of a battle zone as we flip these two masks back and forth. It is not unusual to do this several times in a very short time span; in fact, within seconds we can shift from self-importance to self-pity and back again. Both masks are projected out of our karmic patterns.

The mask of self-importance always says everything is just fine: "I may be insecure, neurotic, and emotionally stressed, but I'm fine. I am happy!" Inside, the person may be screaming or sinking in denial.

Here are some examples of self-important statements:

The eternal negative ego: "I could do better than she's doing if I really wanted to." "He thinks he knows everything; hrmmph, I've been around longer than he has."

The impetuous, arrogant child "brat": "I will do it my way!" "I don't care what the rules are."

The rescuer who wants everyone to be happy: "Just think good thoughts, and nothing bad will happen." "Don't worry; everything will be fine."

The invincible one: "Anything she can do, I can do better." "That would never happen to me."

The opinionated one: "That's my story, and I'm stickin' to it!" "Let me tell you. . . ."

The one who plays one-upmanship: "I told you so!"

Whereas the mask of self-pity is like a ladder that takes us down in our assessment of our self-worth, and lowers our awareness of our true measure (our 10ness), the mask of self-importance makes us think we are climbing up the ladder of our measure, when what we are really doing is staying on the same rung of the ladder. Our awareness isn't developing, and we are stagnating. The Twisted Hairs say it is sometimes better to be in self-pity because at some point, we will hit bottom and have to start climbing up. When we are in self-importance, we don't think there is any up. We think we're already there.

One effective way out of this self-pity/self-importance dance is to stop caring about what others think and begin assuming responsibility for being who you are. Do everything as though it were the last thing you will do. Do it knowing you are getting no reward for it. If you no longer care about others' perceptions of you, you can more readily accept yourself for who you really are. You can remove the masks and set yourself free.

Shattering the Mirrors of Self-Reflection

The mask of self-pity underlies every one of the masks we wear, but we can't see our self-pity in the mask. If we would only wake up and look into the mask, we would actually be looking into a mirror and see the reality of the pity reflected back at us. This process of recognition and removing the masks is called *shattering the mirrors of self-reflection*. When we can shatter the mirrors of self-reflection, the Twisted Hairs say we will learn what we forgot, because we will remember why we chose to forget, and we will remember who we are. This is power.

It is very important that we reverse the process of the image makers in order to discover our true nature spirit and attain freedom. This is our most difficult task, for the responsibility and success of freedom is the greatest fear of the shideh. Reversing the process means the mold must be broken and resculpted, and the armor chipped away. In other words, we must recreate ourselves as our true nature mysterious character, which is formless. This is our life work.

Jan: *I would like to share with you an experience that, in one blinding moment of illumination, shattered my mirrors of self-reflection. I* felt *and* knew *my true nature.*

Thunder Strikes was working with a small group of seven apprentices, of which I was one. He was preparing to take us into a ceremony that would aid us in removing the masks to reveal our true nature. To accomplish this he would engage us in shamanic theater or drama within a ceremonial context. As he could see *into our luminosities and our energy fields, and knew us very well, he* saw *the roles that would break the grip of our shideh and our karmic pretender egos. The persona that I was to assume was that of an aging actress, a has-been past her prime who had attained a moderate degree of success in Hollywood appearing in B-grade movies, but had never become a big star. I was to dress the part, assuming whatever mannerisms and behaviors I thought would deepen the character assigned to me. The other apprentices had also been assigned characters particular to them.*

I was going through a difficult period in my life and welcomed this opportunity to gain some understanding of what was going on. On the appointed evening, we all arrived, some of us dressing and acting the parts assigned, and some of us choosing not to take the leap into their assigned persona. I came dressed with a red wig, bright red lipstick, and heavy eye makeup, with garish dangling earrings, gold sandal pumps, and a bag that clashed with the dress I was wearing. Everything glittered. I topped off the ensemble with an aging mink stole and gloves, and a garish bracelet. Attempting to "flood" my character, I was the epitome of gauche glamour!

During the evening I constantly dropped names, alluded to friendships and intimate tête-à-têtes with the likes of Clark and Kirk and Cary, and held the facade of being someone important. The character was difficult for me to maintain because I am not an actress by any stretch of the imagination, and I waffled between a sense of purely acting out a role and feeling acute embarrassment and humiliation as though I were really the character. Having to maintain attention on the ceremonial alchemy while staying in character was an additional challenge.

After four or five hours, we concluded the ceremony. I drove home and shed my costume and the persona. At this point, I still had no clue how this role-playing would reveal my true nature. I have been an apprentice of this path for a long time and have done many ceremonies on my self-growth journey. I was aware that the seven days following a powerful alchemical ceremony can be full of insights, sudden illuminations, upheaval, and change, as the ceremony continues to work inside you on many levels.

So it was that four or five days later, as I was engaged in some mundane task, lightning struck and time stood still. In that breathless moment, a space opened up around me, and I split attentions, becoming aware of two of me present at the same time—a solid physical me and an energetic projected me that I could feel and see with my mind's eye. For the first time in memory, I felt in my physical body what it was like to be natural, clear and clean, free of all baggage, free of all the brain chatter and pretense—centered and whole. I felt pure and light, natural and joyful, intimately connected with everything around me.

Next to me I saw and felt my fraudulent, phony pretender self, wearing masks that kept changing, and expending huge amounts of energy to maintain a facade. This pretender was me and yet a total stranger. There I stood, the pussycat exposed for what it was, like pulling back the drapes and discovering the reality behind the Wizard of Oz.

My first thought was: "You mean, that's not who I really am? You mean I don't have to continue to keep that facade? I can stop spending all that energy to maintain that persona?" I felt two sensations simultaneously: incredible relief at being unburdened of a tremendous load, and dismay and revulsion at the duality. On the one hand, I was floating with the joy and lightness of being at the realization in that moment, and on the other hand, I went into shock and extreme fear.

This epiphany lasted for an instant in real time, but my experience seemed to stretch to infinity. It came in a flash of clarity, and then I was snapped back into slow thought and time like a rubber band. Incredulity quickly set in, and the clarity began to fade.

I must explain something here. We can explore and integrate concepts, ideas, and situations with our minds, and do it quite brilliantly, but true knowledge cannot be seen or heard or conceptualized or pretended. Not until knowledge is felt in our bodies, actually in our cellular structure, do we really know. When this happens, both our substance and our behavior change. It was one thing for me to listen to Thunder Strikes talk about our true nature versus the karmic pretender ego, to understand them as mental concepts and to be able to discuss them with others quite comprehensively. But until I experienced and felt those concepts in my physical body, I did not **know.**

My whole world was shattered. I wasn't who I thought I was. How could my true nature be so different from who I thought I was? If I wasn't that pretender, then who was I? I was faced with an empty canvas challenging me to create myself in my own image, to de-armor and then resculpt myself into my natural jaguar self. But how was I to accomplish this? My mirrors of self-reflection had been shattered, and a new awareness was blossoming. Even as I pondered this, I felt the acuteness of the experience fading, and I was the same Jan in real time, still at the effect of old karmic patterns, character blocks, and masks.

Then I sank into major disillusionment: Why did it take so many years for me to get to this realization? I'm too old to change. Why did my spirit personality have to go through all that molding, sculpting, and armoring to cover up who I was, only to discover who I was and then have to undo all that had been done and start over again? Why did my soul choose those parents? It was all a mistake. (Do you hear the self-pity?)

Shortly after this experience, I went out into nature and did a flowering tree ceremony, very simple yet powerful. The tree will balance any negative energy we may wish to give away or release. It also functions like a rod or conduit that connects us with spirit. I asked the four questions inherent in this particular ceremony. Prior to this time, whenever I did this ceremony, I would get specific answers from spirit, guiding me and helping me to find direction and solutions to problems. This time, however, was very different. The dialogue with spirit went like this:

Q: Who am I?
A: Anything you want to be.
Q: Where did I come from?
A: You came from the dark into the light.
Q: Why am I here?
A: You decide.

Q: Where am I going?
A: Anywhere you want.

*I think the Universe has a sense of humor. Our Dharma Book is truly
an open and blank book, and we can write any story we choose. This
doesn't mean that my life has become a piece of cake. On the contrary, I
have often felt like a shipwreck survivor drifting in a life raft without com-
pass, rudder, or map. Nevertheless, I know I am the one writing the story.
Having had the experience of my mirrors of self-reflection shattering, exposing my true nature, I would never be the same.*

Authoring a New User's Manual for the Journey

Whereas spirit comes into substance form with a script from
our Karma Book of Life, containing lessons we must learn in order
to evolve into dharma, our Dharma Book of Life contains blank
pages. Once we have resolved our karmic issues and learned the
lessons, we close our Karma Book and open our Dharma Book. Opportunities now present themselves to us and we can choose to engage or not. Suddenly we feel as though we have set out on a
journey into the unknown with no road map, no user's manual, and
no directions.

We spend much of our lives doggedly following someone else's
road map, even as we are convinced it is a map of our own devis-
ing, heading to a destination we also erroneously think is of our
own choosing. When we wake up to reality, close our Karma Book,
and open the Dharma Book, we see clearly, perhaps for the first
time, who we truly are. We now confront the opportunity to
choose our destination in sobriety and draw our own map. It is totally up to us. We have to create the road map and the user's manual for our unique individual journey into dharma.

This can be a very confusing time because those moments of
clarity can disappear as suddenly as they appeared. One day you
are different, and the next day you are the same. If you are effectively de-armoring your armored body during this time, you
are resculpting a new one as well. You are exploring unknown

territory. At times the shideh is kicking and screaming, pulling you back into your shadow and resisting change. At other times your hokkshideh takes command and propels you forward into the Light and your shining self.

During these times you may feel like you are getting worse instead of better, becoming more dysfunctional than ever. In fact, what is actually happening is that you have become more awake and aware of your dysfunctional karmic patterns, of how you wear the masks of self-pity and self-importance. You are like a jet plane that is approaching the speed of sound and pushing the sound barrier. The barrier resists, the plane squeals and squeaks with the stress, until suddenly the plane breaks through and streaks beyond the barrier. And just like those first jet pilots, when you break through, you are flying into the unknown.

9

Conquering the Blocks to Character Development

One of the major challenges that presents itself as we create our new road map is getting past the blocks, the potholes in our path. As noted earlier, the major barrier to our evolution, which stops our actualization and productivity, is our attachment to the perceptions of others. We have a tonal personality focus rather than a nagual focus of soul consciousness. We are attached to the perceptions of others to guide us, and we look to them for our empowerment. This is an illusion. "When you see the Buddha on the road, kill him," goes the saying. Following the Buddha's perception (that is, attachment to the perceptions of others) will only give you an illusionary empowerment. You must experience your own perception within Sacred Law.

The shideh utilizes eight major blocks to keep us in line and to insure its survival. These blocks are repression, fear, guilt, blame, doubt, insecurity, shame, and resistance. The Twisted Hairs consider these blocks the faces of evil. Shown on the accompanying wheel (see Fig. 9-a), they are a product of our molding, sculpting, and armoring; they are major contributors to the *pretender voices* (brain chatter) and our *pretense experiences*. They keep us in our *false pretender self* and maintain the command of the karmic pretender ego.

Every block is an energy vampire. The more you are trapped by these blocks, the more energy you expend. They shut off your ability to experience authentically and stop you from getting the lesson from

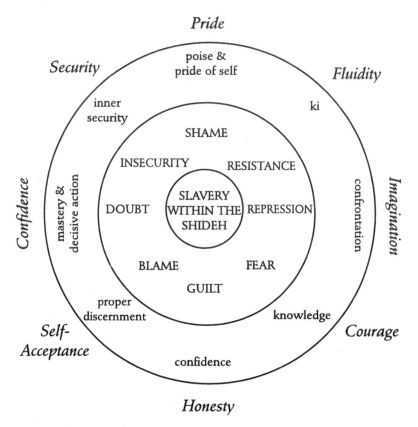

KEY: THE BLOCKS   our allies   *Our Orende Gains*

Fig. 9-a   The Blocks to Character Development Wheel

the experience that presents itself; thus, you incur stress and more karma. In other words, the opportunity will come around again, only more difficult the next time, until you get the lesson. The trickiest part of the pretender voices, however, is that the more knowledge you gain, the more they use it to hide themselves from you.

Fortunately, you can enlist *allies* to help you defeat these enemies, and in so doing eliminate pretense and produce the *orende gain,* which is a gain in your energy level, your impact and attraction. You gain personal power in the confrontation not as power over someone or something (except the block), but as a co-empowerment, an engagement for mutual benefit and welfare. When you conquer the blocks, you experience transformation into the embodiment of your true nature spirit personality, and you begin to experience the gains as essences of your soul in the process of refining your character.

Sophia Thin Sticks, one of the Zero Chiefs on the Twisted Hairs Council, says, "See the blocks as bullets." We are shooting the bullets of fear, shame, and so on, into the world, and they ricochet back at us. We are the victims of our own bullets.

Not everyone is trapped by all the blocks all the time. As you juxtapose your patterns alongside the examples here, you may find that you are at the effect of the blocks only some of the time. But there are probably at least several that consistently trip you up and sabotage you.

Repression

The *repression* circle produces armoring in the human being and includes all the blocks, which get dumped on top of the four aspects of repression. Our pretense experiences dominate, and the pretender voices are in control. Pretense experiences are also a function of emotional imbalance, and they cause us to repress our excellence, our beauty, creativity, passion, and lust. Projected perception is our illusionary world filtered through our emotionality, our molded, sculpted, and armored patterns, and our pussycat beliefs rather than the jaguar concepts of self.

Example: Ruth's boss has been impatient and cross with her the last week or so, and actually cut her off in a discussion yesterday. Ruth first is convinced that she must have done something wrong to upset him. Then she falls into self-pity and keeps saying to herself, "I'm doing the best I can. He favors Joe because he let Joe have the floor in the meeting yesterday. He doesn't like me. He's not fair."

So this becomes her story—her "reality." It is a pretense experience. If she *confronted* her boss and asked what was going on, she might discover that his child has been taken to the hospital, or that his wife is divorcing him, or that his ulcers are acting up; in other words, that his actions have nothing to do with her. Her perceptions of him are projected out of that pretense experience, and the pretender voices of the blocks reinforce the perception that she projects out into the world as reality. She lives in a fantasy world.

The ally is *confrontation,* which teaches us how to increase our self-worth. Our greatest pretenses occur where we have no recognition of our measure of self-worth, and it is only through confrontation that we assess this realistically. Furthermore, if we don't constantly engage and confront the blocks, they will continue to appear over and over again.

Confrontation energy is often maligned and misinterpreted as conflict, and many people try to avoid it. Confrontation is necessary for growth, change, and evolution—for life itself. When you are willing to confront, you are committed to engaging fully with whatever presents itself to you in the Here and Now with true feelings and clear energy in motion. Through your willingness to engage and confront fully, you create your own destiny by opening your vision with *imagination.* The gain is expanded *imagination,* through which you can express your uniqueness and create something original—your life.

Fear

Fear is the first energy that shuts off our natural self and our ability to be in our domain of power. We operate in fear produced by socially, politically, culturally, and religiously correct thinking and behavior. All this correctness rings the death knell to individuality and personal freedom. Freedom does not mean license, which violates Sacred Law; it does not mean personal gain or benefit by destroying or damaging someone or something else. Freedom requires personal responsibility and accountability.

When the little child inside you doesn't have a way to connect to the outside world and know who it is, fear immediately forces it into pretense. We experience fear when we step into the unknown and don't know. There is no harm in not knowing, which means you are receptive and willing to learn, to be creative, and to engage with the unknown in order to make it known. Ignorance, on the other hand, means you think you know, but you don't, and you still act like you do. So *knowledge* is your ally and your weapon in overcoming and defeating fear. You gain *courage* through that confrontation, and raise your measure of self-worth.

We will spend more time with the block of fear than with some of the other blocks, because fear is the most energy draining of all blocks and most dramatically erodes our self-concept. While in the womb, the fetus is connected to the mother through the umbilical cord, which is its energy pipeline. All its needs are met through this cord; it is in a protected environment and still connected to spirit. The child experiences fear for the first time when the umbilical cord is cut at birth, separating it from the mother. This separates it from the connection that has provided its survival and sustenance for nine months.

No longer fed through the umbilical cord, the child feels hunger (a hollow, restless feeling) for the first time, but it doesn't know what hunger is. If the hunger is not satisfied, that energy moves up the chakra line (the energy centers or vortices up the center line of the body) from the *one-point* or COG (our *center of gravity*, located three finger-widths below our navel, the place where our energy is focused when we are "centered") to the third chakra in the navel, and the child experiences *fear*. Fear is always our response to the unknown, an energy that must be dealt with and experienced. If the child is not fed, the energy continues up the chakra line to the heart chakra. The child doesn't know how to cope with the fear of the unknown, so it experiences *anger*, which is the inability to cope with the fear of the unknown.

Now, if the baby still isn't fed, its one-point will move into the fifth chakra, the communication center in the throat. It is trying to communicate but doesn't know how. It will experience *stress, anxiety*, and in the most severe form, *hysteria*.

If the baby still is not fed, the energy moves into the sixth chakra (the third eye in the middle of the forehead). The baby's voice breaks; it gets quiet and goes into *depression*. As a balanced energy, depression is a demand to go into deep introspection and regain the one-point and rebalance yourself. If you stay in depression, however (self-pity loves this place), you will not be able to restabilize. As long as you allow the one-point to move up your body, you are like a tent pole: The higher it goes, the more you get off balance.

This is our first experience of fear and we will continue to react to the unknown and to unknown energies this way throughout our life until we understand what is really going on and conquer the block. Using the ally of *knowledge,* we will gain *courage.*

Task: How to Restabilize Your One-Point and Find Your Balance

When you find yourself losing the one-point, stop and take a deep breath. Focus on your one-point. Curl your tongue back against the roof of your mouth and relax. Let your mind focus downward towards the Earth. This pulls your energy back down the chakra line and anchors you once more in the one-point. You stop the energy drain and regain your center.

Guilt

The Twisted Hairs say that, after fear, *guilt* is the next most energy draining of the blocks. It is an emotional trap forced upon us by our image makers, and it is one of the greatest armorers. We often feel guilty when we *think* we did something that was not socially or behaviorally correct. Guilt is a result of our inability to hold our philosophies and strength of mind with authority, to be responsible for our actions and exhibit spiritual maturity.

We often confuse guilt with *remorse,* which is the willingness to forgive ourselves and others for being human enough to learn through mistakes, the willingness to pay for what we have done. Remorse is the energy that allows dharma to exist. You won't get the lesson without remorse.

Every time you feel guilt, you are blocking your ability to give without expectations. You may be afraid your give-away will be rejected or not good enough. Guilt is often induced by parents as a way to control their children's search for individuality and autonomy. It is not done with bad intent. Parents love their children and want them to have the best and be the best. They do the best parenting they know how to do. Unfortunately, this often takes the form of manipulation and invalidation of true feelings and honesty.

The ally of *confidence* allows you to have no concern for others' perceptions or opinions of you. You will never sacrifice your principles to be liked, approved of, or accepted. Confidence is the ability to live as a sensual and intimate person with your significant others, giving of yourself whether or not it is accepted. The resultant gain is emotional *honesty*, precious and powerful.

Blame

Blame is an unwillingness to take responsibility for your actions and the inability to be spiritually accountable. When you blame, you push your guilt outward onto others, and you do not engage. You step back and put the onus of responsibility and accountability on someone or something else—life in general, others, the "system," or ultimately God. Or you put the onus on yourself, but you don't accept responsibility for it or take steps to solve the problem.

Any time you blame, you are actually refusing to accept that which you have chosen to have appear in your life in the first place. The key to breaking this block is the willingness to engage with full commitment, without pretense or projection. You need the ally of *proper discernment,* which is to know what, when, where, and how you are responsible for your actions. The gain is acceptance—*self-acceptance.*

Doubt

Doubt is a huge block for most people. Physical doubt freezes the body's ability to move and act, which often takes the form of procrastination. Doubt erodes our trust in our body knowing and feelings, throws us into confusion, and shuts down our ability to act decisively; it can even elicit panic. Doubt makes us afraid to make a mistake; we will quit rather than fail. Most any action, however, is better than no action. Confront, engage, and be spontaneous in the moment. Take *decisive action,* and you will gain *confidence.*

The key to decisive action is mastery of the physical. When you have developed many different skills to a level of excellence, when you have learned how to handle yourself in many different situations (whether self-taught or under the teaching of a master), you develop autonomic body response. You act instead of react. You stay at cause in your own circle of power. "Just do it!" is your motto. (See the Doubt Shout ceremony at the end of this chapter.)

Insecurity

All the molding, sculpting, and armoring create our world in the form of a *box,* which is defined by the limitations and boundaries that our image makers and, ultimately, we ourselves build to contain the known, where we feel safe and in control, free from *insecurity.* When people want security, they think that the smaller the box, the more secure they are. Some of our strongest fears are here because we are afraid to change, break down the walls of the box, and enter the unknown.

Self-deception can erode our faith in ourselves and in our skills and abilities; it propels us into incorrect decisions and actions. People often choose dogmatic religious belief systems to give them the illusion of security. Insecurity encourages us to wallow in self-pity and self-importance.

Interestingly, we must summon our own *inner security,* our own truth and trust and faith in self, rather than trusting other people to provide security for us. Break the pattern and expand your boundaries and limitations into a better self-sustaining pattern that works, and you gain the best kind of *security.* (Of course, there is really no such thing as permanent security, in that nothing in life is a guarantee.)

Shame

Shame is fostered by a lack of acceptance of your naturalness. If you do not accept your natural way of doing something, you will feel shame. Shame is our guilt projected inward; it engenders indecisiveness and a sense of inadequacy. It fosters incompetence and inconsistency. Above all, shame is fueled by a fear of failure.

To defeat this block, use *poise* and *pride of self* as allies. Accept your weaknesses and strengths, and learn when to use your weaknesses as strengths and your strengths as weaknesses. In this way, your weaknesses become strengths and your strengths become stronger. Wisdom is knowing when to do which. *Pride* is the internal realization that you do something well and you don't need external reinforcement. Self-acceptance is the epitome of pride.

Very often people who "strut their stuff" are criticized for showing off. The boxer Muhammad Ali, although recognized as a great athlete, was criticized by many for being what they considered egotistical and vain. On the contrary, Ali *was* great, he *knew* he was great, and he reveled in his mastery. At the same time, he didn't take himself seriously, and he entertained us with his gift of humor. It is actually self-importance that pretends humility and plays down your excellence. Your give-away, your Beauty as a balanced human being, is to be the best you can be and to give that away to the world. That is your legacy in this lifetime. So know yourself, and use what you know. Shine, and let the world see your light.

Resistance

When you are caught in the block of resistance, you pull back from and deny opportunities that present themselves to you to engage with. You constrict and restrict your energy flow, and your parameters of engagement are defined by your need for emotional acceptance, the need to fit in, belong, and conform. You resist engaging with anything that jeopardizes your being loved or liked. When you resist, you do nothing that will antagonize a friend or someone in authority because you are seeking their acceptance.

Ask yourself, "What is the key to my resistance? Why am I

afraid to change?" The key to the block of resistance is your un-willingness to grow up and take responsibility for your world. Your resistance to chaos and change increases your stress and the likeli-hood of meeting death prematurely.

To overcome this block, enlist the aid of the ally of *ki*, which is your energy flow and the power of your soul force. Allow yourself to be fluid. Ki allows you to reengage with life and align with chaos. It slows down the aging process. You can increase the flow of ki in your body with high-level orgasm, proper breathing exer-cises, yoga, and physical exercise, particularly aerobic. Training in the martial arts is also an excellent way to develop your ki. An old analogy is also good here: Use your ki to be fluid and bend like a blade of grass in a wind, not like an oak tree that rigidly resists the force of the wind. The gain is *fluidity*.

Pretender vs. Commander

We each have a particularly strong proclivity for getting tripped up by one or two of the eight blocks. These are the strongest for us and sabotage us the most. Which is your strongest block? Look at all the blocks besides repression (which contains within it all the blocks) and find the one or two that stop or sabotage you most of the time. Which pretender voice do you focus your attention on the most? Which of your pretender voices scream the loudest? Atten-tion is power, and if you listen to your *pretender voices,* they will dis-tract your attention and cause you to give your power away.

Your greatest limitations in life are your pretender voices, which speak from all the blocks. They are blabbermouths and do not shut up. When your pretender voices are talking at you, you are only ca-pable of projected perception. What you see is mostly illusion, shadows, refractions, and distortions, not true reflections. You live you life as a pretense experience, not engaging authentically, sitting on the sidelines watching life go by, wishing, wanting, and hoping. Or you blame everyone but yourself for what is happening to you. There is nothing more important in life than assuming authority and taking responsibility for your actions.

The opposite of the karmic pretender voices are the dharmic *commander voices,* which speak from heightened perception and sobriety. When they are activated, they engage in a vibrant and valid experience in the Here and Now, in the moment, with spontaneity and full responsibility, knowing that life is a choice.

We have largely become a victim society, blaming other people or circumstances for why we are how we are. "Well, my mother beat me when I was six years old. I'm a victim of abuse, and I can't help it if I am the way I am." To get out of that pretense requires a full commitment to yourself and your own self-growth and development. That is what studying and working in a true spiritual path of heart can accomplish: It guides you out of the shadow by taking you into the shadow. It teaches you how to shut off the pretender voices, stop the projected perceptions, get out of the pretense experiences, and find the light within the dark.

What follows are examples of karmic ego pretender voices. Do any of them sound like your voices?

Why go after what I want when I'll never get it anyway?

There is always something wrong with me.

I'm not ready.

People will think I'm stupid if I make a mistake.

No matter how hard I work, it's never enough.

You can't make me; I will do it my way by myself.

That's not fair.

I did it, why can't you?

If you really understood me, you would know how I feel.

I give up!

I can't handle it.

Mistakes and weakness make me feel vulnerable to others.

I don't want to change.

What if I fail?

I'll never be happy.

Nobody's good enough (and neither am I).

I have to figure it out all by myself!

I'll do it when I'm ready.

I'm doing the best I can, so leave me alone.

I will only engage in challenges that make me look good.

If only ...

I don't want to deal with it.

I don't know.

Am I good enough?

Do you love me?

Sex = love = pain.

Task: Silencing the Pretender Voices

Walk around the Blocks to Character Development Wheel (again refer to Fig. 9-a), and list as many of your pretender voice statements that apply to each block as you can. Then go around the wheel again, but this time create commander voice statements for the allies that you can use to override and silence your pretender voices. Starting with fear, at each place find a commander voice that will prevent you from succumbing to the block.

Jan: Let me give you some examples. Doubt and fear are my two strongest blocks.

Some of my doubt pretender statements are: "It's not important." "I'll do it tomorrow."

Some of my decisive action ally commander statements are: "Right now I'm the best I have ever been!" "Let it shine!"

Some of my fear pretender statements are: "I'm afraid I'll make a mistake and people will think I'm stupid." "I'm not good enough."

Some of my knowledge ally commander statements are: "Nothing ventured, nothing gained." "I call my fear by name and look it square in the eye."

As you learned earlier, the shideh wants freedom while at the same time wanting security and safety. It wants change but isn't willing to take responsibility for it, so it fights to stay in control. The pretender voices get more and more clever at dodging and avoiding our attempts to rout them out and demote them to minor roles. Interestingly enough, they never totally disappear, but by elevating your ally voice to the level of commander, you can demote the pretender voices to inconsequential status. This transformation doesn't happen overnight; it takes a great deal of digging and commitment. The pretender voices are tenacious and fierce and require intense engagement and confrontation. How much are you worth? Is your transformation into the freedom and autonomy of your true nature spirit personality worth the effort?

Using Ceremony to Help Conquer the Blocks

The following two ceremonies will help you to confront the blocks, enlist the aid of the allies, and silence your pretender voices.

Task: A Nature Walk/Talk

This first ceremony is offered by Stella Many Names, a matriarch on the Twisted Hairs Council. Go out into Nature as often as possible, preferably once a week, either into the open country or into a large park in the city away from people. Your intent is to talk to the animals, the plants, the wind, the elements, and spirit. Go with no agenda, no expectation of outcome. Give yourself enough time (at least an hour). Be an objective observer witness of yourself walking. Walk for a while, allowing yourself time to relax. Then:

1. Listen to your inner dialogue, and slowly silence it.

2. Observe the way you carry your body. When you're in Nature, you walk differently, more naturally. Your whole carriage

shifts. How does it shift for you? How does your physical body move differently than it does when you are with people? Pay attention to that.

3. Feel any energetic changes in your body.

4. Pay attention to your connectedness to the things around you —mineral, plant, animal, spirit. What attracts you?

Once you observe these four shifts, you will begin to be more aware of your natural self. You may find that you are walking naturally in a gait of power. Your head comes up, your shoulders come back, you're natural and relaxed. You may have a certain agility and quickness that you don't usually have.

When you come back into society, have the courage to be exactly the way you were in Nature. Do this in just one arena in your relationship with others this week. Your greatest limitation in life is your karmic ego pretender voice. As soon as you come back from your Nature walk and encounter another two-legged, the pretender voice will try to disempower you because you are worried about their perception of you. Stop it. Stella says, "Treat people like trees." A tree doesn't judge you. If you treat people like trees, you won't worry about what they think of you, your stress will lessen, and life will get a lot easier. You access the ally whenever you remove the stress of needing to be liked or loved.

Task: Finding Your Doubt Shout

Thunder Strikes: *This ceremony was taught to me by Guboo Ted Thomas, an Australian aboriginal shaman. They have a saying: "When in doubt, shout it out!"*

A ferocious, willfully intended shout is one of the strongest tools for cutting through any challenge that life offers, any situation you must confront when your pretender voices are going crazy, particularly your doubting voice. The doubt shout is also a major stress reducer.

When you use your doubt shout, several things happen:

1. Your physical body centers itself in your one-point, and you feel very grounded and centered. This is your shamanic root of power.

2. Immediately your body fills with energy.

3. Your mind becomes very clear and shuts off the inner dialogue.

4. Your senses become much more acute.

5. Your true nature self, your higher self, kicks in, and you step into heightened awareness and begin to determine from spirit.

You will be doing an Ancestor Speaking Ceremony, asking the ancestor spirit beings to help you hear your doubt shout. Ideally, find a place in Nature or a large city park where you will not be disturbed. However, you can also do this in your backyard. Engage with a warrior's intent, that is, your whole attitude and approach is one of "I am going to establish a firm body mind-set that will allow me to engage no matter what!"

1. Walk around the area, and make your connection with the plants, trees, wind spirits, and all of Nature in that place. Say a short personal prayer of thanksgiving to the spirit of this place and to the ancestor spirits who dwelt there for this opportunity to do ceremony.

2. Face the South direction, then do the following to awaken the spiritual ancestors of that direction: Stamp your left foot on the ground twice; then clap your hands twice. Stamp your right foot twice; then clap your hands twice. Stamp your left foot twice; then clap your hands twice. Then clap six more times.

3. Speak the following in a respectful manner: "This is [your name] speaking. I call to my ancestor spirits who have loved me Since Always to come from the direction of the South, and let me hear clearly, distinctly, and accurately my doubt shout of self-empowerment." Then stay in the silence and listen. Close your eyes

if this helps you to stay focused and quiet. You may hear your shout from that direction, and you may not. In either case, after several minutes, move clockwise to the next direction—Southwest.

4. In the Southwest, repeat steps 2 and 3, except now you are asking your ancestors to come from the Southwest direction. Repeat these steps all around the wheel, moving clockwise, ending in the Southeast.

5. If after one walk around the circle, you have not heard your doubt shout, go around the circle again. However, the answer may come much faster than you realize. What sometimes happens is that the shout comes quickly, and you doubt that you could get it so quickly, or that it could really sound like that. So doubt will try to talk you out of your doubt shout! After all, that pretender voice is fighting for its very life.

You may hear your doubt shout in only one direction or from several directions. It is important to remember which direction you heard it from and in which direction it was the strongest and most powerful, because that will tell you where you are in greatest misalignment and where the shout can help you break through the block in that direction as well.

6. Practice shouting your doubt shout. When circumstances don't allow you to shout it out loud without disturbing others, you may shout it silently to yourself. In that case, it will sound slightly different. However, whenever possible, shout it out loud, REALLY LOUD! If your doubt shout comes to you sounding like *hee-ahh'*, shout it up from deep in your belly: ***HEEEE-AHHHH'!*** In a way, this is a form of primal scream, but here you are focusing your intent clearly on banishing doubt.

Your doubt shout is not always exactly the same each time you use it. The martial arts shout *kiai* (kee'-aye) is the perfect example of the doubt shout from a different tradition. It means "to rid of demons" or "to banish negative spirits." When men in military airborne units started parachuting and had to face their fear of jumping into space, their doubt shout became "Geronimo!" to give them courage on the way down. Humans have always shouted in some way as they enter into battle. We must do battle with our inner pretender voices and the tyrant voices of our image makers that seem to sit on our shoulders and offer "shady" counsel. The doubt shout can propel us into action and give us the confidence to defeat these saboteurs and banish them from our reality.

Section Three

What Is This Planet
of the Children?

Our Alignment With Nature

About Section Three

We leave the maturation of the spirit personality in its Sun-Dance Journey for a closer look at the environmental context and the elemental energies we birth ourselves into here on Grandmother Earth. It is time now to take a look at the forces of Nature that are part of the mold we are born into on this Planet of the Children, and the balance of energies that we are naturally aligned with when spirit comes into substance.

When the spirit personality emerges into human form into the mold of its image makers, it, too, is born into the arms of the Goddess Beauty, the forces of Nature and Grandmother Earth. All these forces define our world and our very existence. They feed us, they nourish us, and they dance within all the Sacred Laws. Our molding, our sculpting, and our armoring shut off our conscious connections to these powers and to the Earth. This retards our growth and the development of our character. It is time to explore this sacred matrix of Nature and realign with it.

10

The Powers of the Four Directions

In the Universe and in Nature, wheels harmonize with one another in songs of co-empowerment. Just as the alto, soprano, tenor, and bass voices of a choir weave rich harmonies, so do the *Powers of the Four Directions*. Each direction on the sacred Wheel of Life resonates in a particular harmonic, and all things that sit in that place do so because they are uniquely interconnected, share the same energetic, and work together. Their song is sung in the special "key of life" of that direction.

We have become so far removed from the natural world that we have lost our appreciation for the magick of these natural forces and their importance in the balance of our lives. The early tribes and all Earth peoples have always known the importance of harmonizing with Nature and the Powers of the Four Directions. They experienced intimate connection and relationship with these spiritual forces and knew them as teachers and guides.

Among many Earth cultures steps were taken to ensure the child's connection to the Earth and the natural forces, even before birth. While the infant was still in the womb, they performed ceremonies and rituals inviting these powers to align with the infant. At birth, the oldest matriarch or patriarch would take the child outside and, lifting it up to the sky, announce this new being to the four directions and the powers of the Universe, giving the little one away to the Great Spirit so that it would always keep its connection to these natural forces. Our separation is a tragic loss, and an important part of our journey is to find our way back to that connection. In this way, we rediscover ourselves.

Among the early tribes, *Wakan Tanka* was the most common name for the Mystery, the Everything. Tribal peoples recognized that there are eight spiritual forces, eight spiritual entities that are one and the same, dancing together on the Medicine Wheel. The East mystery or spirit, the key of the mystery, was Grandfather Sun, whom we call Sohotomah. In the West was Grandmother Earth, or Eheytomah. These are Twisted Hairs words of spiritual power that acknowledge that this is not just the physical sun; it is Grandfather Sun as a spiritual energy and part of the Great Mystery. In the South was the Earth Mother, Quetzal, the spiritual energy of all the plant world. In the North was Earth Father or Father Sky, Coatl, the spiritual energy of all the animals.

Those four were considered the holders and keepers of the Powers of the Four Directions. Without them, there could be nothing else—no life, no human beings. So they were commonly referred to as the four great life bringers, or the keepers of the Powers of the Four Directions.

Then there was the "As Above" into the world of spirit, and the "So Below" into the physical world of physical form. The noncardinal directions were called *movers,* turning the Wheels of Life, the sacred circles or hoops of existence, and making evolution possible.

The force of Nature in the Northwest is Thunder (Ah-keech'-nah) (spelled phonetically), which establishes the clear pattern, the direction, and timing of a storm. Thunder is called the *awakener* because it snaps us awake into sobriety. In the Northeast is Lightning (Woh-nee'-nah), the strongest form of electricity and the very symbol of chaos. Rain holds the place of the Southwest, and Wind holds the Southeast direction. In the Center is the Thunderstorm (Ki'-chee Mah'-ni-hey), the key catalyst that births *all* weather changes.

There was no single word for wind or rain. The Earth peoples had such an intimate connection with these entities that every different form or personality had a different name. For them, rain had spirit and it came in many guises, in many ways. Soft female rain (Wah-nee'-nah) was gentle, warm, steady, and cleansing, but often not enough to soak into the ground and give nourishment to the plant children. Hard male rain (Wah-ke'-tah) came in driving, pounding downpours that caused flooding. Child rain sustained life, soaking into the soil, and feeding the plant roots so that life will bear itself and rebirth. East was the sudden cloudburst called sun rain (Chees'-hay) because it came quickly from a cloud overhead while the sun was still shining on the land. In the Center of the wheel was the deluge of major proportions (Kah-tee'-quah).

Jan: My mother always enjoyed walking in the rain. Even in a hard rain, she would don her galoshes and raincoat and off she would go. As a youngster, I thought she was crazy. Who wants to get wet? "Listen to the rain talking," she would say. Now, many years later, I understand her connection and find myself enjoying walking in the rain.

Many energies resonate in each direction (see Fig. 10-a). The wheel harmonizes the Powers of the Four Directions with a color, an element and elemental energy, a season, a world, a human aspect, a heavenly body that guides it, a self-expression, a shield (which you will learn about in Chapter 18 as part of your energy body), and a manifestation through which the Twenty Count and the Great Spirit communicate. Pay particular attention to the elemental energetic. The Center of any wheel is always the catalyst that drives all other aspects of the wheel.

Songs of the Four Directions

The Great Spirit's highest thought is the human soul. Here we explore the songs of the Powers of the Four Directions in each of the cardinal directions.

South

The powers of the South nurture the heart of the human soul,

Fig. 10-a   The Powers of the Four Directions

NORTH

Color: white
Element: air
Season: fall
World: animal
Human Aspect:
mind, mental aspect
Heavenly Body: Stars
Self-Expression:
wisdom, logic, alignment, harmony,
balance, meditation, contemplation,
knowledge, harmonic resonance
Manifestation: science and math,
philosophy and religion

WEST

Color: black
Element: earth
Season: winter
World: mineral
Human Aspect:
body,
physical aspect
Heavenly Body:
Earth
Self-Expression:
introspection,
change, death,
intuition
Manifestation:
magick

CENTER

Color: purple/amethyst
Element: the void
World: spirit
Human Aspect: soul-sexual
Heavenly Body: Black Hole
Self-Expression:
breath, chi/ki
Manifestation:
womb, the egg and
seed of all creation

EAST

Color: gold,
yellow
Element: fire
Season: summer
World: human
Human Aspect:
spirit,
spiritual aspect
Heavenly Body:
Sun
Self-Expression:
illumination,
enlightenment,
pleasure, beauty,
medicine
Manifestation:
art/writing

SOUTH

Color: red
Element: water
Season: spring
World: plant
Human Aspect: heart, emotional aspect
Heavenly Body: Moon
Self-Expression: trust and innocence
Manifestation: music

and the element of water leads this song, as it is our primary teacher of the energy of *giving*. Water shows us how to be fluid and open in our emotions, not stuck in emotionality or emotionalism. Whether water flows gently in a quiet stream, meanders around rocks in its path, or rages in rapids and waterfalls, it demonstrates a nonresistance, a giving or surrender to the contours of the landscape, not as giving in, or submitting as a victim of something stronger, but rather as surrendering to the free-flowing expression of itself. Water will not be denied. It gives itself to all empty spaces in its path despite the landscape, whether open or filled with obstacles.

The plant world gives us beauty, oxygen, and food. It gives us life and teaches us to be openhearted, to love and to give unconditionally, no strings attached, no baggage. Sister Moon influences the ebb and flow of the waters on the planet and of the red blood rivers of our body. Trust and innocence here do not mean naiveté or ignorance or weakness. Rather, trust is knowing that we are an integral part of the interconnection and interdependence of all things and are a part of something much greater than ourselves. Innocence means to simply be who we are, to be in our own essence, like water.

When we are in alignment with these powers and honor them in our lives, the little girl and little boy inside us embrace the world with open joyful hearts in trust and innocence, and it is through them that we create our music, the heart communication of the Twenty Count and of the Great Spirit.

West

The powers of the West nurture the body of the human soul, and the element of earth takes the lead in demonstrating for us how to develop strength and stability in our bodies. The mineral world contains all the forms and textures of the earth element, which provide the solid substance of the planet, the body of Grandmother Earth, and demonstrates how *to hold and transform energy*. It also provides the basic sustenance for life, absorbing and holding the potent light rays of the Sun which Grandmother Earth takes deep into her body, into her magma. Through magick and alchemy, she transforms that fertile energy and births her children, the myriad and magnificent forms of life on the planet.

When we are in alignment with these powers and honor them, our inner warrior can go deep within through the process of introspection, and access our intuition and the strength of our bodily knowing. Wisdom and knowledge are not seen or heard; they are felt in our bodies. When we welcome death and change as part of our evolution into excellence as human beings, the body of the Great Spirit and the Twenty Count is expressed through magick and alchemy.

North

The powers of the North nurture the mind of the human soul. The element of air or wind shows us how to be mentally clear and flexible and teaches us how to *receive* with our mind. Whether as a gentle breeze or as a fierce hurricane, this element aligns with us to clear the cobwebs, fog, and toxic smog that often masquerade as pretense brain chatter and dogmatic belief systems so that we can access the wisdom of our sacred mind and see reality for what it truly is.

The animal world, also known as sweet medicine, offers perfect examples of inner balance and harmony. Animals naturally receive energy, and in doing so they can adapt and align with Nature and natural forces. Animals teach us to accept ourselves for who we are because they are so in alignment with who they are.

The stars, and our fascination with them, challenge us to stretch beyond our limitations, to use our imaginations to explore the unknown. Their siren song lures us off the planet. In looking back, we see the beauty and magnificent uniqueness of our home, which prompts a greater appreciation and wisdom in our relationship with her.

When we resonate with these North powers, our inner adult seeks to live in harmony with all peoples and align with Nature, the

Goddess Beauty, instead of warring with her. Only then can our philosophies promote the development of sciences and technologies that reflect the strength of mind of the Great Spirit.

East

The powers of the East co-empower the spirit of the human soul. The element of fire is called the *determiner* of energy that fuels our expansive imagination, our *fire within* that burns with passion and artistic originality, and represents our true nature spirit personality. It is the fire of spirit that seeks to grow and to learn, the desire of the soul to return to the before as one with the Great Spirit. Fire also symbolizes for us the spark of Grandfather Sun that empowers us to be spiritual determiners seeking illumination and enlightenment as luminous beings. The world of balanced humans—and the key word here is *balanced*—teaches us how to determine with our spirit and be in dominion with all things, preserving and protecting the balance and harmony of life on the planet.

When we honor these sacred powers of the East, our spirit child within experiences joy and aliveness, explores the edges, leaps into the unknown to find illuminations there. It is through our art and literature, through the inspired artistic expression of this spirit child that the spirit of the Twenty Count and the Great Spirit communicate.

Center

The Void in the Center of the Wheel of Life is called the Black Hole of Creation within which that first Sacred Breath, the spiritual-sexual Quodoushka union of WahKahn and SsKwan, birthed all forms of all things of the Everything. It is the *catalyst* that ignites the fire, the prime mover of all else in all the directions on this wheel and all wheels. It is our sexual catalyst energy, our life force, our soul. Balanced sexuality and orgasticness are the key to our alignment and balance in all directions on the wheel. They open our hearts with intimacy and fluidity; raise the orende, prowess, and strength of our bodies; expand our minds with flexibility and clarity; fuel our imaginations and spark our creativity and originality; and catalyze our spiritual evolution towards the freedom of formlessness and resurrection. The free-will expression of our sexual soul force energy catalyzes the Everything's ever-evolving experience of itself.

11

The Worlds of Grandmother Earth

J **an:** *Several years ago, a number of apprentices and I accompanied Thunder Strikes into the Arizona desert for teachings and ceremonial experiences in Nature. Our Warrior Task Assignment was to move through the desert landscape at night, stalking the shadows and listening with every fiber of our being—not just our ears—to the plants, the animals, and the rock people, for they had much to teach us, he said.*

I am afraid of the dark. Terrified. Every slight noise, every rustle of leaves, every whisper of wind, every shadow, is a monster waiting in ambush. I have stood frozen in one spot for interminable minutes because a gust of wind rustled a sage bush, causing its branches to rub and scrape against one another.

I left the campsite with the others of my party. Slowly we separated, following whatever direction called to us. I walked tentatively, startled by every sound or imagined sound. My heart pounded, and my breath caught in my throat. My fear mounted as I forced one foot in front of the other, cringing from everything around me. I feared what I could not see. Finally in desperation, no longer able to force myself to move, I slumped against the steep rock walls of an escarpment and wrapped my arms tightly around myself.

I remembered something Thunder Strikes had told us to do if we needed to ground ourselves. I pushed back against the cliff face, tried to envision myself sinking into the rock, and asked it to embrace me and talk to me. I asked it to help me settle my fear and dissolve the overwhelming isolation and separation I felt. Meanwhile, the myriad of desert sounds continued their onslaught on my nerves. I prayed to Grandmother Earth and asked her to help me connect with her, to feel at one with her and her children.

I hunched there shivering for a very long time. Slowly, I began to calm and feel my body relax into the rock. I looked around me trying to make out details in the moonlit landscape.

Suddenly, I felt a shift in my body and my perceptions, and I realized the sounds that frightened me so were really the sounds of consciousness. Grandmother Earth was alive. She was breathing. The plants were breathing. The rocks and boulders were breathing. And as I sat in wonder, I found myself, quite without conscious thought, inhaling and exhaling rhythmically with them. I was no longer separated or disconnected. I was no longer a stranger in this place. I was an intimate part of this great living, breathing matrix. What joy! I leaped up and skipped off across the desert like a child, laughing and singing.

The power and aliveness of such moments defy any attempt to describe them. But that experience validated for me my connection to Nature, to the Twenty Count, to all things. And I saw clearly that this natural connection is a sacred thing.

Learning to Communicate

We talk a lot about alignment and connection. Volumes are written about human alienation, separation, and poor communication, yet collectively we still wallow in planetary static and conflict.

Where do we go to learn how to communicate better? A new seminar? The latest guru teaching about human behavior? A national authority on communication and cooperation in the workplace? No. Our wisest choice is to go into Nature as an empty cup and let the worlds of the Earth show us a thing or two.

Plants, animals, minerals, and the world of spirit are our most powerful and authentic teachers (see Fig. 11-a). They can lead us deep into our inner silences, where they introduce us to and teach us about our true nature—our authentic natural self. Those of us who accept Nature as our mentor continue to discover unlimited

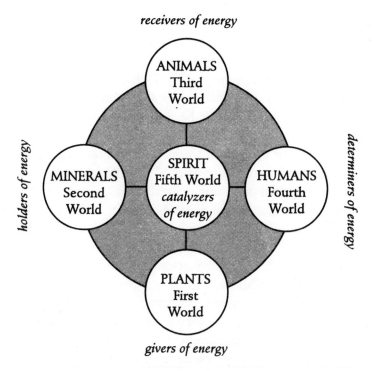

Fig. 11-a   The Worlds of Grandmother Earth

inner treasures. No seminar, as beneficial as it may be, can begin to equal these teachers. It is not enough to read books either. You have to accumulate your own experience. Don't feel satisfied because you have listened to a shaman or medicine person talk about nature spirits. Get out in Nature, and do your own connecting. *Feel* what it's like; experience it for yourself. The tragedy of our generation is that so often we settle for information alone. True knowledge and wisdom come from direct personal experience. The Internet, as magnificent as it is, is contributing to the massive collection of data and information, and helping to create the illusion that information and data are knowledge. This does not develop wisdom, and it cannot replace direct personal experience.

The Language of Nature

We can learn to unlock Nature's voice, the language of life, inside us. For most of us, however, this process entails a serious attitude adjustment. The original Dr. Dolittle is not just a fanciful, make-believe character. He is a role model to emulate. As part of our attitude shift, we must be willing to become students of Nature.

Next, we must discard all the paraphernalia we drag with us that separates and insulates us from Nature. Many of us spend our vacations in national parks and beautiful natural areas, but we are not in any way connected or aligned. We are afraid of insects and snakes, startled by animal noises in the night, or irritated by both hot and cold weather. To feel safe, we feel we need our Airstream trailer or our superdeluxe tent. Surprisingly, even many of those adventuresome folks who trek in the wilds with just the minimal needs on their backs, while enjoying the scenery, often pass through unmentored because they are not aware that they are the student passing through the landscape of the teachers. A disease of our society is that we have forgotten how to get below the surface of things.

Learning to Listen

The key to developing a greater facility to communicate is to listen, to hear what the other worlds are telling us and awaken them inside ourselves. We possess a direct connection to the other four worlds of Grandmother Earth: We contain minerals in our body; we are animal in that we are two-leggeds; we are the water and nutrients of the plant carried in our blood; and we come from pure spirit at birth and return to pure spirit at death.

People just haven't learned how to listen. We usually speak and listen from our brains, filtering everything through the chorus of our pretender voices and brain chatter. Furthermore, language— words—as our primary means of communication limits our experiences and separates us, thus contributing to the chatter that prevents us from hearing.

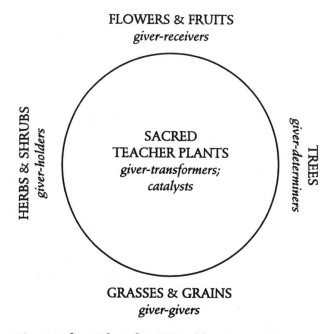

FLOWERS & FRUITS
giver-receivers

HERBS & SHRUBS
giver-holders

SACRED
TEACHER PLANTS
giver-transformers;
catalysts

TREES
giver-determiners

GRASSES & GRAINS
giver-givers

Fig. 11-b The Plant World: Givers of Energy

We are like walking radios tuned to only one station. We must get rid of the static and develop the wide band of receiving and broadcasting stations that are an intrinsic part of our natural self. To do that we need to know more about the nature of each of the worlds, their essence or give-away, and their role in the matrix of life here on Grandmother Earth.

The Plant World: The Givers of Energy

Sacred plants are *givers* (see Fig. 11-b). They give oxygen, nourishment, and beauty so that all other life on the planet can flourish. They literally give life.

Grasses and Grains

In the South are the *grasses and grains,* which, like Grandmother Earth's skin, hold the sand and soil in place. They are like her hair, protecting her skin and preventing erosion. They are the *double givers,* in that they hold nutrients, water, sunlight, and carbon dioxide, and give all that as nourishment for other life.

Herbs and Shrubs

In the West are the *herbs and shrubs,* the *giver-holders.* They hold healing qualities from which humans get food and medicines.

Flowers and Fruits

In the North are the *flowers and fruits,* the *giver-receivers.* They give away their beauty, and their scent, which is air in the North of that wheel. They also receive. All alchemists know that if you put flowers and fruits in any kind of magickal circle—church, lodge, marriage ceremony, funeral—they receive or absorb any negative energy that might be present. If the atmosphere is impure, flowers and fruits will wither and rot quickly.

Trees: The Standing Nations

In the East are the trees, called the *Standing Nations,* the *giver-determiners.* Trees have always been used as power symbols, and all magickal lodges, religions, and spiritual paths refer to the human being as the *tree of life.* They communicate most directly with human beings because they are in the same place on the wheel that we are—in the place of determination—and the aura of a tree, particularly that of the Joshua tree, is similar to that of a human.

Trees determine the weather, for they are the lungs of the Earth. They carry memory of the ages and of Grandmother Earth's story of herself, and the Elders say that the dying and destruction of the ancient grandmother and grandfather trees are slowly erasing that memory.

Trees determine the nature and variety of vegetation that grows around them by determining the amount of light that reaches the ground and the nutrients and acidity in the surrounding soils. Growing around the tree are those plants that need shade and thrive on that type of soil; those that need sunlight grow away from the tree. Furthermore, within two hundred feet of any toxic plant will grow its antidote. Mugwort, for example, is an antidote for poison oak and can be found growing nearby. Thus, the plant world keeps its balance. The growth and proliferation of medicinal plants that provide sources for our healing are determined by the sacred trees. It is no accident that such a large percentage of medicinal plants are found in our lush rain forests.

Since we depend on plants to give us life, food and oxygen, when we clear-cut forests, for example, we are truly destroying the determiners of life on this planet. This applies to all the worlds of Grandmother Earth. Human beings live on this planet because these worlds make life possible, and they are necessary partners in our evolutionary journey. Destroy them, and we destroy ourselves.

Sacred Teacher Plants

In the Center are the *teacher plants,* which are *catalysts* and *transformers.* They are also called hallucinogenics. *Hallu* means "sacred," and *genic* means "ancestor" or "spirit." So they are sacred spirit teachers. *Hallucination* means "the sacred gathering of energy," so a hallucination is a sacred gathering of images that teach. They help us to experience altered states of consciousness and to open to other realities. However, this is so only when a teacher plant is gathered, prepared, and consumed in a sacred ceremonial manner.

Connecting With the Plant World

A little child learns about the world through observation—miming, mimicking, and copying. In Nature, we are the child, and the plants, animals, minerals, and spirit are the teachers. Plants, animals, minerals, and spirit always communicate openly—no mind talk, no chatter—resonating in the various chakra centers of our body. We can learn to hear by feeling their voices inside ourselves.

To start learning this new language, get into Nature away from urban noise and confusion. If you can't do this, a large city park with lots of trees will do. Take the opportunity to wander in this place. This is actually a walking meditation. Don't *decide* where to walk. Quiet your mind; just walk and listen.

Walk as though you are playing a game in which an invisible friend is pulling you gently by a slender silver thread connected to your navel. Follow it. After a while you may begin to feel "drawn" to a particular place or plant without knowing why. Take the time to send energy to that plant, appreciating its beauty and its give-away.

Be aware of thoughts and insights that come to you that are not your thoughts. You may suddenly *know* something but don't know how or why you know it. Just accept it. Don't let your mind kick in to question your sensations, feelings, or *hunches*. If distracting chatter intrudes, just let it pass through you and move back into your inner silence.

You may begin to feel delight and the joy of *discovery*. The dictionary defines *serendipity* as an aptitude for making desirable discoveries by accident. There are no accidents. Serendipity happens when you open up and let yourself be guided by spirit and by that innate inner connection to all things around you.

Task: Talk to the Trees

Connect directly with a tree that has attracted you or *pulled* you to it. Put your arms around the trunk of a tree, sit in the tree, connect physically with it in some way. Offer a prayer and perhaps some tobacco or corn *paho* (fine cornmeal). This is a way of saying thank-you and honoring the tree for its gifts and its beauty. Talk from your heart—maybe saying something like this: "I'm new at this. In fact, I feel awkward talking to you. I've been told that you can communicate with all the worlds, so talk to me and teach me how to hear your voice."

Then be quiet and listen. It's that simple. If you don't feel a connection at first, don't give up. You have to relearn, remember actually, how to listen as you did as a small child when you were still closely connected to all things in the Great Round of spirit.

Be a Tree

Then practice being that tree you are talking to. Move your body and arms, mimicking its limbs bending in the wind. Let your body take on the structure and form of the tree. Don't let your mind determine what this should look like. Go inside and listen. Feel what it feels like to be a tree. Let its voice, resonating inside you, guide you into the shape of its spirit. And whatever you do, don't be inhibited by the thought that someone might see you acting like this! Your actions might intrigue them. Then you can become their guide.

When you take your leave of the tree, thank it with an offering of tobacco, corn paho, or a strand of your hair. Practice this, and you will experience a powerful connection not only to Nature but to every other aspect of your life. Learning this new language doesn't require long journeys, expensive equipment, or great amounts of time. All it takes is practice with an open heart, receptivity, and a strong desire to rediscover the shining of your true nature.

Next, begin to align with the trees and plants in your garden and the plants in your house. Don't water them once a week and let it go at that. Pay attention to changes in your plants. Do changes in weather affect them? How? Talk to your plants and really nurture them.

The Mineral World: The Holders and Transformers of Energy

Thunder Strikes: *People have said to me, "Okay, I can accept that plants are alive, but come on, you have gone too far if you expect me to believe that rocks have a consciousness. How can I experience them that way?"*

Let's take a closer look at the properties of the *mineral world* (see Fig. 11-c).

Sands and Soils

The *sands and soils* sit in the South on the Mineral World Wheel as *holder-givers*. They are the skin of Grandmother Earth, holding everything in place. Sands and soils absorb and hold the light and

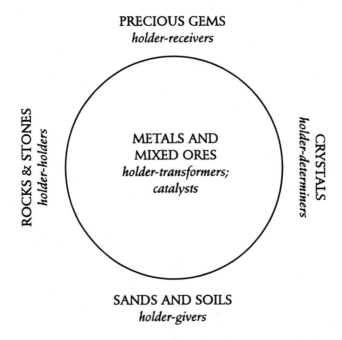

PRECIOUS GEMS
holder-receivers

ROCKS & STONES
holder-holders

METALS AND MIXED ORES
holder-transformers; catalysts

CRYSTALS
holder-determiners

SANDS AND SOILS
holder-givers

Fig. 11-c   The Mineral World: Holders of Energy

heat from Grandfather Sun, eventually transforming it and giving it as nourishment for plants.

Rocks and Stones

Rocks and stones are *double holders* in the West. They are the muscles and bones of Grandmother Earth. A rock is alive; it talks to you. The *Stone People* hold the energy in a Medicine Wheel and give their alchemy to you in ceremony. In the sweat lodge the heated stones hold the heat of the fire and then release it inside the lodge. When water is poured over them, they sing their give-away song. This transforms the space and makes it possible for us to purify and heal ourselves.

Precious Gems

The *precious gems* are *holder-receivers* in the North. We put them in our jewelry, in breastplates, in amulets, in talismans, so they will hold what we as humans determine they will. Jewelry is extremely powerful if it is properly made alchemical jewelry.

Crystals

In the East are the *crystals*, the *holder-determiner* brain cells of Grandmother Earth. A crystal chip in a computer is programmable and allows the computer to create and to run complex programs. Silicon dioxide chips are the essential elements that drive our electronic age, used in everything from coffeemakers to space flight guidance systems.

Thunder Strikes: *The crystal skull I work with is also programmable, but by Magickal Law, not science. When I access it, holographic images appear in the tenth chakra above the crystal skull, and it talks and teaches.*

In order to meet the demands of our high technology, industry mines thousands of tons of gigantic crystals from the Earth. The ramifications of this are awesome. The crystals are an integral part of the Earth's electromagnetic field and impact our psychic-kinetic connection to the worlds of Grandmother Earth. Given that crystals are the Earth's brain cells and affect this electromagnetic field, they are positioned or located in a particular pattern throughout her body, not randomly scattered. The Elders explain that this positioning can be compared to the hypothalamus part of our brain, which controls our four inner rivers through hormone secretion.

Brain/mind research has shown that stimulating different parts of the brain with electrical sensors produces every one of our responses such as blinking eye, erection, twitching muscle, laughter, and emotions. As we systematically remove the large crystals from the body of Grandmother Earth, we are in effect performing a lobotomy on her brain. The brain cells of the giant crystals combined with her skin cilia—her plants and trees—coordinate the flows of all rivers and, subsequently, all seasons, so this can have a huge impact.

Metals and Mixed Ores

In the Center of the mineral world are the *metals and mixed ores,* the *catalyst-transformers.* South of Center is copper; West of Center, iron and lead; North of Center, silver, plutonium, and aluminum; East of Center, gold and titanium. In the Center is brass and uranium. The Center of all wheels is the catalyst energy. Consider this. We take uranium, titanium, and plutonium—that is, we take the soul, spirit, and mind of Grandmother Earth—and we threaten to destroy her and her children with nuclear energy and waste.

Task: Strengthening Your Connection to the Mineral World

Lie on your stomach on a large boulder. Spread your arms and legs out, and focus on your navel. As you breathe through your navel into the rock, experience the energy flowing between you and the rock. How does it make you feel? Communicate with the rock as you did with the tree. Remember, communication will come through your body sensing and your chakras (the energy vortices of your luminosity), through your intuition, and through your heart, not through your mind.

You may also want to take a class from someone who is an experienced practitioner in the use of crystals for balancing energy in the body. Learn how to use crystal energy for your own healing.

Locate a Zen garden in your community to visit. These gardens are arranged so that there is instant communication that speaks as a wholeness. A Zen garden has impact because of the artistry of the arrangement, to be sure, but it also communicates strongly because of the alchemy, because of the consciousness or essence of the rocks and plants. This environment stills your brain chatter. You feel a part of it. Everything else outside is eclipsed, and the rest of the world falls away. So what is it doing to you? It is actually shifting you into a slightly altered state of awareness and consciousness, letting you feel more connected. Very often you may feel a need to go inward; you will feel your body relax and let go of stress. The plants and rocks are speaking to you through pure energy-to-energy translation.

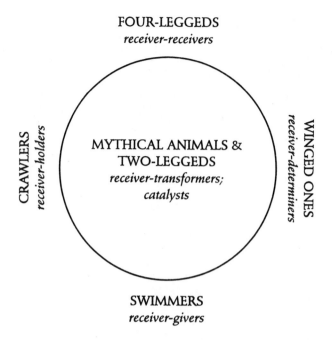

FOUR-LEGGEDS
receiver-receivers

CRAWLERS
receiver-holders

MYTHICAL ANIMALS &
TWO-LEGGEDS
receiver-transformers;
catalysts

WINGED ONES
receiver-determiners

SWIMMERS
receiver-givers

Fig. 11-d *The Animal World: Receivers of Energy*

The Animal World: The Receivers of Energy

The third-born children of Grandmother Earth are the *animal world,* or *sweet medicine,* in the North (see Fig. 11-d). Animals are receivers of energy. They have much to teach us.

Swimmers

In the South are the *swimmers,* the *receiver-givers.* They move through the water, the South of the Elements Wheel, and teach us how to be fluid with our emotions. Fish receive through water whatever energy is present and hold it in their flesh. The highest incidents of food poisoning in the world result from eating seafood contaminated by pollution in the water. The cetaceans—dolphins and whales—are the greatest receiver-givers and holders of genetic memory on this planet.

Crawlers

In the West are the *crawlers,* those whose bellies are closest to Grandmother Earth and who often move through her. They are the *receiver-holders.* The snake is closest to the Earth, receiving energy from the Earth, then giving back to us knowledge of the perfect alchemy of Earth.

Thunder Strikes: *When I'm in the desert and can't find water, I find a rattlesnake and talk to it with my larien (psychic gifts). It will tell me where water is. It has never failed to do so. You first have to know how to speak to a rattlesnake and not be afraid of it, but I'm not suggesting that you try that as a way to connect with the animal world. That's graduate school stuff, so to speak, but I share it here to emphasize once again how out of alignment we are as a species, how we have forgotten that we have this intimate, natural connection and ability to communicate with all forms of life.*

Four-Leggeds

In the North are the *four-leggeds,* the *runners* who are *double receivers.* They are in perfect balance within themselves and with everything around them. They know when the weather is going to change or a storm is brewing or a natural catastrophe is about to happen. They receive energy, very often absorbing human emotions. If your pets are in the area where you are doing body work, healing work, crystal work, medicine work, or magickal ceremony, they will soak up every bit of negative energy. Your animals will literally die for you.

Thunder Strikes: *The elk is the greatest energy receiver of all animals— the energy magician. When I was about twelve years old, I went off into the country alone to hunt. As the day progressed, black menacing storm clouds gathered, and by midafternoon the storm broke with intense thunder and lightning and downpour. As I tried to find a place to take shelter, I caught sight of a big bull elk standing exposed on a high ridge not far away. I stopped frozen in my tracks, breathless, as I saw jagged lightning strike his* *antlers and his whole body take on a glow. It was as though he was being recharged by the lightning. This lasted for what seemed minutes, although it was probably only seconds. I was sure I had seen a magickal elk. I took off as fast as I could run, totally oblivious to the fact I was carrying a gun which could easily have attracted the lightning to me and fried me in my shoes. I couldn't wait to tell my clan uncle and my grandmother of my great good fortune in seeing a magickal elk!*

I burst into the house and blurted out my story. My grandmother, Spotted Fawn, and my clan uncle, John Two Crows, laughed and howled until they almost split their sides. Once they collected themselves, they explained that the elk is the keeper of thunder and lightning and a master choreographer of energy in the animal world. I had seen it in its moment of power.

I received another teaching years later from Stella Many Names, one of the matriarchs of the Twisted Hairs Council. She said that when you are given the gift of a sweet medicine teaching, and if you know the medicine of that animal, you can approach it in its space, or territory. She said if I had stayed and approached the elk, it would have taught me how it transformed the lightning, and I would have known it as my dharma animal and the giver of my Elder Council name, Thunder Strikes. These encounters present opportunities for major illumination and transformation.

Winged Ones

The *winged ones* are aligned with spirit, and they are the *receiver-determiners* in the East. They are masters of movement in alignment with the wind energies, so they can fly the currents of the mind. In every aspect of their being they symbolize the way our mind receives.

The winged ones also represent our fierce desire to fly. Even in earliest cave drawings there are two connections made to the animal world by shamans and sorcerers: first to the horned ones and second to the winged ones. Early humanity equated freedom with the symbol of the winged ones. The greatest thing our mind can conceive is its individual, autonomous freedom, and birds represent this at the highest level, symbolically and in practice. They also give us their wings and feathers as medicine objects that can direct or move energy.

Mythical Animals and Two-Leggeds

In the Center are the *mythical animals,* which are *receiver-transformers.* The unicorn, the pegasus, the dragon, the thunderbird, and other mythological archetypes transform our myths and our dreams into sources of understanding and power. The mythological animals sit in this place along with the ancestors because they are stored within our ancestral memory. We sit as unbalanced *two-leggeds* in the very Center of this wheel, but if we can grow up and become balanced humans, then we can evolve to our own circle and become "human beings."

Animals as Teachers

Animals are powerful teachers and have much to offer us because they possess natural balance, harmony, and alignment. They do not have doubt, blame, shame, insecurity, and all the other blocks we experience. A wolf does not worry because it is not an eagle. A fox does not experience jealousy because another fox is bigger and has longer, shinier fur. They don't yearn to be something else. The animal simply knows what it is and instinctively knows its purpose. Animals teach us to accept ourselves for who we are because they are so in alignment with who they are.

One way to align with and communicate with the animal world is to go to your local zoo. Spend time with an animal that you are attracted to, particularly one of your *totem animals,* for they are key to your own unique naturalness. Do not stare into their eyes, as that is a signal of aggression or danger; rather, gaze at them indirectly or with soft focus. Send your energy and your communication softly, with respect and honor. Ask that animal to receive the energy and send its energy back. They communicate in images, so see what you get. Observe the animal in its catness, its deerness, its rabbitness, its crowness, its wolfness. What makes it what it is? If the opportunity presents itself, imitate the body movement, mannerisms, and sounds of the animal, just as you did with the trees. What does it feel like, look like, act like in your own body to be a jaguar, a bear, an eagle?

When you study an animal this way, you realize it has a medicine teaching to give to you. Awaken those attributes in yourself, exemplify them in your life.

Thunder Strikes: It is unfortunate that so many people today do not have the opportunity to observe animals in their natural habitat. When I was a youngster, part of my education, guided by my clan uncle John Two Crows, was to sit for hours in a "blind" near an animal trail or watering hole and observe the animals. I learned many things about myself.

Over time, you will want to get to know your own personal totem animals. We encourage you to explore this arena by reading Sun Bear's book *The Medicine Wheel* (New York: Prentice Hall, 1986). His sacred vision, his Earth wisdom, and the love of Grandmother Earth that Sun Bear shared during his life were instrumental in bringing back the sacred Medicine Wheels and reawakening people's connection with the Earth Mother. (See Appendix B to find your birth totem animal and Appendix C for a ceremony to help you connect with your totem animals.)

In their natural habitats animals maintain harmony and balance. They exhibit alpha/beta behavior and assert their territorial imperative to maintain that balance. That same behavior is exhibited by humans as well, since we are still two-legged animals, but we don't create balance and harmony with our alpha/beta behavior. More often than not, we dominate and try to take control, thus upsetting the balance in the environment. When we enter the picture, we destroy the whole balance and suffer immeasurably for it.

Thunder Strikes: As a kid, I hunted rabbits for food and killed those that were diseased for bounty. I made medicine over my box of shells each time and killed the rabbits in a sacred way. To approach an animal in a sacred manner means to have a healthy respect for the animal's natural instinctive ability and to honor its sacrifice, its give-away to us. That is why I was taught never to take the first plant I came to or kill the first animal I encountered when I was hunting. If we take only what we need and no more, we never interfere with the animal and plant worlds. They will stay in their proper ecological balance.

Humans often insist animals are like people, and we impose our human values and emotions on them. Pets do mimic our behaviors. They absorb the energy we give off as well as the energy in the overall environment. So when you think your pet needs to see an animal psychologist, leave your pet at home and make an appointment for yourself. They are mirrors for us to look into and see ourselves more clearly.

The key to our own survival adaptability is our ability to see through animals' eyes, to encode their natural instinctive ways into our bodies. You see, we already possess all that "knowing," but we have lost access to it, and we must focus our will to find it again, to do what animals do naturally. We can focus our will to develop a particular trait or characteristic as part of our personality. Animals are called *sweet medicine* because they teach us the sweetness of our free will and our determination.

Our Relationship to Plants and Animals as Food

The food you eat comes from the plant and animal world. Plants and animals have done a sacred give-away of themselves to provide nourishment for you. The food—plant or animal—has a consciousness as well as a substance form. When you eat the substance form, it releases its spiritual essence, which is what really nourishes you. In this way, it gives you life.

There is such a thing as *dead food* and *live food,* even though both may be cooked food. The manner in which your food is prepared affects how and to what extent its essence can be transferred to you for your sustenance and health. Food prepared in fast-food restaurants and take-out chains or available in the frozen-food section of the supermarket is essentially *dead food.* It has not been prepared with loving care; it has been thrown together on a rushed assembly line, and too often we then scarf it down on the run. Families less and less often sit down to a lovingly prepared meal and truly focus on and appreciate this nourishment, this give-away that comes to us from the worlds of Grandmother Earth. More and more, our meals are squeezed into our work schedules—between meetings, band practice, our workout at the gym, picking the kids up from school, or going to the movies. Remember, *everything* is energy. The energy we radiate into the food we eat is what we carry into our bodies.

Task: How to Align With the Food You Eat

You can make a powerful connection with the worlds of Grandmother Earth through the food you eat in the following way: When you sit down to eat, look at every single plant and meat on your plate and envision it alive in its natural form. Reflect for a moment about the preciousness, the sweetness, of that food usually taken for granted. Then, very clearly from your heart, say thank-you, and honor the way in which it died in order for you to be nourished. Declare your intent—to gain the greatest amount of energy and nourishment possible from the food.

When you do this, you receive much more than just calories and vitamins; the plants and animals co-empower you through their give-away. In this way, you engage in a process of connection and communication that transcends physical substance form. Do this for a week, and then go back to your old routine and notice the difference in your energy. This is a step for you towards alignment. This also applies to people who say grace at a meal. Usually this is spoken as a prayer to God or Creator/Creatress for the blessing of the food. In addition, however, offer your prayer of thanksgiving directly to the plants and animals that feed you.

Finding Our Balance With the Food Chain

We need the balance of male and female energy that comes from eating both plants and animals. This is about alchemy, knowing your way of balance.

Thunder Strikes: *As a result of my experiences in Vietnam, I needed to be a vegetarian for a long time to cleanse my body of toxins. I needed to go inward and be receptive to my feminine energy. When I went back out into the world, I found I needed to add meat to my diet to nurture the active-conceptive masculine part of myself, to create balance again. The key is to be so intimately attuned to your body that you can hear it talking to you. Your body will tell you what it needs.*

Many people refuse to eat meat because they see that as killing life. What they fail to realize is that eating plants is also killing life. Plants are givers, and animals receive plants as food. When you eat meat, the animal is helping you receive the plant, for an animal is a walking plant, in a sense. Remember, death gives life. The animal's sacrifice empowers us, nurtures us, heals us, and teaches us how to receive. We determine how that give-away is honored and respected by the way we receive it. To deny that gift is to deny one of the important roles they play in the web of life of this planet.

On the other hand, there are those who refuse to eat meat not because they see it as intrinsically wrong, but because they are offended by the cruel and inhumane way animals are slaughtered and processed today. We now live in a world where we are dependent on our food coming from and through the process of mass production. Through your prayer and honoring of the food that comes to your table, you can determine what happens to its energy. Offer thanks for its give-away, and say a sincere prayer to that animal or plant for the way in which it had to die for you. Let it know that you appreciate what it had to receive in order to finally provide sustenance for you. This heart connection with the spirit of the plant or the animal can reinstate the natural balance and alignment within Sacred Law. This is an example of energy transformation that we determine through our intent and our actions.

At the same time, you can actively lobby for reform in the food production industry and spend your consumer dollars in stores that stock products that are more in alignment with these principles.

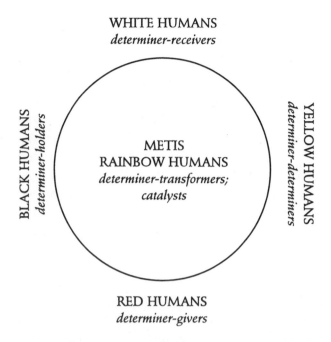

WHITE HUMANS
determiner-receivers

BLACK HUMANS
determiner-holders

METIS
RAINBOW HUMANS
determiner-transformers;
catalysts

YELLOW HUMANS
determiner-determiners

RED HUMANS
determiner-givers

Fig. 11-e   The Human World: Determiners of Energy

The Human World: The Determiners of Energy

Humans are the fourth-born children of Grandmother Earth and sit in the East (see Fig. 11-e). Again, we are two-legged animals in the Center of the receiving world of animals, but we can evolve and become balanced human beings as *determiners,* taking responsibility for our place in the web of life. Human beings are determiners, or directors, because we have choice and free will; we can destroy or nurture our environment.

This wheel tends to create controversy because it distinguishes between *red, black, white, yellow,* and mixed races, called *metis.* Furthermore, in these modern times, unique cultural and racial distinctions are blurring as technology shrinks the globe, and the world community continues to become more homogenous. This Human World Wheel teaches the traits and gifts of humans as determiners of energy and honors the unique beauty of the gifts and

the give-away of each race of people that the soul seeks in its evolution and chooses as part of the mold for our spirit personalities.

The Twisted Hairs Elders say that each of us is a spiritual metis,
as we have reincarnated into each race many times. (They say that
since each spirit personality, guided by the cycles within Sacred
Law, reincarnates a minimum of 144 times to evolve to the point of
resurrection and enlightenment, our spirit personality has incarnated into each race a minimum of thirty-six times.) Furthermore,
we all have red blood, black pupils, white bones, and yellow mar-
row in our bones, and we carry the gifts and give-aways of each of
the colors within our cellular memory. All we need to do is access
that memory to realize we are metis; we are all brothers and sisters in the larger family.

Red/Brown Humans

As an incarnation in this race, we have the opportunity to align
with the energies of the South—learning how to flow with the waters and be as the plants to give of our self in life and in nature. We
learn to align with the heart and the fluidity of emotions and our
heart connection with Nature.

Black Humans

We incarnate into this race with the opportunity to integrate the
attributes of the West—learning how to hold and transform energy
within our body, to develop mastery, and to experience our body
as the sacred temple it truly is.

White Humans

We incarnate into this race with the opportunity to learn to receive like the wind in the North, to develop multiple perceptions,
and to use one of the greatest gifts of humanity—an open and
imaginative mind.

Yellow Humans

We incarnate into this race to learn the power of fire in the East
in order to embrace spirit and gain moments of illumination.

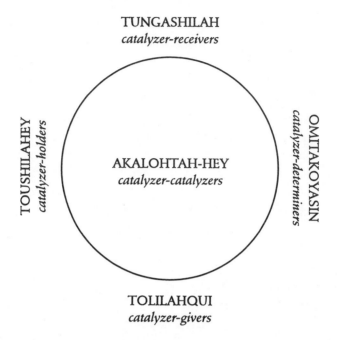

TUNGASHILAH
catalyzer-receivers

TOUSHILAHEY
catalyzer-holders

AKALOHTAH-HEY
catalyzer-catalyzers

OMITAKOYASIN
catalyzer-determiners

TOLILAHQUI
catalyzer-givers

Fig. 11-f The Spirit World: Transformers of Energy

The Metis

In the center are the *metis*, the rainbow humans of mixed blood. These are the ones who bring to us the gathering-together circle of the teachings and the opportunity to exercise the unique gifts of all the great races and powers. When we come into physical form as metis, we integrate the opportunities of the combination of racial attributes we have inherited. Ultimately, on a spiritual level, we are all metis.

Ancestor Spirit World: The Catalyst Energy

The *ancestor spirits* sit in the Center of the worlds (see Fig. 11-f), for it is the journey from spirit into substance and substance back into spirit that makes transformation and evolution possible. We are the culmination of all the potential of all our ancestors, and we owe them honor and respect. We have the opportunity and the obligation to develop our excellence to actualize the potential of our ancestry and carry the Beauty and power of that legacy on to the next seven generations.

Tolilahqui

Tolilahqui are the little people. They came here with the elementals to prepare the planet for habitation by humans. They work with the *Sasquatch*, considered by Native Americans to be rulers of the animal world, who use the little people as communicators and balancers of ecology. Only when they were present could humans be birthed into this world. They delight in mischief and teach us the gifts of laughter and humor.

Toushilahey

Toushilahey are all our spirit selves and personalities from every lifetime Since Always and For Always. Our task is to gain freedom from the cycles of reincarnation and resurrect into enlightenment.

Tungashilah

Tungashilah are all the blood relations of our toushilahey.

Omitakoyasin

Omitakoyasin are the spirits of all ancestors of all humans on this planet Since Always and For Always. People who enter into your circle of life experience have done so because you have dreamed them there. In some way your souls have established an agreement that allows you to empower each other's evolution. We are all related.

Akalohtah-hey

Akalohtah-hey are those ascended masters who teach us from the spirit world and act as guides for us on our soul's SunDance Journey.

Our technologies and scientific advances, our modern conveniences, and our electronic ease of communication have created lifestyles that foster the illusion that we are masters of the worlds of Grandmother Earth. Humanity's arrogance will prove its undoing. Separation *is* an illusion as we are all part of the web of life. Destroy one part, and the web collapses. The Earth Mother will survive, heal, and rebalance herself through her Earth changes in alignment with the Cosmic Law "Death Gives Life." It may take a million or so years, but that is merely a blink in her time line. We may not survive, however; extinction is certainly an option for the human species. The choice is ours.

12

An Elemental Balancing Act

We contain the elements of *air, fire, water,* and *earth* within us, and we live and breathe with these elemental energies every moment of our lives. These were introduced to you in the Introduction and again in the wheel for the Powers of the Four Directions. Here they are presented again, so you can take a closer look at how each element, including the center *void,* correlates with the five aspects of your being (see Fig. 12-a).

When we talk about proper expression of elemental energies, or elemental balance, we are referring to a balanced choreography of energy—what it takes to be in alignment, harmony, and resonance. How do we use our energy? How do we relate to people and things? How do we interact with aspects of our inner being and with all things in our environment?

If the internal energies in our Magnetic Attracting Thought (MAT) space are out of balance, we pull energy from other spaces and disrupt other energies, for example, other people and everything in our environment. Elemental imbalance is a primary cause of stress and all its manifestations in our lives, and occurs when we are not in alignment with what the emotions, body, mind, spirit, and sexual energy were designed to do best.

To draw from the Twenty Count analogy, imagine again sections of an orchestra. *Mind* is the winds section, and its proper energetic is one of *receiving. Heart* is the percussion section, and *giving* is its proper energy expression. The *physical body* can be likened to the string section, and it plays its part when it *holds and transforms*

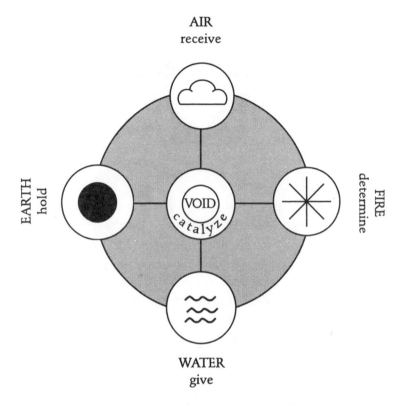

AIR
receive

EARTH
hold

FIRE
determine

WATER
give

Fig. 12-a   The Elements Wheel

energy. *Spirit,* the conductor, is in proper alignment when it is *de-termining,* or *directing. Sexuality* is the energy and vibration of the music, and it *catalyzes* energy. Imagine the orchestra performing a beautiful symphony, all instruments playing their parts in harmony with one another, resonating and following the cadence of the per-cussion section. We hear a perfect choreography of sound. Sud-denly, each instrument starts to play one of the other parts, or whatever they feel like playing, ignoring the beat and rhythm and totally disregarding the direction of the conductor. The result is noise, dissonant and without meaning, ultimately playing to an empty house. So it goes with two-leggeds.

Our Emotions

Our emotions sit in the South, in the *giving* place. Emotion means *energy in motion* or *e-motion*. It does not mean emotionality or *emotion-null,* which means the negation of emotions. The most natural emotions in the Universe are the bliss, joy, and ecstasy of pure light energy within the stream of livingness, the flow of soul consciousness. All other emotions are learned responses, products of our molding, sculpting, and armoring from the time we are born. Yet when expressed as pure, giving movements of energy, emotions are part of our beauty and our imagination.

It is important to distinguish between feelings and emotions. If you pinch your inner thigh really hard, you feel pain. If you stroke your inner thigh, you feel pleasure. Feelings are physical sensations in the body. Emotion, on the other hand, is *how* you express the feeling: what you say about it, how you label it, and what story you tell about it based on past experiences. That type of emotion is emotionality or emoting. If you are pure energy in motion, you acknowledge your body is experiencing the feeling of pain or pleasure; that is all.

Water and plants are the purest givers of energy. If you are not giving with your heart, you are out of alignment with the water and the plant world. The nature of water shows us how to be fluid and flow with our emotions. This doesn't mean we don't get angry or sad or have energetic outbursts, but if we express our emotions properly, we move the energy through and out of our body, with no residue or leftover charge that hangs around and grows into something else. And as long as we *give* our emotions *with tenderness*, they are true, clear, and clean expressions of who we are naturally. We are balanced.

Misuse of energy in the five aspects can cause major repercussions in our physical body, leading to sickness, disease, illness, and even death. If we try to hold, receive, determine, or catalyze with our emotions, then we get into trouble. Let's look at some imbalanced uses of our emotional energy.

If we hold with our emotions, our energy becomes like stagnant water. We are literally stuffing this energy in our body and slamming the lid on it, so we don't express the emotions we are feeling. We are constantly emotional, often wallowing in emotionality, and taking everything personally whether or not it is directed at us.

Jan: *I acted out this pattern a lot when I was married. If my husband got upset or angry about something, or was out of sorts, I just knew it must be because of something I had done or said. And I would recapitulate past events to try to figure out where I went wrong. What agony! What a waste of energy!*

This energy imbalance can manifest in the body as obesity, addictions around food and water, alcoholism, high blood pressure, and cardiovascular problems. When we hold with our emotions, the drums in our orchestra are trying to be the strings.

On the other hand, if we try to receive with our emotions, we become an energy vampire, in that we pull energy from others to ourselves, expecting others to take care of us and our needs. Often, we demand that others "make it right" or "make it better" or "fix it," sapping their energy in the process, unless they know how to confront our imbalance. We need to have people around us all the time. Physiologically, this often manifests as obesity, anorexia, bulimia, neuroses, high blood pressure, hypertension, sugar diabetes, or constant depression, among other symptoms.

What is the difference between holding with our emotions and receiving with them with regard to weight problems? With bulimia, for example, what exactly is happening? If we receive with our emotions, that intake of energy feels like body substance with weight, so we tend to feel fat. Such individuals think they are fat, so they constantly purge themselves. They receive so much with their emotions that their emotions become overamplified. They constantly regurgitate to get rid of the "weight" of their emotions. Why doesn't this apply to holding with the emotions and obesity? Obese persons are holding by stuffing themselves, taking in and not releasing. Receiving, on the other hand, is amplifying a misconception or illusion to begin with. Bulimics also don't think they deserve, so they have to regurgitate everything.

If we try to determine with our emotions, we become a brat or a tyrant, and we overwhelm others with our demands. We demand attention through our emotionalism; we "get even" or throw a temper tantrum to get our way.

Jan: An acquaintance of mine often determines with her emotions. When she gets confused and begins to feel she is losing control, she goes into a dramatic tizzy, and people come running to her rescue. She makes decisions and sets priorities as emotional reactions rather than taking decisive action as a pure expression of energy. She is typical of people who wildly exaggerate and play out the drama of their emotions to stay in control of their perceptual reality.

The extremes of this energetic imbalance are the sociopath, the psychopath, and the schizophrenic.

If we catalyze with our emotions, we tend to develop fanatical personalities, or become hypochondriacal or hyperactive. This energy imbalance in the extreme can also create suicidal tendencies.

Our Body

Our body sits in the West and is meant to *hold with intimacy* and then, like the Earth, it must transform and stabilize itself. This means you must take in the energy you need for stability and good health, always keeping a reservoir of energy for emergencies, and then giving away or releasing what you do not need. Regardless of gender, you receive or pull in energy from your left side and release energy or produce results with it from your right side.

Think of yourself as a battery. Energy is put into the battery from one direction, thus charging it. It discharges as it sends energy to the starter, the clock, the radio, or other parts of the car, while the running engine continues to recharge it. If the charge and discharge are not balanced, the battery will become overcharged or undercharged and malfunction. Our body is no different. Much of our energetic dysfunction, in all aspects of ourselves, is an imbalance of our body charge and discharge. When you hold and transform energy properly in your body, you are utilizing energy for good health.

This has to do with the polarities of the electromagnetic energy in your body. You can test this polarity by holding a pendulum over your hands, which are vortices of energy. With a steady hand, dangle the pendulum over the open palm of your left hand. If your energy flow is balanced, the pendulum will rotate counterclockwise. Turn your palm over and then hold the pendulum over the back of your hand; this will reverse its motion.

In the palm of the right hand, the proper energy motion is clockwise. Turn the palm over, and it reverses. It is through your receptivity to your creativity that you are able to actualize tangible results in your life. If your polarity reverses or is not moving properly, this indicates the energy that you are taking in through your left side and charging the body with is not balanced by your discharge of energy through your right side. Relate this to how you utilize your physical energy in your daily activities. Do you produce results? Do you get a return commensurate with the energy you expend?

People in the caregiving professions, such as nursing, psychotherapy, counseling, and social work, need to guard against holding energy with their bodies without transforming and discharging it. They are constantly exposed to negative energies around their clients, and it is necessary to take steps to prevent it from sticking. Holding with the body can also lead to rigidity.

On the other hand, people who give with the physical body tend to substitute working, physical rewards, and money for loving, hugging, holding, nurturing, and physical closeness. They expect their body to do it all for them, so they will exhibit some of the same symptoms as those who are workaholics and totally dedicated to career. There is a difference between the people who determine with their body and those who give with their body. People giving with the body exhibit a more "shotgun" approach in their output of energy; they tend to overextend themselves in many areas. They physically give, give, give. People determining, or directing, with the body, on the other hand, are more focused. They often become workaholics or alcoholics; in other words, they have an addictive personality.

This also happens when people hold with their emotions and give with their body. This is the root cause of all addictive personality paradigms, combined with fear of human sexuality or sexual freedom. In this case, people give their energy away, whether to another person or to a work schedule or to food. For example, consider the father who cannot give love with intimacy to his children, so he works overtime or holds several jobs to give them physical, material things as a way of showing his love.

Receiving with the body produces a lethargic victim syndrome in which we have no energy to do anything. This also weakens the immune system, which can exacerbate body stress and cause a complete physical breakdown. This is a basic syndrome at this time, one form of which has been tagged as chronic fatigue syndrome and is at almost epidemic proportions in our society today. We are constantly tired, we have no energy, and we have no reservoir of strength. We tend to sleep and eat a lot. This often produces the couch potato.

If we determine with our bodies, we tend to act as a bully, engage in physical abuse, or overpower people with our physical presence to stay in control or have our way. Such individuals often become obsessive-compulsive, like chronic workaholics, constantly physically structuring and controlling their world. Ironically, this includes the bully as well as the overachiever and the Olympic athlete, whose total focus is physical structure and control of the body. Determining with our bodies produces extreme aging very quickly. Fortunately, this is rare.

If we catalyze long enough with our body, we die. This happens when people continuously progress from one disease and illness to another. They may become extremely accident-prone and create an accident of such magnitude that they can become quadriplegic (most of the time, however, this is not a conscious choice). They create physical crises in a desperate attempt to establish meaning in their life and a sense of identity for themselves, and their need becomes so great that it dominates everything else in their life.

Our Mind

In the North, we *receive* with the mind *through clarity and caring.* Our mind should be like the wind, clear and open. To dance in balance here means to have the ability to be mentally flexible, to see reality from many viewing points. Approach everyone and everything as an empty cup. Be receptive, and let your cup be filled without judgment or prejudice. Then take a sip, test it, and integrate what works for you. Take another sip, test it, and integrate again. Hold with your mind and you come with a full cup, full of your belief systems and personal philosophies, and fixation on a particular point of reason to the exclusion of others. This develops tunnel vision, which often causes people to be judgmental, bigoted, prejudiced, and dogmatic.

If we give with the mind, we are asleep to reality in the environment and can often be adversely affected by it. We constantly deal with the way things should be, can be, must be, or ought to be. We can become "poor me" victims. We may create illusions in our heads, give them out as "truth," and paint the world with them.

People who determine with the mind often get depressed, despairing, or disappointed because things aren't the way they want them to be, like a director who can't get the actors to do what she wants them to do.

People who hold with their mind are similarly frustrated. However, with this particular energetic, they hold tightly on to an idea or concept of how something should be, and instead of changing their attitude or shifting their viewing point, they rigidly keep trying to make it work. They often drop one activity or project and move on to another, jump from one social cause to another, or experiment with one spiritual path after another. They typically keep changing jobs, trying to find the perfect combination of elements, rather than dealing with the cause of their dissatisfaction. As long as they are doing this, they will never get to the heart of their problem and solve it. This keeps them in constant distraction.

Catalyze with the mind, and we become a lord or queen tyrant, the dictator. This pattern often occurs in combination with determining with the emotions. Such people insist, "It's my way or the highway!" Catalyzing with the mind can contribute to borderline personalities, schizophrenia, and sociopathology, and in the extreme, dictators who practice genocide. This energy imbalance also produces an extremely regimented discipline with the body, such as the physical fitness freaks who obsess over their body and work out as the end-all and be-all.

Our Spirit

In the East, we *determine* with the spirit *through passion and lust*, which is our creativity. Spirit is the *fire* within us which, properly choreographed, directs or determines what the mind receives and determines wise and decisive action. When we try to determine with our minds, we go into total mind constructs of pain and illusion. Only spirit can see the big picture and knows what we are here for—what our vision and sacred dream are. Spiritual determination allows us to live the Magician's Law: "Love of Will and the Will to Do Is the All of the Law." This entails the will to do what must be done.

It is obvious that Michelangelo painted the Sistine Chapel with creative passion and lust fired by sacred vision. Few people are willing to delve deeply enough into their well of vision and artistic originality to discover such power and beauty. Many people are unhappy in their career or vocation and wish they were doing something else, but they are afraid to risk their security. They are afraid they will alienate friends and family, or they may feel they must do what is expected of them. "All my life I've really wanted to ... but ..." Are you doing what you really, passionately desire? If not, why not? If you are, congratulate yourself.

If we try to give with our spirit, we are essentially just giving away our vision. We often fall asleep, not very aware of what is going on around us; we imagine the world in a haze of illusion and fantasy. You might say that we seem to be "in outer space." Giving with our spirit puts out our fire. Water puts out fire.

If we hold with spirit, we will tend to become disillusioned and lose hope. People who hold with their spirit have lost sight of the bigger picture, a vision of what can be, the potential of something greater than what is in front of their nose. They are caught in doom and gloom.

Receiving with spirit is just the opposite. These people can have a vision, a passionate desire to attain greatness and accomplish something special, but they never make it happen.

If we catalyze with our spirit, we burn out.

Our Sexual Soul Force Energy

In the Center of the Wheel of Elements is the void element, which is aligned with our sexual catalyst energy. It is our soul force, which literally *catalyzes* our life and *sparks* all other aspects of ourselves, giving us our identity as a human being. This is the major source of our communication of truth through our integrity and an open heart. Some of our greatest imbalance and pain is also created here due to the influence of our image makers.

If we give with our sexuality, we manipulate and bargain with our sexuality within our relationships. Here is an example of what this looks like: A man demands sex as part of his rights as a husband or significant other; a woman manipulates by giving sexual favors to get what she wants. Withdrawing or refusing to be sexual when the other partner desires it is often a ploy to gain a bargaining advantage.

Determining with sexuality creates sexual deviancy. These are the rapists, the child molesters, and the spouse beaters who are being controlled and driven by their anger and rage expressed sexually to get even. On a far lesser level, determining with our sexuality is caused by the fear of freely expressing our sexuality. This is the underlying imbalance and addiction of the addictive personality paradigm. Instead of becoming the rapist, we express our anger by punishing ourselves. Our spirit becomes dead with alcohol, or heavy with food, or lost with gambling.

If we receive with our sexuality, we stay in a continuous fantasy, frequently alone, never or rarely ever experiencing it for real.

How to Realign Our Energies

Most people switch the North and East energies and the South and West energies, and they tend to lose their balance in their emotions first. There are a number of ways you can begin to learn about and align with the elements of air, fire, water, earth, and the void. Obviously, being in Nature and connecting with the many forms these elements take is an important part of alignment. In addition, the willingness to engage in confrontation and take decisive action are key to balancing your energies. This bears repeating here.

If you avoid confrontation, you will surely fall out of elemental balance. When you are engaging with others, the correct spiritual determination is the willingness to engage directly in a confrontation with the mirror they present to you. If you are not willing to meet them, if you refuse to confront their energy, you will go into reaction instead of decisive action. When you react instead of act, you will always be at the effect of other people's energy, whether negative or positive. This will throw you into elemental imbalance every time.

Any decisive action is better than a reaction. It takes much more energy to start your car than it does to keep it moving. Get going, then learn to make decisions in motion, not standing still. Why? You will already have met and engaged with other people's energy and can read their energy more clearly if you are moving than if you are standing still energetically. You cannot operate from a stationary position. You are waiting for a learned response to come from the brain to tell you what to do, and that waiting limits you.

What does this have to do with self-worth and self-deservement? In any given moment you carry within you a measure, an assessment of worth and what you feel you deserve. Suddenly others present you with new stimulus, a mirror to look into, and an opportunity to engage with them. Look into the mirror they present to you, and during the experience, present to them the most valid assessment of your self-worth. Let them see themselves in that mirror. Then, after the engagement, measure and reassess your self-worth and what you feel you deserve before you go on to the next experience. If you are not conscious of your measure, you will be unconscious in the confrontation. You react and get thrown out of balance.

Commit to confronting and engaging others with consciousness. You will expand, evolve, and increase your measure, your life force, your illumination. Someone once asked, "What happens if two people meet with decisive action? Isn't that a war?" The answer: "No. Wisdom ensues." You will walk away feeling touched by spirit. This develops charisma. It will definitely increase your magnetic attraction.

Task: Aligning With the Elemental Energies

Spend time working with the Elements Wheel to explore and identify how you engage the elemental energies. How do you align with the elements externally and internally? Examine how you give, hold, receive, determine, or catalyze with your emotions, body, mind, spirit, and sexual energy. Where do you create imbalance by misdirecting these aspects of yourself? How does this imbalance affect your relationships with family, friends, work, and your physical environment?

Another simple, but extremely effective, technique to help you achieve elemental balance is to tap your wrist every time you catch yourself out of balance. You may have a very sore wrist by the end of the day, but after a few days, you will begin to notice that although you still may catch yourself out of balance, you realign much more quickly. You will feel a difference in your energy.

This takes discipline, and discipline gives us freedom. Commit yourself to the experiences that present themselves to you, particularly those that offer the greatest attraction, because they are your greatest opportunities for growth. Part of discipline is the ability to be unaffected by the pretenses and projections put on you by others. Again, we recommend you start a journal and record your observations. Then, one step at a time, begin to reprogram your energy patterns so that you create greater balance and harmony in your life and in your relationship with those in your immediate environment.

Section Four

Are You the Star in Your Movie?
How We Journey Through the Cycles of Our Lives

About Section Four

The journey of the spirit personality of our soul in the *life round* is described in cycles traversed around the Great Medicine Wheel of Life. We determine whether these are cycles of evolution, growth, and learning, accomplishing our transformation from karma into dharma, or whether we stay stuck and stagnate, continually repeating our karmic patterns like a fox chasing its tail.

The *Star Maidens Circle* is the *Key Driver Wheel* of the Sweet Medicine SunDance tradition, and it is the primary focus of this next section. The Twisted Hairs say this wheel came from the stars, from the Pleiades, called *Star Maidens* or *Sskwanasie*. This Key Wheel is a *master cognitive map* to guide the spirit personality of the soul on its SunDance Journey. Along with the *Infinity Movement*, it provides a powerful tool for discovering our shining light within our shadow. It shows us how to rewrite the drama of our lives, this time casting ourselves as the award-winning star.

13

The Star Maidens Circle

The *Star Maidens Circle* is the *Key Driver Wheel* from which all the wheels and teachings of the Sweet Medicine SunDance Way are birthed (see Fig. 13-a). To the people of Turtle Island, it is the equivalent of the Philosopher's Stone of the North Power and the Holy Grail of the Northwest Power, both of which represent our stretch for the excellence of our true nature spirit personality. The Star Maidens Circle is one of the most powerful teachings of the Twisted Hairs, and one of the oldest.

The Star Maidens Circle Is a Master Cognitive Map

The Star Maidens Circle describes the experience of living life as a process of spiraling to enlightenment through constant connection with the Twenty Count. On one level or another, everyone is dancing the Star Maidens Circle simply by being alive. The moment we are born, we proceed around this Medicine Wheel, experiencing life from each direction in our own unique way, in our dark shadow side (*dark mirrors*) as well as in our light side (*light mirrors*). Each direction is one of the eight parts of the whole of how we pattern ourselves and our relationships in the world. The characteristics of each direction on this wheel are reflected in the same directions on all the other wheels in the Sweet Medicine SunDance teachings.

The Star Maidens Circle defines our Book of Life. It is a *cognitive map* that traces the patterns of how we do what we do because of the molding, sculpting, and armoring of our image makers. It

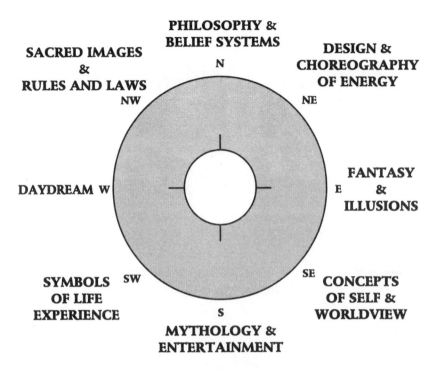

Fig. 13-a   *The Star Maidens Circle*

describes how we put limitations on ourselves. It then guides us to eliminate or alter these patterns, embrace change and our personal dream, and bring fulfillment to our lives as the true nature spirit we are. It is a very practical tool to help the needy, wounded, abandoned child in all of us grow up and heal the angry, vengeful, manipulative adult. By working with the Star Maidens Circle, we begin to realize how to rewrite our script and direct a movie of transformation as we become balanced human beings. The purpose of studying the Star Maidens Circle is to wake up and grow up, and this can happen only if we are willing to take full responsibility for our lives—Here and Now.

The teaching of the Star Maidens Circle shows you how you can edit the screenplay in process. Through constant rewriting and editing, you can create a masterpiece, a "dream-come-true" classic with yourself as the star.

Jan: *Through this process, I can star as the jaguar that roars, not the pussycat my image makers carved me into.*

The first walk around this Wheel of Life in a clockwise direction is called the *neutral position,* because it describes the directions of the wheel in a static, frozen position, allowing you the opportunity to clearly understand the dark and light sides of each direction before you begin to work your own patterns on the wheel. In addition to the neutral position, there are nine *spins,* or movements around the wheel.

Each direction of the walk around the wheel also holds a *Warrior's Attribute,* a strength or gift you acquire as you refine your character and step into the light side of that direction in balance and harmony (see Fig. 13-b). As you walk around the Star Maidens Circle, consider the qualities of the Warrior's Attributes Wheel, which overlays the Star Maidens Circle. Then overlay some of the other wheels you have learned about in previous chapters. Watch for the correlations. Observe in the South, for example, how the emotions and elemental energy of giving, or the need for emotional approval, or the block of guilt, affect you and your life experience in the South of the wheel. And so on around the wheel.

The Neutral Position of the Wheel

Although you may enter a wheel from any direction to study and work with the experience of that wheel, we will walk the Star Maidens Circle starting from the Southeast because we carry the qualities of that direction with us into every other direction on the wheel.

Southeast: Our Self-Concepts and Worldview

No matter where you are journeying on the Wheel of Life or what you are doing in the "real" world, the self-concepts you carry

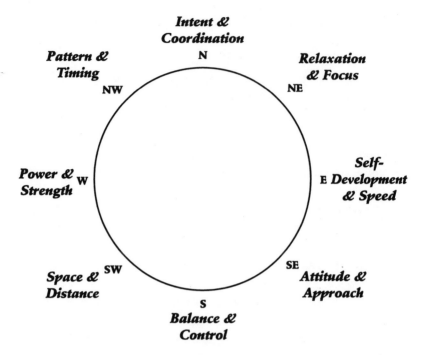

Fig. 13-b: The Warrior's Attributes Wheel

inwardly and subjectively color or affect all of your life experiences. They were formulated from the mold you were born into, and inherent in this are the questions: "Who am I? Where did I come from? Why am I here? What is my path with heart? Where am I going?"

The metaphor that helps to answer these questions is the warrior with his/her bow, quiver, and arrows. The bow symbolizes the self, that which aims for the target—life. This includes both the shideh and the hokkshideh. The quiver is the Warrior's Circle of physical and spiritual resources—the worlds of Grandmother Earth, the elements, the five aspects of self, your image makers, your knowledge, skills, tools, credentials, as well as your molding, sculpting, and armoring. The quiver contains seven *dark arrows,* seven *light arrows,* and seven *rainbow arrows.* The arrows represent your choices and decisions about how you express your energies. You shoot these self-concepts at yourself, at life, and at others. They offer a metaphor for choice—you choose which arrows you will shoot—and this determines how you process your experience of life all the way around the wheel.

When your shideh and karmic pretender ego are in control, the seven dark arrows—*attachment, dependency, judgment, comparison, expectation, the needy child syndrome,* and *self-importance*—throw you off balance and out of alignment. The dark arrows keep you in your karmic circle, mired in low self-esteem and a negative, distorted view of the world.

The seven arrows of the light—*self-awareness, self-appreciation, self-acceptance, self-pleasure, self-love, self-actualization,* and *impeccability (warrior's freedom)*—teach you how to be balanced within the self. These arrows teach you that true understanding and empowerment come from focusing on the reflections within yourself. They teach you self-reliance and show you how to transform your karma into dharma.

The seven rainbow arrows—*illumination; introspection and natural intuition; trust, innocence, and perfection; wisdom; open heart-to-heart communication; balance of our male and female energies;* and *abundance and prosperity*—are magickal arrows, gifts given to you as a result of right actions. Every time you pick up a light arrow and break a dark one, a rainbow arrow comes back to you. This is a process of transformation.

Here in the Southeast, you also formulate your worldview as a synthesis of the other seven of the eight directions. It is your external concept of the world outside yourself within which you carry your concepts of self.

Needs, Wants, and Desires

Key to developing a high level of self-esteem and a healthy worldview is your ability to drop the dark arrows and pick up the light arrows. In order to accomplish this, you need to know the difference between your needs, wants, and desires.

Needs: You may often choose to incur long-term pain for short-term pleasure to satisfy what you consider to be essential needs that are not needs at all. There are legitimate *reality needs* that you must have or suffer tremendously: food, water, shelter, clothing, sleep, dreaming, orgasm. But you may often include the need for love, approval, security, recognition, and acceptance outside yourself, and you suffer immeasurably if you don't get them. You may need help to extricate yourself from the pain incurred by these needs.

Wants: A *want* is a wishful yearning for that which is not a need or a true desire and may or may not change you or enhance your well-being if you were to acquire it. Wants are distractions. To want is to think you don't deserve the thing you want. In order to satisfy a want, you may experience short-term pain for long-term pleasure, and unlike a need, if you can't get what you want, you don't lose much energy over it.

Desires: *Desires* are your highest level of energy awareness where you meet your reality needs, determine which of your wants are really desires, and let go of the rest. You turn your attention to feeding your hungers, which are really desires of your soul to enhance your character. You develop your excellence and increase your value assessment of your self-worth and what you deserve. Feeding your hungers becomes your first and primary priority, and you eliminate all distractions, so that you are happy and joyful, and your life reflects ease and abundance.

The key to attaining this higher level of awareness lies in your willingness to engage with life fully, to confront life's challenges and testing, to be willing to make mistakes and fail in order to learn and grow. Your confrontations help you to mature and to become stronger and more powerful every day.

In the Southeast are *attitude* and *approach*, the primary Warrior's Attributes you always carry with you. You cannot do anything about the past except learn from it. You cannot do anything about the future but be prepared for as many possibilities as you can. Therefore, change what you can change. Those things you cannot change, change your attitude about. When you shift your attitude, your perceptions of the world shift. When your perceptions of the world shift, reality changes. *When all else fails, shift your attitude!* When we drop the dark arrows and pick up the light arrows from our quiver of resources, we step into proper attitude and approach as an act of empowerment. So your attitude and approach will influence your perceptions all the way around the wheel, thus having a major effect on your reality and way of being in the world. They will determine whether your journey is a struggle or a dance of Beauty!

South: Mythology and Entertainment

Out of our concepts of self, we create a story or screenplay and cast ourselves in the character we have been told we are. So the jaguar casts itself in the role of a pussycat and creates pussycat stories. This is the place where we create our mythologies, our stories of our life experience, our pretense experiences and projected pretenses that have helped to answer the question "Who am I?" These mythologies and stories may be painful tragedies or lighthearted comedies, high drama or low farce, but they are essentially survival stories that describe or mask the pain of the molding, sculpting, and armoring in our journey to adulthood. Incorporated into our mythology is our core personality, our moods of stalking, and many other aspects of our character.

So the jaguar that was sculpted and armored into a little pussycat picks up the seven arrows of the dark in the Southeast and begins to construct a story about itself and give it a name. Between birth and nine years of age, something happens that causes us to title our life movie. This "something" consists of critical events as well as the constant molding, sculpting, and armoring of the image makers.

***Thunder Strikes:** My movie title was "The Tough Little Boy Gets Going." This came out of my early school experience. I had been raised in a very traditional way, particularly by my Cherokee grandmother, Spotted Fawn, and my clan uncles. When I entered the White Man's school, the rules*

changed and the attitudes were very different. Many of the teachers con-
sidered non-whites to be less than human, and I found that I had to fight
to hold on to the values and view of the world I had been raised with. My
mythology helped me to survive.

Jan: *The movie title that grew out of my experiences was "I Don't Need*
Anyone. I Can Do It Myself!" My early years through my teens were
tightly controlled by my parents. I was rarely allowed the opportunity to fol-
low through on my own initiative or do anything on my own without their
permission, their guidance, and their constant interference. Even when I ini-
tiated an activity, they would invariably insist that it be done a certain way
and put their rules and limitations on it. To the extent I could, I tried to find
subtle, unnoticeable ways to make the things I did my own, to feel I was my
own person. My mythologies and my movie title reflect my need to view my-
self as independent and self-actualizing.

What is the title of your movie? Now, as we reach adulthood,
it becomes essential that we do a major rewrite, because these stories no longer serve us or describe who we are as adults. If we hold
onto them, they will anchor us in the past. Because our shideh resists change and strives to stay in control, it holds on to these stories, refusing to rewrite them. Instead, it replays them over and
over, even the most painful ones, reinforcing the mythology of the
pretender ego, and reassuring itself that it knows who it is. These
stories are often narrated by our pretender voices, and often we replay them as a form of entertainment. The little kid in us believes
that if it changes its survival-adaptive pain game, if it rewrites its
story, it will open the door to the unknown, which it fears will
cause even worse pain.

Our mythologies can be either dark or light. If you are caught
in the dark mythology based on the entertainment pain game, you
are stuck in the needy, wounded, abandoned child who will not
take responsibility and grow up. You entertain yourself with tonal
fear, anger, stress, and depression.

The South is the direction of the emotions, and if at any time you are in an emotional situation, your stories will take on the flavor of total survival—you against the world. Your emotions cloud your perceptions, and you will need to use your expanded imagination to stay out of the emotional traps of the South.

Your higher self knows you are much better than your story, and as you begin to break the mold and start the process of resculpting yourself, you begin to see which parts of your stories are fiction and which are fact. Weaving a superhero or archetypal hero into your mythology becomes a means of emerging out of your dark side. You are becoming acquainted with your true nature spirit, making a realistic evaluation of your strengths and weaknesses.

Through a process of recapitulation (see Appendix A), you discover what really happened; your stories change and become mythologies in the light that serve to empower you. Then the cliffhangers in your movie become challenges and adventures, opportunities to evolve and refine your character. When we accomplish this shift, we incorporate strategies for overcoming the blocks to character, for silencing the pretender voices, and finally for closing our Karma Book, opening our Dharma Book, and writing our Rainbow Light Warrior story.

In the light, you are connected with Grandmother Earth and all of Nature in a state of trust and innocence. Balance, particularly emotional balance, occurs when you rewrite the dark side into the light side. When you do this, you acquire the Warrior's Attributes of *emotional balance and control*.

Task: Write Your Stories

Choose three of the most emotionally traumatic events that you can recall in your life and write out in detail your story about each one. When you have finished, look at the common theme running through each of them. Look at the entertainment you got by the way you wove these stories around these events. What vicarious thrill or satisfaction do you get telling the story? Look at how you might shift your attitude and take a new stance so that you stop being at the effect of your dark-side mythologies.

Southwest: The Dream and Symbols of Life Experience

This is the place of the process of life itself as a dream. Our soul dreams our spirit personality present in the physical, and the only way we can perceive or experience life is through symbols and our translation of these symbols. How is this so? Our mind uses symbols as building blocks in the following process:

1. Symbols coalesce to form a thought, then ...

2. Thoughts form into ideas, then ...

3. Ideas merge into an image, then ...

4. We use images either to define and limit our perceptions and experiences or to stretch our imagination into the unknown; then images coalesce to form ...

5. Opinions, which form ...

6. Beliefs, which we formalize into ...

7. Philosophies and religion.

We carry the Southeast and the South into the Southwest experience, and that predetermines how we interpret symbols—open or closed. The box defines who we are, and we set limitations inside the box that determine how much freedom we allow ourselves. We put life experiences that we are afraid of outside the box along with symbols of these life experiences. They are *closed symbols,* or doors we will not open.

Jan: An example of a closed symbol for me is the snake. My intense fear of snakes prevents me from engaging with them (even harmless little ones) and learning more about them to overcome my fear. When a friend invited me to taste rattlesnake meat cooked at a fine restaurant, I almost gagged. I couldn't get beyond the closed symbol, the emotional charge, in order to engage in something as harmless as tasting snake meat. How would my fear be transformed if I were willing to engage with that closed symbol? I know it would change. I know that would be a benefit. But I cannot bring myself to open that closed symbol. This separates me from experience.

Too much of our life is dictated by our closed symbols. When we see life through closed symbols, we do not see reality. In fact, the closed symbols define our pretense reality. Behind every closed symbol is a dark mirror which hides a monster—our greatest fear—something that threatens the survival adaptability of our needy, wounded, abandoned child. Our little child believes that a dark monster is on the other side, one that will eat it if it opens the symbol to look at the mirror. So the child will not open the closed symbol and confront the monster. Furthermore, it deliberately alters its perceptual view because looking into a closed symbol might force it to rewrite its script. Closed symbols, then, are the filters or darkly colored glasses through which we view reality, unwilling to look at anything outside of that point of view, or *point of reason.*

Jan: *I will relate to snakes only to the extent that this relating does not force me to open my closed symbol about snakes. The moment I might have to engage in a direct experience, I'm out of there!*

Other examples of some culturally closed symbols are oral sex, a woman as president of the United States, skin color, short people, tofu, and parachuting.

A shock or trauma creates closed symbols and dark mirrors. In many interactions, they are produced through our belief systems. The more rigid the belief system, the more trauma we will experience when the belief system is challenged or threatened. Opening these symbols and looking into these dark mirrors will create a major death/change experience and a major transformational shift. The blocks are the gatekeepers of these closed symbols. Again, the willingness to confront these blocks and enlist the aid of the allies will help you open the closed symbol and confront the monster behind the mirror.

A closed symbol provides an opportunity to learn, grow, and change. If you are willing to look into it and get a pure reflection, not a distorted image, you will realize that the monster on the other side of the mirror is your own shadow and fears, which eclipse the pleasure and joy, the aliveness and vitality, in your life experience.

Your ability to look at the closed symbols is influenced by your self-concepts and your mythologies. When you are eclipsed by the closed symbols, you have very little concept of self-actualization. Life becomes rote pattern, and you are caught at the effect of the image makers and the tyrants of life. You begin to adopt a concept that says, "I can't do anything about these tyrants. I can't change anything." You *blame* others for what is wrong with your world. Your view of reality is faulty, and you do not take responsibility for your life. You are stuck in self-focus, and your personal dream is at risk because you live your life at the expense of others and through the experiences and perceptions of others. You have no sacred dream. You are not living life; you are watching it pass you by.

In the light in the Southwest, every time you are willing to confront and conquer a monster, you experience a surge of energy. What comes out of this is knowledge, higher orende, and an expanded self. When you experience the Southwest in the light, your life is a ceremony, and you have a sense of fulfillment because you remove the boundaries that restrict your experiences. In doing so, you gain clarity about your personal and sacred dreams, and you make a positive impact on the collective dream of humanity.

The Southwest Dream Wheel of the Star Maidens Circle

This is a wheel within a wheel in the Southwest of the Star Maidens Circle (see Fig. 13-c).

In the South of this little wheel is your *personal dream,* which is really the desire to live life to its fullest. This includes meeting all your reality needs and providing a minimum of security and comfort in your tonal, physical lifestyle along with the opportunity to acquire knowledge and skills. Your health is one of the major aspects of your personal dream. Your emotional balance and control affect your ability to actualize your personal dream.

In the North is the *sacred dream,* which has nothing to do with your profession, vocation, or career, or the way to make your

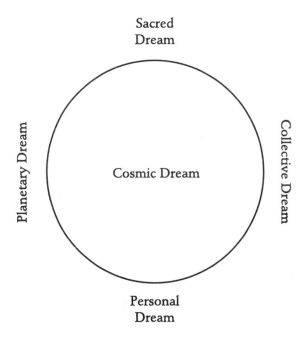

Sacred
Dream

Planetary Dream

Cosmic Dream

Collective Dream

Personal
Dream

**Fig. 13-c   The Southwest Dream Wheel
of the Star Maidens Circle**

money. It is your spiritual growth. It is what you have come here to do in this lifetime, the legacy you leave behind. You can merge your personal dream into your sacred dream, and one may be a part of the other, but they are not the same. Your personal dream represents your work; your sacred dream represents your give-away, your sacred service to life and others.

The *collective dream* in the East is how we as a group, subgroup, culture, nation, or planetary family of humanity dream ourselves into alignment or misalignment with Sacred Law. Do we dream a dream of evil and destruction, or do we dream a dream of beauty, prosperity, and peace with individual, autonomous freedom? Do we feed the Dark Horse or cheer on the Gold Horse?

In the West lies the *planetary dream*. Basically, this is Grandmother Earth's dream of her ecological balance and survival and her evolutionary excellence. Grandmother Earth will do whatever is necessary to survive, including destroying in order to recreate. Your personal and sacred dreams should be as much in alignment as possible with Grandmother Earth's dream.

The Warrior's Attributes in the Southwest are *distance* and *space*. When you open closed symbols, you see reality for what it is. You are able to hold your space and are comfortable in any arena of experience, willing to engage to make the unknown known. You can close the distance between you and challenges, or expand the space to widen your experiences. You make things happen instead of sitting on the fence, watching or waiting for something to happen. You take decisive action to expand your box and change your life. You stop blaming as an excuse for not doing.

West: The Daydream

The *daydream* here is not the usual concept of gazing out the window in fantasy and reminiscence. It is your material, physical, tonal, three-dimensional world in the Now. This embraces your reality needs, your level of comfort and security, of abundance and prosperity, including your acquisition of tools, skills, and knowledge. In the West, you are dealing with two basic realities: constant struggle for survival and relationship alignment. Alignment is ebb and flow, a rhythm. Survival is a battle.

When we are in the dark mirror of the daydream, we are caught at the effect of tyrants and image makers, unable to be present because we are preoccupied with the past or overconcerned about the future. We fear not having; then we blame others for not being able to get what we want; and then we experience shame because we can't have what someone else has. We play the victim, convinced that what will happen tomorrow is because of what has happened to us since birth.

In the dark mirror, we are walking asleep, refusing to take responsibility for ourselves or the actualization of our personal dream. Often this is because we are living our life for others' approval, acceptance, and recognition. We are afraid of death and change, particularly physical death, but also the many little deaths that are necessary for us to grow and actualize our desires. It is essential for us to be willing to go inside to that inner "body knowing" and trust our intuition to find the answers and the self-knowledge we need to make the necessary changes.

To be in the light side of the daydream is to be fully present, to assume authority in your world, and to take responsibility for your actions within Sacred Law. When something needs to be done, you do it the best you know how, with as little effort as possible. The major factor that keeps us in the dark here is our reluctance to assume authority, to assert, "I can change my world," and take responsibility for that. The victim syndrome is a dangerous trap in the West.

If you are in the light side, you manifest your ideas and you are open to change and movement. You keep your attention focused because you understand that attention is power. We so often lose our focus, constantly distracted by the clamor and cacophony of our daily lives, yet our happiness is dependent on where we focus our attention. Distractions erode our ability to take decisive action; they trip us up and allow doubt to enter and lurk about. Doubt causes us to hesitate, to question our priorities and our desires.

We play a dangerous game of sabotage here in the West. We strive and struggle for the "good life," for credentials, promotions, status, money, and security. The irony is, however, that many successful and wealthy people who are out there every day actualizing and getting wealthier and wealthier are supremely unhappy. Why? They are living the pretender life of their molded, sculpted, and armored self instead of the sacred dream of their spirit personality. All their accomplishments are not evolving the destiny of their soul.

Whether you like it or not, your soul will not be denied, for its sole purpose for being here as a spirit personality in physical form is to grow and evolve. It is not here to build a bigger house, become president of the corporation, own a summer cottage, bask at Club

Med, or retire at sixty. The sacred dream of your soul is not your career, how much money you make, or even the contributions you make for the good of the collective. These may satisfy your desires and bring you the fulfillment and joy of accomplishment and plea- sure, but they should not be the defining meaning and purpose of your life. They do not define who you are. They are adventures and rewards on your journey, not your destination.

Power and *strength* are the Warrior's Attributes in the West. At- tention is power, and power is a feminine energy that manifests as an ease of living. When change comes, you already see where change is trying to go, and you are willing to add your energy in or- der to go where it wants to go. This is soft power that operates within the law of "Maximum Efficiency With Minimum Effort." The Twisted Hairs say you *catch minimal chance* and ride the chaotic wave. *Minimal chance* is a term that refers to fleeting moments of opportunity that present themselves, like the ideal moment when a surfer has to catch the wave and ride it. If you are awake, aware, and alert enough to catch these waves of opportunity, you can ac- commodate change smoothly without losing your balance and in- curring stress. These are moments of power. Constantly asking "Why?" or "Why me?" keeps you from power. Stay present in the Now, and you will attract power to you. To understand power align with the four elements.

Northwest: Pattern, Rules, and Laws; Sacred Images; Law of Cycles

This is the place of *rules and laws, rights and wrongs, morals and ethics*—all the paradoxes and dualities of life. The Northwest is also the place of the Law of Cycles and the seasons, Grandmother Earth's patterns of form. Our patterns of behavior, our karma and dharma, sit here as well.

Your Book of Life, the movie script your higher self wrote for you to experience in this lifetime, sits here. This is the place of your *sacred image,* which represents the full development and full ex- pression of your true nature spirit personality. It is your stretch of excellence in this lifetime. When you live as your sacred image, it is possible for you to actualize your sacred dream. Your first sacred image is of life itself—how you relate to all existence as sacred. The second sacred image is of you, yourself, as a sacred thought of the Great Spirit—as a Magnetic Attracting Thought (MAT) space within which a physical form has been dreamed or thought. And the third sacred image is of you within life—as an interconnected, interdependent, and interreliable part of the sacredness of all life. In order to stretch into our excellence, we must follow Sacred Law.

The Northwest is a breaker place on the wheel because it is the most conflicted place. In the dark side, we stay stuck in pattern and endless repetition, trapped in our box of do's and don'ts, rights and wrongs, the boundaries and limitations of our mythologies and stories. We are unduly influenced and controlled by the image makers, frequently violating Sacred Law in order to fit in, belong, and conform. It is here that we make soul contracts known as our *children's fire*. If we break these, we incur karma. On the other hand, if we honor and fulfill our contracts to the best of our ability, we increase our chances of closing our Karma Book and opening our Dharma Book, free at last to be who we really are. When we are willing to break old patterns of behavior and develop new ones, push out and ultimately break down the walls of our box of limitations, we change karma into dharma.

We all want beauty, pleasure, and ease in our lives. However, we create pain and struggle for ourselves because we constantly fight change. Either we refuse to accept that change is inevitable, or we want to make change safe and convenient; we want guarantees that the new pattern will be better than the old. We are determined to do it "our way." There is nothing wrong with wanting to do things in our own unique way; that is part of our artistic originality and our beauty. But many of us, stuck in our little boxes of experience, safe in the redundancy of our entertaining pain games, try to birth these new patterns without giving up the old ones. We try to swim in the middle of the stream without stepping off the shore because we are attached to the familiar.

In the dark mirror in the Northwest, we are also under the illusion that we can disregard the cycles of Nature, of the Earth, of the Universe, and of Sacred Law. Our energy orchestra is often out of control, for we refuse to open up and listen to the determination voice of our higher self. Life is a choice, and this is our script. There are no ghostwriters here. We make things happen because we want them to happen. Change is inevitable. It is our warrior's ally. Dying means making the changes that will empower us, help us step into our sacred image and make our sacred dream a reality. A spiritual warrior's motto is: "Today is a good day to die."

Pattern and *timing* are the Warrior's Attributes in the Northwest. As you move into the light in this place and begin to recognize your patterns and unmask your pretenses, you develop the timing to know when to break or change the patterns that no longer serve you and establish new ones that empower you. Timing also helps you to know when to change a pattern. In other words, when the chaotic wave hits, you must be awake to see the pattern and perfect your timing to ride the wave that will take you out of your predictable pattern. In the light, you will always break a pattern the minute you understand that it is no longer right for you, and you are willing to take responsibility for the change.

North: Philosophies and Belief Systems

We formulate our philosophies and belief systems, our *frames of reference* or *points of reason,* in the North. This is where we develop the meaning and purpose to our life. We have an *anchor belief* and several *core beliefs* behind which sit our frames of reference, which feed our opinions. Our core beliefs are rooted in our molding and sculpting, particularly by parental and religious image makers.

In the dark side of the North we are mentally inflexible, rigid, and locked into one point of view because our core beliefs are so strong. We give meaning to the world strictly from our opinions, every one of which we can justify, and believe that anyone who doesn't share the same point of reason is wrong. Beliefs are products of our past. Fear and denial press us into a core belief or inflexible point of reason. A core belief is related to our physical body and our fear of death, and the belief can be so strong that shattering it can cause death.

An example of an underlying core belief is "sex = love = pain." This belief comes from a low self-concept and low self-esteem. The North feeds back into our South mythologies and pain tapes. Shame works here in the North to keep us locked in tunnel vision.

You can dance in the light in the North by having an open mind, receptive to many different points of view and opinions. Be an empty cup, and test and question. Believe in nothing, find your own validations, and embrace as truth only knowledge that works for you.

The Warrior's Attributes here are mental *intent* and *coordination*. In the light side, a positive self-concept is important, and multiple viewing points are essential. You have a very flexible, clear state of mind with which to coordinate your thoughts and ideas. You recognize that the only beliefs that are valid are beliefs in the Great Spirit and in yourself. Clear intent can be likened to the range finder in a camera. When your intent is out of focus, you will not actualize in the world because you cannot see clearly what it is you desire to do or where you want to go. Clear intent, like a sharp camera focus, will make the difference between success or failure.

Northeast: Design and Choreography of Energy

This is where we *design and choreograph our energy* and actions. It is the place of perfect male/female balance, where we set priorities and make decisions and choices. Here we answer the question "What am I going to do?"

In the dark side, we are asleep and make decisions from self-importance and self-pity, with focus on personalities and events. We wear the mask of self-pity, not realizing it is a mask. The block of resistance is strong, as are the pitfalls of procrastination, laziness, fear of success, and self-sabotage that distract us from doing what needs to be done.

In the light, you can identify your desires and your *hungers*—what your heart, mind, body, spirit and soul yearn for. Establish feeding your hungers as your highest priorities. Very often we are confused about what we really desire, and we are not sure where to put our focus. We lose our attention because, still seeking outside validation and clues from others, we want to be sure that what we do will not make anyone dislike us or hate us. No wonder so many people are disillusioned and dissatisfied.

Relaxation and *focus* are the Warrior's Attributes in the Northeast. Once you have clearly identified your desires, set your priorities, and supported them with your choices and decisions, you must then focus and relax. Struggle distracts your attention, diverts your focus, and depletes your energy. Relaxation and focus allow you to function with "Maximum Efficiency With Minimum Effort." Relax, and just do it. It is like: "Ready, aim, fire!" This requires commitment, discipline, and follow-through. Like a laser beam, sharp focus helps you to zero in on the target, but you will not hit the mark if you are stressed and tense. Relaxation is critical to hitting the target and getting the job done. When you can achieve this, you create a momentum that propels you forward with greater energy, giving you the ability to live your life at a higher level of accomplishment.

East: Fantasy and Illusions

The East is the place where you look into your mirror of self-reflection and experience leaps in self-growth. Here is expansive imagination, your creativity, and the realization of your sacred dream and vision. You play out the fantasy of your self-concepts in the finished award-winning movie everyone is going to see.

In the dark, this is the place of fantasy and illusion; in the light, it is the place of open and unlimited imagination, and artistic originality. Fantasy is essential if you take an open and unlimited imagination into action to find your vision, which holds the greatest possible stretch of your potential in this lifetime, what you will do, and where you will go to evolve and expand the space of your soul. This includes your service to humanity and the planet, and it is the unique movie of how your story will be different from anyone else's. The fulfillment of your vision forms your legacy in this life-time.

Fantasies are openings into your mirror of self-reflection, but frequently they become distortions. Fantasy becomes illusion when you model your life on the distorted glimpses in the mirror, which will not lead you to decisive actions.

It is critical to learn to utilize our fantasies properly. When caught and consumed by the illusion, we are living our life accord-ing to someone else's expectations of us. We are living our life for the benefit of others without regard for reality; we are caught in the web of our pretense experiences and projected perceptions. For ex-ample: In the West of the wheel, in the daydream, a man may hate his job in his father's business, he may know his father wouldn't mind if he did something else, but he decides he will take over from his dad someday anyway. Here in the East he still hates his job, but he is convinced that this is what he was meant to do. This is a case of *reality* vs. *realness*. The irony is we derive a certain amount of pleasure and vicarious thrill in the fantasy, a payback that reinforces the fantasy and may take us deeper into illusion, away from our sacred dream.

Thunder Strikes: *One day some years ago I was walking past a lot where a house was being built. A brickmason was constructing a wall along the front of the property, so I stopped to watch him for a while. Finally, I struck up a conversation with him. I asked him if he liked what he did. Was this something he had always wanted to do? He said his father and uncle had been brickmasons, and he just kind of fell into the trade, although as a young man he had dreamed of being a naturalist and traveling around the world. When I responded, "It's not too late. You can do what you want to do," he shrugged his shoulders and said he was doing okay and, besides, making a change now was pretty risky.*

Your dreams are the yearnings of your spirit personality, and when you give up on your dreams, part of you dies inside. Your spirit personality withers, its growth retarded. Your shideh turns to fantasy and illusion to create a vicarious experience or to convince yourself that what you are doing is what you are supposed to be doing.

In the dark side, if you have no fire or passion and lust; you have no hope and no vision, only illusions. Illusions go much deeper than fantasy and are a dangerous trap. You may think your spirit has received a special message proclaiming that you are absolutely right and everyone else who differs from your point of reason is wrong. Every time you are in the dark side of fantasy, you will not produce results. Every time you are in illusion, you lack imagination. You have no seed to plant in the ground to grow.

In the light side, you are realizing your dream while at the same time keeping your reality needs at the level of abundance and prosperity. You are awake and aware of your spirit personality, your ideas, and your vision, and you act on them.

The Warrior's Attributes here are *speed* and *self-development*. This is where you determine to stretch and grow, to open to your creativity and imagination, or to shut down and walk asleep. As you focus on your vision with clear intent, your speed of self-growth will increase, you will push out the walls of your *box of self,* and you will embrace your life and your brilliance. Your spirit child will dance for joy.

This first basic teaching of the Star Maidens Circle is essentially a presentation of information and preparation for working with the Medicine Wheel as a tool for personal transformation. The Sweet Medicine SunDance paradigm overlays wheels on top of one another, and the interconnections of the energies and attributes can take you into deeper understanding and integration. The *Infinity Movement* discussed in the next chapter is the tool that allows you to accomplish this.

14

The Infinity Movement: The Key to Personal Transformation

T he *Infinity Movement* is a map within a map, for it defines the path of our journey around the Star Maidens Circle. A working understanding of this movement is the key to unlocking all Wheels of Knowledge as well as all the patterns of how we perceive reality. Not only is it a critical tool in our process of self-discovery, it is also a tangible, workable means of answering questions and solving problems in every arena of our lives. It explains why we do what we do, where we walk on the dark side and where we dance in the light, and how we choreograph our energy and run our behavior patterns.

The Eight Steps on the Infinity Movement

There are eight *Steps of Process* on this Infinity Movement (see Fig. 14-a). We will walk you through this process, first explaining each step as simply as possible. Then we will invite you to "tag along" as we walk someone through the first three movements or spins to illustrate how it works.

It is important to keep in mind that we move through these steps of the Infinity Movement many, many times each day—every time something catches our attention or enters our awareness, every time we must make a decision, every time our five senses communicate to us the status or conditions in our environment, and so on. This is our process of integrating stimulus input and

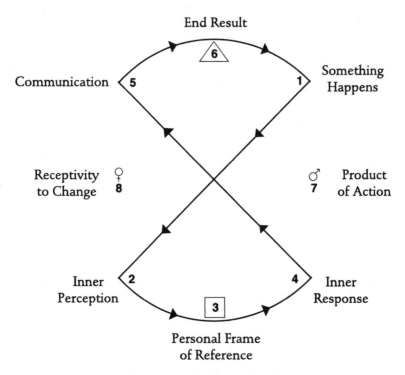

Fig. 14-a   The Infinity Movement

perceptual data. Furthermore, Steps 1 through 3 are all internal sub-jective movements that happen in milliseconds.

Step 1: Moment of Magnetic Attraction or Stimulus Input

Something happens, your attention is attracted to it, and you fo-cus on it. This is the starting place of your perception.

Step 2: Internal Perceptual Engagement

You take this into your perceptual filtering process. You tap into your intuitive "inner knowing" and your well of knowledge to begin to define the nature of this attraction. This step is about how you perceive and begin to make sense out of what has just happened.

Step 3: Personal Frame of Reference

At this point, you rely on what you know to be true. You continue to apply the filters of past experiences, beliefs, and so on, as you examine how you feel about what has happened and assess its meaning. Notice that the 3 in the figure has a box around it. You put your perceptions and your definition of those perceptions into a box and label it. This is the internal "Aha! Now I know what this is." When you are working this infinity movement, you always put the boxed 3 in the direction of the problem or the direction you want to examine. This is called the *sitting place* of the problem or event. You sit here with it and work the movement from this place.

Step 4: The Moment of Determination

This is the most critical moment in your process, for this step is your internal determination to take action as a result of what transpired in Steps 1 through 3. You answer the questions "What am I going to do about what happened?" or "What am I going to do to solve this problem?" You shift into your active-conceptive aspect and step into decisive action or reaction.

Step 5: External Impact

At this step, you understand the impact of your action. Your action, also known as your give-away, has communicated a message out to other people and the world about you. The impact of your action, how it is perceived by others, is reflected back to you. This is known as your *dancing place,* or place of power.

Step 6: End Result of Your Action

This is the final outcome, the effect of the impact at Step 4. Note that the number 6 in the figure has a triangle around it. The 6 in the triangle identifies the area where you apply your imagination to find a solution to the problem you are dealing with. In other words, this direction holds the way out of the box around 3. The triangle is like an arrow pointing to the way out. It is important that you pay attention to the feedback you receive from others. This *mirroring back* is invaluable in identifying your patterns and helping you see how you may be violating the Elemental Energy Laws.

Steps 7 and 8

These are the masculine and feminine energies at work in each of the previous six steps. These two points also identify the specific areas where the significant female and male image makers exerted the greatest influence on you. These steps refer to the result of your action and the effect it has on your pattern.

Step 7: Male, Active-Conceptive Energy

The pertinent question here is: "Am I taking responsibility for my action or not?" This energy carries the seed of all action, the focus behind the action, and the product, or result, of the action. Here you answer the questions: "Does my action produce something viable? Does it move me along in my self-growth and development? What effect does it have on my pattern of behavior or action?" To better understand your pattern of active-conceptive energy, look to the male figure in your life who most influenced how you run masculine energy.

Step 8: Female, Receptive-Creative Energy

This refers to the intent behind your focus of energy. This is also heavily influenced by a primary female image maker in your life. Energetically, there is a looping back inside to be receptive to changes that might be necessary to break patterns and embrace change and new ways of being.

The Nine Spins of the Star Maidens Circle

The Star Maidens Circle is the map and the Infinity Movement is the key that lead us out of our *box of limitations,* from pain and struggle into expanded awareness, pleasure, knowledge, and ultimately, enlightenment. It takes nine spins, or movements, to accomplish this. You will be guided through the first three. As you follow along, refer back to your walk through the directions on the

Star Maidens Circle and the corresponding Warrior's Attributes so that you can become more and more familiar with them and how they relate to your patterns (see Chapter 13). Learn the essence of each step in order to use this movement as a powerful weapon in your quiver of resources to forward your own stretch of excellence and self-growth.

First Spin: The Circle of Foxes

The fox occasionally becomes distracted by its tail, and begins to spin around and around trying to catch it. Our initial spin, or movement, is called our *dark-side shideh spin,* which is based on what we learned from our family and other image makers during our childhood. In a sense, it is our sleep walk, because we are unconscious of the fact that our "reality" is really our projected pretenses, the illusions of our pussycat survival stories, our striving for love and approval, and so forth. As we journey into adulthood, our shideh's travel bag is filled with the dark arrows and the dark mirrors, and we take our cues from others to define our identity. We have not silenced the pretender voices because we probably haven't even discovered that all that chatter is not the voice of our true nature. Furthermore, we do not exhibit the Warrior's Attributes when we are stuck in dark patterns.

For the purpose of this illustration, we will use the name Susan to illustrate the birth pattern of someone who is a Gemini; therefore, her *birth sitting place* is in the Southeast on the Star Maidens Circle. (To identify your birth sitting place on the Star Maidens Circle, refer to Appendix B.) Your original sitting place is significant because that is the place where you have some particularly important learning to do in this lifetime with regard to the properties of that direction.

Susan's Dark Shideh Birth Pattern

We place Susan's boxed 3 in the Southeast to begin her dark shideh story, the patterns of her *Circle of Foxes* (see Fig. 14-b). Follow closely with the Star Maidens Circle in each direction.

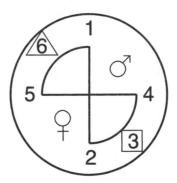

Fig. 14-*b*   *Susan's Circle of Foxes* (*Infinity Movement*)

Step 1: When something happens, Susan's attention is immediately influenced by her focus on the 1 place, which is where she always begins her process. Her 1 place is located in the North of the wheel, so she perceives this "something" filtered through a lens colored by her belief systems and philosophies and what she sees as the meaning and purpose to life. If she is caught in the dark here, she sees what happened through *tunnel vision,* through a narrow or single-minded viewpoint; or she may be righteously stuck in a rigid belief system that wields the dark arrows of judgment and comparison. Her viewfinder is already prejudicing her attention.

Step 2: The reality of what happened has already been distorted in Step 1. In order to gain knowledge about what happened, Susan now goes inward into introspection and sees how it fits with her stories and mythologies in the South. What happened pushes her pain tape buttons, and she is off and running, entertaining herself with her stories about her needy, wounded, abandoned child. This often triggers emotionality, and she loses her emotional balance and control.

Step 3: In this step, Susan's perception of what has happened and how she feels about what happened is shaped by her concepts of self and her worldview in the Southeast. If she has an *inferiority complex,* for example, or doesn't feel good about herself, or harbors fears of confrontation, and so on, her attitude about what happened will be negative. Given her Steps 1 and 2 in the dark, she is certain not to feel good about what happened in relation to herself and how she sees herself.

Step 4: Here Susan determines how to respond and what action to take from the East place. She steps into the dark side of fantasy and illusion, and if she makes her decision based on how she wishes it could be or thinks it should be rather than based on the reality of what actually happened, her action will not be creative or original and will not solve the problem. She is blind to her spiritual vision and what she needs for her self-growth. Consequently, she will probably choose to do something that causes pain or stress rather than something that solves the problem or gets positive results. She may choose to do nothing at all, in which case she stays stuck in her pattern and saddled with an unsolved problem.

Step 5: Susan's action communicates her choice from the direction of the West. She resists change and doesn't take the time to go into introspection to seek answers. Because she often focuses on the past or worries about the future, her action will not have an impact. If she is not producing the results she wants, she often blames others for what happened.

Step 6: The outcome of Susan's action plays itself out in the Northwest. She stays stuck in pattern, trapped in her box, and at the effect of others' rules and laws, do's and don'ts, and so on. In the process, she denies her stretch of excellence into her sacred image. This is her *working place,* directly opposite her *sitting place.* The working place gives an opposite viewing point of the sitting place; it holds the opportunity for Susan to break her sitting place patterns and move out of her Circle of Foxes. However, the feedback from others as a result of her actions is another stimulus input. If she is still stuck in her dark side pattern here and at the effect of what is happening, she will chase her tail right back to Step 1 and continue to run her Circle of Foxes again and again, ad nauseam.

Step 7: Susan's masculine energy sits in the Northeast. Here, she needs to ask the questions: "Does my action help me set clearer priorities? Does my action solve the problem or create a new one? Am I taking responsibility for my actions?" Procrastination, laziness, stress, fear of failure and of success, lack of focus, distraction—all or some of these may be part of Susan's dark shideh pattern in her masculine energy in the Northeast.

Step 8: Susan's feminine energy is influenced by the qualities of the Southwest. If she is adversely affected by what happened, or if she feels abused or victimized by it, she is not receptive to her personal dream and her sacred dream. She is also not receptive to changing her pattern. She experiences little joy and aliveness because she is afraid to open her closed symbols and look at the monsters lurking behind the dark mirrors.

Now, it is your turn to walk your Infinity Movement through your birth pattern, your dark side shideh story.

Task: Write Your Dark-Side Shideh Story

Place the boxed 3 of the Infinity Movement in your birth sitting place and write your Circle of Foxes story using only the dark mirrors of the Star Maidens Circle. It is important to look at the *darkest* of your dark patterns in this spin. Don't hold back! Carry a good amount of humor with you, and try not to take yourself too seriously. When you begin to see your negative patterns more clearly, and to recognize how they keep you stuck in your molded, sculpted, and armored self, you will be ready to do the *Dance of the Coyote.*

Resist the temptation to skip past this exercise because your life doesn't seem to be so dark in all places and in all aspects. That may very well be true. Nonetheless, there is darkness in all of us that we are completely unaware of, and our shideh and karmic pretender ego work overtime to cleverly prevent us from looking too deeply. Working your Infinity Movement helps you explore your shadow to discover the darkest of your dark side. When you are willing to journey there, you discover the light of your undiscovered self— your magickal mysterious character.

Second Spin: The Dance of the Coyote

The coyote is the trickster, and in this spin he takes you on a tour around the Star Maidens Circle following your same birth sitting place pattern. But this time, he points out all the light mirrors, turning everything 180 degrees opposite your walk on the dark side. He is saying, "Let's take this trip again, but this time let's walk on the sunny side of the street!" You're not asked to do anything different; just see how your pattern would look if you were walking it in the light—what a powerful dance that could be! Being a clown, the coyote will help you to see the folly of your dark stories and your self-pity, and encourage you to lighten up.

Task: Write Your Light-Side Birth Sitting Place Story

Again, place the boxed 3 of the Infinity Movement in your birth sitting place. This time, write your story using the light mirrors of the Star Maidens Circle. By looking at the light empowered side of each direction, along with the Warrior's Attribute you pick up in the light, you get to see your dark patterns from a different perspective. You may very well discover additional dark patterns you did not recognize in your Circle of Foxes movement. Once you have done this, you are ready to do the *Walk of the Wolf*, which enables you to begin breaking or altering old karmic patterns and begin to form new patterns that serve you.

Third Spin: The Walk of the Wolf

The wolf teaches courage, honor, and commitment. This animal shows us how to heal ourselves and gain wisdom, and guides us to our path with heart so we can develop our highest potential. The *Walk of the Wolf* requires discipline, courage to face the unknown, and willingness to change, so that you can stop sabotaging yourself, edit your movie, and start living your life fully.

Identify your *dancing place* (5 of your sitting place movement). Place the 3 in that direction. Notice how that puts the 1 of the Infinity Movement into your birth sitting place (where your original 3 was). This spin puts the light of 1 (the focus of your attention)

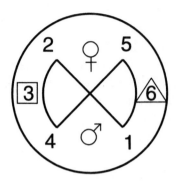

Fig. 14-c   Susan's Walk of the Wolf (Infinity Movement)

into the dark of 3. This is the first spin that shows you how you can change your patterns. In keeping with our two metaphors: This is where you begin to rewrite your script casting yourself as the star; this is where you become your own sculptor and begin to resculpt yourself into the jaguar.

Susan's Walk of the Wolf

Let's take Susan's molded, sculpted, and armored self that has been running around the circle of foxes and see what she must do to *break pattern* and begin to grow towards the light of her true nature spirit personality as she takes her Walk of the Wolf (see Fig. 14-c).

Step 1: Something happens. What must Susan change? Her new focus is in the Southeast. In order to step into the light mirror, she must affirm her worthiness as a person. She must have a good attitude and approach towards herself, life, and others. In doing this, she picks up the light arrows of self-awareness, self-appreciation, self-acceptance, self-pleasure, self-love, self-actualization, and impeccability.

Step 2: Susan goes inside to see what her new internal reaction needs to be. She needs to reassess her concern about do's and don'ts and how much she abides by others' rules because she wants to be loved and liked. She needs to realign her actions with Sacred Law and the cycles of Nature. This will help her to establish some new patterns and enhance her ability to catch the proper timing to change.

Step 3: This is Susan's new frame of reference. If she is able to break an old pattern and create a new pattern in the Northwest, then here in the West she can take responsibility for her part in what happened. As a result, she will experience better health, and more stability in her physical world, and begin to be more present, productive, and fulfilled in the Now.

Step 4: The Southwest is the place where Susan needs to determine a new action to take. Since, in her dark-side story she kept plenty of distance between herself and closed symbols, here she must be willing to get "up close and personal," open the symbol, and shout to the monster in the mirror, "Identify yourself!" She sees her own face in the mirror, and with that comes insight and illumination. She will feel a surge of energy, and suddenly, life is wonderful!

Step 5: Susan's action communicates her message to others in the light mirror in the Northeast. She arrives at a new understanding of how she communicates to others. She learns how to reduce stress and focus on relaxing and keeping her priorities in alignment.

Step 6: The new result happens in the East. Here Susan stretches her imagination to embrace her spiritual vision and to nurture her spiritual self-growth. She explores her creativity fully and is not afraid to express herself through her own unique artistic originality.

Step 7: In the South, Susan must look at what she needs to change in order to act more decisively and get better results from her actions. She needs to rewrite her myth and her story, which will bring more emotional balance and control into her life.

Step 8: In the North, Susan must find a new way to be receptive to multiple viewing points and to examine closely her belief systems that prevent her from seeing other points of view. The process of redefining life's meaning and purpose for herself will also clarify her intent and strengthen her mental coordination.

Task: Break Old Patterns and Create New Ones

Place the 3 of the Infinity Movement in your sitting place. See where the 5 is located. Then place the 3 where the 5 was originally. Let the wolf guide you through this spin as you discover what you must do to break your old patterns and create new ones of balance, harmony, and alignment. (Keep in mind that Susan's story represented only one version of this walk. Your story, utilizing the energies and attributes of each direction, will be uniquely yours.)

Once you have developed your ability to apply the Infinity Movement, start to overlay the other wheels you have learned— the Elements Wheel, the Blocks to Character Development Wheel, and others. You can use a shortcut to give you a clue as to where you will find the solution: It is the direction where 4 sits in your original birth sitting place spin (which is now the 6 place in your Walk of the Wolf spin). Work the complete movement, however, as that shows you what must change in each step of your process.

Using the Infinity Movement to Solve Problems

Give yourself a pat on the back and smile. You have stepped out of your dark pattern and onto a path of empowerment and actualization. You can also use the Infinity Movement to solve problems. Put the 3 of the Infinity Movement in the direction on the Wheel of Life where the problem is evident (see Fig. 14-d).

For example: You are having financial problems, and no matter what you do, you can't seem to produce results or establish financial stability for yourself. This has to do with the energies in the West. Put the boxed 3 of the Infinity Movement in the West, and work the movement to see what your dark-side pattern is that is producing the problem. Then work the other movements to find resolution and solution.

Here's another example: You are overly busy, but you seem to get distracted and can't stay focused on one thing long enough to finish it, and you are getting more and more stressed. This sounds like poor choreography of energy and an inability to set clear priorities. Put the boxed 3 in the Northeast, and work the movements.

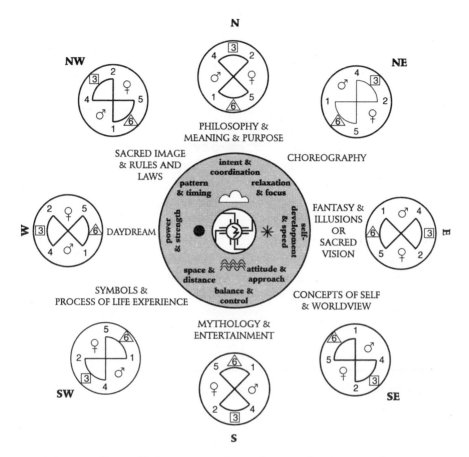

Fig. 14-d   Infinity Movements for Each Sitting Place on the Star Maidens Circle Wheel of Life

Another example: You feel your relationship is one-sided and that you do all the giving, but you haven't been able to assert yourself and ask for what you need and desire from your significant other. Is this a self-esteem/self-deservement issue? Do you have a poor self-concept? Put the boxed 3 in the Southeast, and work the movements. Do you see your pattern? What does using the Infinity Movement show you about the changes you need to make?

Fourth Spin: The Flight of the Eagle

In this spin, your Infinity Movement stays in the same position as it was in your Walk of the Wolf, with your focus Step 1 still in your original sitting place. (For Susan, her Step 1 stays in the Southeast.) With the knowledge you have gained working the first three spins, you are now in sobriety, awake, aware, and alert to reality. You are no longer living in reaction to events or at the effect of others, waiting and watching. When something happens, you step into decisive action. You have developed a *stop button* that immediately stops the pain tapes from playing and shuts up the pretender voices. You begin to open a strong line of communication with your hokkshideh, your higher self, aided by the gift of the eagle, the messenger between your higher self and the Great Spirit.

Very few people evolve beyond this level, so we will only briefly describe spins 5 through 9.

Fifth Spin: The Pace of the Bear

This spin is really a refinement of what you have gained and integrated so far. Now you begin to truly resculpt your life into a work of art called the *art of controlled folly.* You begin to live your life authentically, as your true nature spirit personality, but often you choose to wear a mask that makes it appear as though you are conforming to politically and socially correct rules of conduct. Most important, you wear the masks consciously, never forgetting you are the jaguar.

To master this spin, you become adept as a *mask dancer.* You become the chameleon, totally unpredictable and uncontrollable. Your new stories cast you as the hero.

To aid you in your mastery at this level, use the Infinity Movement, placing the 3 into your original working place 6. This spins you 180 degrees, so you can look back across the wheel at your birth sitting place and see clearly your original entertainment pain patterns and pussycat stories. Your pace and rate of self-growth speed up, your orende increases, and your Magnetic Attracting Thought (MAT) soul space begins to expand appreciably.

Sixth Spin: The Stalk of the Jaguar

The jaguar teaches us how to commune with the ancestor spirit world, develop our ability to do *controlled dreaming,* and stalk the dreamscape, awakening memory of other lifetimes.

The *Stalk of the Jaguar* starts in the Southeast, regardless of your birth sitting place, and stalks the dream by moving around the Star Maidens Circle counterclockwise, utilizing only the light mirrors. This allows you to actually *unwind* memory. You develop the art of controlled dreaming.

Seventh Spin: The Flight of the Feathered Wing Serpent

The Feathered Wing Serpent represents the Great Spirit. This spin looks like a lightning bolt, and the movement goes from South to North to West to East to Southeast to Northwest to Northeast to Southwest. Again you work with only the light mirrors in each direction.

Following this lightning bolt movement, you end up in the Southwest, the place of your life's process. This is where the Star Maidens Circle and many of the other wheels you have studied and integrated begin to dream you. To repeat what we said earlier in Chapter 1: First we study the wheels. Then we apply the wheels and experience them in our lives. Next we begin to dream the wheels. When we dream the wheels, they begin to dream us.

Eighth Spin: The Flight of the Hawk or the Explosion of the Phoenix

This spin enables you to discard the last vestiges of your identity as a person, and your true nature spirit personality emerges fully. The hawk is the messenger between your hokkshideh and your shideh. At this stage of your journey, your shideh has finally gotten the message, given up control, and acquiesed to the command of your higher self, thus finding freedom.

This spin focuses on balancing your masculine and feminine energies through two separate movements. First, put the 3 in your original feminine place (Step 8), and work the Infinity Movement to increase your receptivity to your creativity. Then put the 3 in your original masculine place (Step 7), and work the movement to increase the active in your conception. This is necessary in order to plumb the depths of your creativity and manifest it in the world. You create works of power and beauty, whether they be works of fine art or of the art of living.

Ninth Spin: The Flight of the Hummingbird

At this point in your SunDance Journey, like the hummingbird who is the master of choreography, you transcend all directions on the Wheel of Life in that you live in the light in all the directions at the same time within Sacred Law. You have attained enlightenment at the center of the Star Maidens Circle, recreating yourself anew in each moment. You begin to breathe the wheels, and when the wheels breathe you, you become the wheels of wisdom and realize they have always been inside you. This is the completion spin within the 0-9 Law.

15

The Moon Cycles of Life Experience

The teachings of the Star Maidens Circle are used to describe our life experiences in the *Moon Cycles* and can help us to live more consciously and to be better prepared, because they show us the nature of our journey at various times (see Fig. 15-a). We journey from infancy to our Elder years in cycles of three years and twenty-seven years. Every three years, we complete one walk around the small wheel, called a *Circle of Life Experience*. Every four and a half months, we shift the direction of our frame of reference on that wheel, as each Circle of Life Experience is influenced by the nature of its direction on the Star Maidens Circle. This direction indicates the opportunities to grow and learn, the testing and challenge, and the experiences that will present themselves as natural milestones in our journey.

Each Circle of Life Experience is entered through the South and exited through the East. The Southeast, the place of our true nature spirit personality, is bypassed because this is our attitude and approach that we carry with us all around the circle.

The only exception is our very first circle (see Fig. 15-b).

We are born out of the East and travel clockwise around the first Circle of Life Experience. From then on, our travels around the circles create a spiral of evolution. As we leave one circle (from the East), and prior to entering the next circle (from the South), we experience nine months of what is called a *chaotic journey*.

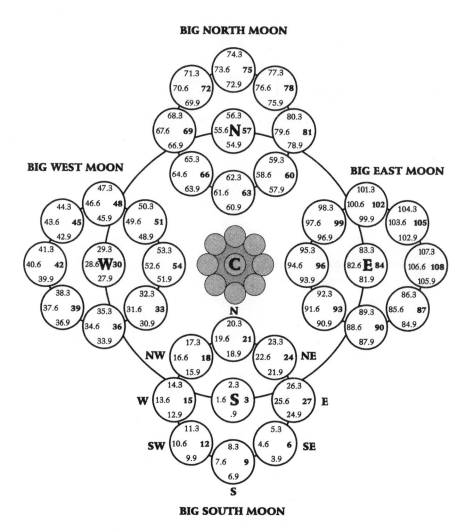

Fig. 15-a   The Moon Cycles

Every chaotic journey is the internal journey past the South-east, and as we begin that journey, we review what we have learned in the Circle of Experience we are exiting. We review our script in light of the question "What is it that I have come here to do?" This provides the opportunity to rewrite and edit our

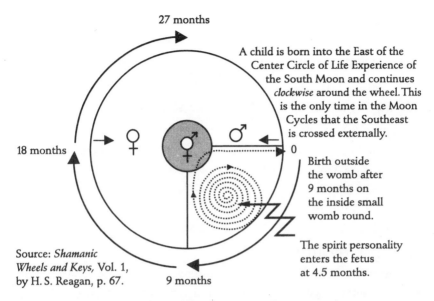

27 months

A child is born into the East of the Center Circle of Life Experience of the South Moon and continues *clockwise* around the wheel. This is the only time in the Moon Cycles that the Southeast is crossed externally.

18 months

0

Birth outside the womb after 9 months on the inside small womb round.

Source: *Shamanic Wheels and Keys,* Vol. 1, by H. S. Reagan, p. 67.

9 months

The spirit personality enters the fetus at 4.5 months.

Fig. 15-b The First Cycle at Birth

screenplay to prepare for the focus of our experiences in the next Circle of Experience. This is a time to appreciate where we have come from and to anticipate the opportunities and challenges that lie ahead.

Nine months later, we enter the next Circle of Experience and begin to travel around the wheel, experiencing life ideally at a higher level on the evolutionary spiral. Knowing the nature of this process gives us the advantage of being in sobriety and being a better actor and director of our movie.

The Four Big Moons

There are Four Big Moons and the Nine Circles of Life Experience within each of those Big Moons (refer again to Fig. 15-a). The numbers in the cardinal directions indicate your age in years and months. For example, 20.3 is read as 20 years, 3 months. These are the *exit ages* at which you will leave each direction and travel further, clockwise, around the wheel to the next direction.

The Big South Moon: The Child Moon

The first twenty-seven years are spent developing your personality and creating your mythology and stories about who you are.

The Big West Moon: The Adolescent Moon

The next twenty-seven years, from age twenty-seven years, nine months, is the time for accomplishing goals, achieving success (in whatever way we define that), stability, and even abundance. You become captain of your own ship. On the other hand, you may relinquish your power and authority to others, waiting for something to happen, and watching life pass you by.

The Big North Moon: The Adult Moon

From age fifty-four years and nine months to eighty-one, you reap the harvest of your life experience in the West Moon. At this point, you will either enter your mature years with ease, grace, and a sense of fulfillment or become set in your belief systems and unwilling to make changes. These years offer the opportunity to devote more time and energy to personal growth, perhaps even to seek adventure and further explore the unknown in spiritual development.

The Big East Moon: The Elder Moon

This is the Moon you enter with wisdom and honor for the legacy you have created, or you can enter with regrets and resignation, waiting for death to come. Few people reach this age today with vitality and eagerness to explore the years ahead, yet these can be years rich with illuminations and enlightening experiences. This Moon brings you closer once again to the Great Light, to the world of spirit, and you begin to prepare for your journey back to the Source. Your departure can be an act of power.

The Big Center Moon: The Wizard Moon

The Twisted Hairs Elders say that if we live our lives as balanced humans, awake to who we truly are, living in harmony and aligned with Sacred Law, we can walk in this Big Moon to a minimum of 135 years of age. It is possible, it has been done, and it is inherent in the space of our soul.

The Nine Circles of Life Experience

We begin each Big Moon in the Center Circle, where our experiences are not influenced by any particular direction. This is a *staging area,* in a sense, where we land from the previous Big Moon and prepare for the next twenty-seven years of our life. In many ways, our preparation here sets a pattern for these years.

Then we enter the South of the Southeast Circle of Life Experience and continue our walk here for the next twenty-seven months, experiencing the dynamics of each direction in turn. As we leave the East at the end of that time, we enter another chaotic journey—a time of change and challenge.

Study the directions. Identify where you were in these cycles at different ages and your age when significant events occurred in your life. What factors influenced you? What did you learn? Did you navigate your stream of livingness in alignment with the energies of that direction, or did you get toppled in the rapids?

Your age plotted on the Moon Cycles is called your *standing place.* For example, people who are 34 years and 2 months (34.2), are *standing* in the West of the South Circle of Life Experience of the Big West Moon. Based on what you have learned about the directions on the Star Maidens Circle, you can see the critical experiences and opportunities for growth for people at this age. The broad arena of experience during this time (Big West Moon) provides the basis for establishing a solid physical, economic, and career structure, honing physical mastery, maintaining good health, and actualizing the personal dream. The energetic of the little South Circle of Experience presents opportunities to recapitulate life experiences and begin to rewrite stories about who they are discovering they really are, in the context of the physical influences of the Big West Moon. The fact that these people are in the West Circle of Influence of the Big West Moon compounds the importance of working with all the energies of the West and developing the Warrior's Attributes of *power and strength,* and incorporating them in the rewrite of their script.

A working knowledge of the Moon Cycles allows you to understand more clearly the energetic forces that are influencing your life experiences right now. They shed light on the pivotal experiences of your past and provide guidance in planning and choreographing your future, because they show you what arenas of influence you will be playing in and what challenges and opportunities will present themselves. These are powerful tools that you can use to rewrite your story and actualize your dreams.

16

The Five Movements of the Book of Life

The *Five Movements of the Book of Life* preserved from the Mayan culture assist us in breaking the mold of the image makers and resculpting ourselves into our true nature, our sacred image of self (see Fig. 16-a). They can provide a road map to assist us in editing our Book of Life and changing our karma into dharma. They allow us insight and direction on how to manifest, with true spiritual awareness, our highest self into the Now of everyday living. We experience these five movements continuously and may find ourselves in more than one movement at any given time.

First Movement: Erasing Personal History
(Trust and Innocence Cycle)

The task here in this first movement is to recapitulate the past, to pull back the curtain and reveal the reality of your life experiences and your true nature. This process reveals the illusion of your shideh, the subterfuge of your *karmic pretender ego* and its emotionally charged *pretense story* and projected perceptions, narrated incessantly by your *pretender voices*. You can erase this story and this image, learn from that past, and then let it go. Here you must accept your mistakes as strengths, for they are your scars of experience, the price you paid to grow and mature. Furthermore, you must see that what has happened in the past does not matter unless you make it matter. This leaves you in the Now reality with the

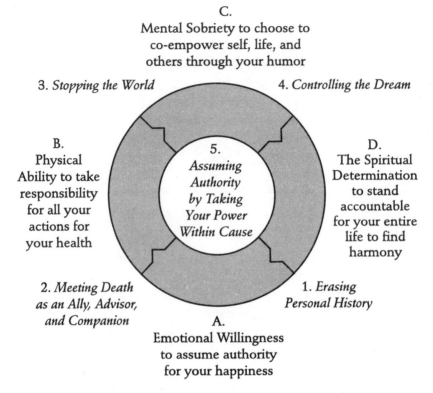

C.
Mental Sobriety to choose to
co-empower self, life, and
others through your humor

3. *Stopping the World*   4. *Controlling the Dream*

B.
Physical
Ability to take
responsibility
for all your
actions for
your health

5.
*Assuming
Authority
by Taking
Your Power
Within Cause*

D.
The Spiritual
Determination
to stand
accountable
for your entire
life to find
harmony

2. *Meeting Death
as an Ally, Advisor,
and Companion*

1. *Erasing
Personal History*

A.
Emotional Willingness
to assume authority
for your happiness

Fig. 16-a   The Five Movements of the Book of Life

opportunity to rewrite your script and recast yourself as who you truly want to be, as who you truly are, and create a life that resonates with joy and harmony.

This process begins with your willingness to take responsibility for your life and for your personal choices, recognizing that who and what you are in the present moment is who and what you choose to be. *Erasing* doesn't mean that you renounce your heritage, throw away all your old photographs, and never see your family and old friends again. It means getting rid of the illusions and pretense stories you tell about your life, getting rid of the insistence that these stories are reality. You dig deep to erase your pain tapes and your ignorance tapes and replace them with pleasure and knowledge tapes. This is the process of de-armoring and res-culpting.

Part of erasing personal history is removing yourself from the need to identify yourself as the child of your parents—recognizing that you have learned the lessons that they gave you as your parental image makers. The key to this is forgiveness, first to your-self, and then to them for any pain you may have experienced in your process of learning the karmic lessons. Only when all is for-given can all be forgotten, and what is gained be integrated into what must become.

Jan: Part of my process of erasing personal history was to finally let go of blaming my parents for "messing me up" or "stealing my light," and to rec-ognize the gifts they had given me as part of our soul contracts. My father gave me lessons about the power of will. Because he didn't allow me to ex-ercise the power of my will, his actions often caused pain, and as a result of the emotional charge and my armoring, I remembered mostly the pain. Now, I can take the power of will he taught me, be thankful for his gift, and integrate it into my character in the light. My mother gave me lessons in unconditional love and compassion, giving from the heart and serving others. As I related earlier, she was often out of balance in the other ex-treme from my father, and I blamed her, too, for letting me down. Now, I can appreciate the beauty of her heart and take this into my refinement of character.

If you put your attention on erasing personal history, you de-velop a very good subjective and objective observer witness. The process of recapitulation allows you to evaluate your life and get good validations of your actions. When you do this, you invite power to come inside you.

As we work our way through these Five Movements of the Book of Life, shattering the mirrors of self-reflection, we encounter and overcome the *nagual enemies* of *fear, clarity, power,* and *old age and death* (see Fig. 16-b). Here in the first movement of erasing per-sonal history, we face the nagual enemy of *fear*. You have already

Fig. 16-*b*   *The Wheel of the Nagual Enemies*

met fear as a tonal enemy, the fear of the unknown that a baby feels in its first dealing with hunger, and learned how we experience it in our bodies and emotions as a reaction to events in our everyday lives.

Nagual fear is also fear of the unknown, but even more it is fear of the unknowable, which is on the far side of the unknown, in the dream landscape and other realities and worlds that you can access in the dreamtime or in states of heightened awareness. Shamans have always journeyed through these landscapes.

This fear becomes in many ways a displaced fear of God/Creator/Great Spirit, Creation, and Nature, a fear of being spiritually accountable. In tonal fear, you can make the unknown known by gaining knowledge, testing, and engaging. When you experience nagual fear deep in the world of spirit, each journey can take you into a different nagual space where the rules change almost every time you enter. Nagual fear is never permanently conquered, for it is present with each new journey.

What would you do if you suddenly woke up in a world where

the parameters of experience and observation would not allow anything that you had ever learned to help you to solve the problems in that world?

For shamans, all journeys into the nagual require them to abandon any prior learned or preconceived ideas of what is and what is not reality, because they must figure it out in the process of the experience. This is their virtual reality video game, except that they do actually enter that reality, not just view it on a mental screen. Shamans Since Always have done it for fun, challenging and testing themselves by learning how to move into, out of, and between these alternate realities. In a sense, erasing your personal history challenges you to do the same thing.

Erasing your personal history demands a willingness to let go of the personality and the life stories that have anchored you in the past and defined your identity, to venture beyond your imagination and plumb the depths of your spirit, because it is a movement towards discovering and exploring the cosmic landscape of your soul. You approach the unknowable.

Second Movement: Meeting Death as an Ally, Advisor, and Companion (Introspection and Intuition Cycle)

Here you see death as a continuous guide. It directs you and helps you see where you need to change so you can make your death changes rapidly. It helps you to leap into the abyss of the unknown, to gain glimpses of the unknowable. It helps you to live life by being in the present, out of the effects of the past, but with constant hope for the future. Therefore, it gives you power and clarity.

So to work on death as an ally, you should seek change and challenges. Look for the things and situations that produce the tonal enemies of fear, anger, stress, and depression, and confront them deliberately. No one can take your power away; only you can relinquish it. Courting death as an ally and advisor will help you take back your power.

Here we face the nagual enemy of *clarity*. Clarity is an enemy because it is what the Twisted Hairs call a *heyoehkah,* a contrary or reverse opposition. This means that you cannot understand and gain clarity except to the extent you are willing to give up clarity and be an empty cup. Clarity is an enemy because the moment we believe in anything, we are not willing to listen; we think we know it all. It is heyoehkah, because we strive for clarity and understanding which is good, but once we attain these moments of clarity, we tend to grab on to them, possess them, and immediately turn them into beliefs, which anchor us and then blind us to any other viewpoints. We then get lost and struggle with disillusion, only to empty our cup once again, become open and receptive, and eventually shift once more into a moment of clarity to gain new insights. Then we latch on to this new clarity, make it a belief, and so on.

Third Movement: Stopping the World (Wisdom and Logic Cycle)

In the course of this movement, you assume authority and take responsibility for your choices, decisions, and priorities in order to die your *little deaths* and expand. This demands spontaneity in the moment, surfing the wave of chaos. At that moment, you stop the world and become a part of chaos, entering into the center of chaotic energy and gaining control. This is called *catching minimal chance,* and it requires a willingness to be spontaneous. You have hit a moment of real death/change experience, power has chosen you, and you have climbed on for the ride. You have stepped into the "Maximum Results With Minimum Effort" law, which is the law of controlling chaos. You become the eye of the hurricane. When you stop the world, you get the greatest return for the least amount of energy. You see what must be seen, and you do what must be done. Your intuition is operating without any fear, and you act decisively from autonomic body memory.

During these moments of power, you become awake and aware and alert, able to see life and the world through many different points of view. You realize that each is just as valid as the other in that they are all projected perceptions. You enlist the support of the allies to battle and conquer the blocks of guilt, blame, shame, doubt, insecurity, fear, resistance, and repression. Stopping the world means you are not living in the past or the future, but in the Now, focused only on that which must be seen and done. Totally absorbed in the present, you act as though each action is your last. You become impeccable, understanding that *self-acceptance and a valid assessment of your self-worth* are essential to your growth and evolutionary process. This moves you out of the mask of self-pity; you stop worrying about how others see you. You become a *strong attraction* and can *make impact* in your circle of influence.

We face the nagual enemy of *power* in this third movement. Power is our ability to stop the world and master change. Our process of stopping the world helps us to eliminate the arbitrary boundaries and limitations of karmic belief systems, concepts, philosophies and religion, and replace them with knowledge, skills, and abilities that always exemplify physical excellence, an eclectic mind capable of holding multiple states of heightened awareness and attention. The inevitable result is that our body is able to change metabolically at the cellular level.

Power looms as a nagual enemy, however, when we try to control and manipulate with it. Power seduces us. It sings its siren songs of self-importance, wealth, fame, and glory. It feeds the greed, avarice, hate, and lust for domination that lurk within our shadow. Conquering the enemy of power in this movement is necessary, or our next cycle back through the Five Movements of the Book of Life will not take us to a higher level of experience and evolution.

Fourth Movement: Controlling the Dream (Illumination and Enlightenment Cycle)

In this movement, we have the power to become the jaguar that we truly are because we wake up and suddenly realize all our stories and beliefs are really the script of our pretender self. We can now cast ourselves as the hero in our movie and increase our magnetic attraction. This also increases our presence in the nagual dream world and enables us to remember our dreams much more clearly. Hence, we can bring the reality and power of the asleep dream into our awake dream.

We attain inner balance and experience harmony and absolute oneness with all things within the Everything and within Sacred Law. We begin to manifest all the powers of the *O'larien*, the powers of the great masters and avatars, and we can choose to live an ascended state of being, free to be in any "dream" at will, free of any limitations of time, space, or mind. We have achieved the death of our karmic pretender ego, embraced the *great teacher* which is our higher self, and become illuminated to our soul as a human. The result is the living embodiment of a balanced human being.

Here we face the nagual enemy of *old age and death.* Our fear of physical death is perhaps our greatest fear. It slows our body rhythms, decreases our energy orende, and, ironically, ages us to what we fear most—premature physical death. Our elder years are a beautiful time if we approach them gracefully, relaxed and with a sense of ease. We can see old age as sickness, disease, and debilitating illness, which leads us to death without honor, without dignity, and without integrity. Or we can experience old age as the years of wisdom and reflection. Those who understand this and are controlling the dream learn to meet death and walk with it in every step of their path, and in so doing they learn to live out their old age in a state of peace and tranquility. Never allowing themselves to be swayed by image makers, they seem to fit in, belong, and conform, when, in fact, they are practicing *controlled folly,* that is, consciously wearing different masks but never falling asleep and believing that they are the mask.

The Elders say that when we end the war with the enemy of old age inside ourselves, we will stop trying to escape old age by creating wars that kill us when we are young.

If you are not willing to die, you can be controlled. If you have no fear of death, you are unpredictable and, therefore, uncontrollable. This gives you mastery of the physical and of your life—your relationships, your economics, your career, your ability to produce results. The warrior's expression "Today is a good day to die" is applicable here. With that attitude, you will do everything as though it were the last action you will ever take. If you are not afraid of your advancing years, you are not afraid to go for broke and put all of yourself on the line. Isn't that the same as being the best you can be, stretching to test your fullest potential? Joy and aliveness are the inevitable result.

Through accepting your own death, you gain control of your own dream and gain an ally—your dharmic self. This is a Sacred Law: "Death Gives Life."

Fifth Movement: Assuming Authority by Taking Your Power (Acceptance and Attainment Cycle)

Here you are able to walk your talk, to give away the credibility demanded by the image makers. Instead, you assume your own authority. The knowledge that you share works.

Authority and power come from knowing what will work in a particular situation. They reflect the ability to see any and all potential changes that might occur, to clearly discern the pattern that is at work and how to change the pattern. Therefore, the Universe gives you power, and you must take it when it is given to you.

The only way to assume authority is to establish your own credibility based on valid knowledge that works for you. If you really believe that you are Dr. So and So, or that you are a licensed whatever, then you will need all those things to assure yourself of your credibility. You will think that the only way you have the power of attraction and can make an impact is through these trappings bestowed on you by the outside world. In reality, your only credibility is the knowledge that works which you give to others. You must look at how much you play in the game of thinking you are what society has acknowledged you for. You give away your power. Some people live only within the levels placed on them. Credibility from the outside really creates limitations and dulls your awareness even further about who you really are.

In this fifth movement you are no longer in a position to be controlled, nor are you controlling and dominating. You maintain your own dominion, becoming self-disciplined and self-accepting, assessing your true measure of self-worth, and walking with integrity. From here you gain knowledge in all the other directions of the Wheel of Life and meet your physical death with power.

You can successfully master these five movements only if you conquer the tonal enemies as well as the other nagual enemies. When you succumb to anger, you lose your attraction. Therefore, you cannot meet death and change. When you go into stress, you cannot stop the world. Therefore, you cannot have *impact*. When you fall into depression, you cannot control the dream. Therefore, your empowerment fades. You have no place to go except inward into introspection. If you go into depression instead, you relinquish your authority. You have given your power away. Therefore, you lose your dominion; you can be controlled and dominated, and you are absolutely predictable.

Thunder Strikes: *My journey through these movements was guided by many teachers. One of the most important teachers for me was a wolf who worked with me in a three-month vision quest during my thirteenth summer. This was a quest for warriorship, to test if I was worthy of initiation into the Cokie (Crow) Medicine Clan. I had the right of access to that clan through my grandmother, Spotted Fawn, and I was being tested to see if I was truly worthy in spirit, and if I could find the totem animal to guide me. This experience would also teach me how to embrace Nature and be at relative ease and peace with her, even in the harsh environment of the Big Bend region of southern Texas.*

The challenge was to completely erase my personal history: to learn who my parents and my brother really were; to discover what I was really here for; to know what my history really was, not my pretense stories about it. The quest would help me to discover what I would do with my life. The challenge was also to find how to exist in a world that I had concluded I did not belong in. I was a rebel, even as a kid, and a half-breed. Inside my heart was an awake Merlin screaming to get out, but I found myself in a world where, if he got out, punishment and ridicule awaited. So I didn't know how to stop the world and get on with my life.

Late one evening I lay next to my campfire in a half-awake, half-asleep twilight zone. As I was dreaming about becoming more accurate with my bow and arrow, a big gray wolf approached the fire, and I sensed his presence. Since animals are afraid of fire, I was perplexed that the wolf was approaching me. At the same time, I grabbed my rifle to defend myself. All the while I was still in that hazy, half-asleep space.

Then I felt the wolf dreaming into me with such wise and benevolent eyes and heard him say, "I'm not here to harm you; I'm here to walk with you."

I experienced an almost orgastic sensation that swept up my body, and in that moment I knew what I was out there for. This was the moment I had been waiting for! Then doubt set in, and I questioned whether the wolf was really there. Was I in a dream state, or was this reality?

The wolf came close enough for me to touch him, and I heard him say, "Yes, I'm here. This is a dream, but I'm bringing reality to the vision of your dream."

I thought, "Can I touch you?"

"Good," he replied. "You understand how to communicate to us animals with respect. Yes, you may touch me."

At that point I jolted fully awake and realized I still had the gun in my hands. I apologized and laid it on the ground. When I started to speak out loud, he kind of tucked his head down.

He said, "When you communicate with your verbal words, they contain a harshness of judgment, so it's difficult for me to listen to you. Instead, communicate by thinking with me, and I will always be inside you." He was teaching me the voice of power.

"Aren't you afraid of fire?" I asked.

"How can a wolf with power be afraid of power? It is my inner light," he said. He told me the most important discipline for humans to approach pure spiritual determination is the discipline of humor, the most neglected of the five huaquas.

I called him Lobo. From that point forward, on many nights he curled up and slept by my side. My major task was to stalk him when he left, which developed my hunting and tracking skills in ways I couldn't learn from another human. I learned how to look at the mineral world to understand physical transformation and how to listen to the wind spirits and winged ones. I learned the true meaning of emotional giving.

Lobo taught me the gaze of power, how to probe the game for food, but also how in war to probe the enemy without them knowing you are there. I learned to develop multiple thoughts and split attentions and do this rapidly because the wolf does this easily. This skill proved invaluable during my experiences in Vietnam.

Lobo showed me how to stop the world and gain back control of the dream by assuming authority for everything that would happen in that dream. Most important, he showed me how to assume authority for being different and being forced into positions of leadership I didn't really like.

To stop the world, you simply stop projecting your pretenses on it, and instead step into sobriety and act decisively with everything and everyone you engage with. When you accept the interconnection, interdependence, and interreliability with all things, you are not separated from the mental and spiritual essence of the communication between any form of any living thing. Then you begin to control the dream when you start walking your path of heart, your path of character refinement and spiritual awakening. Lobo showed me that this must include adversity, struggles, strife, and pain, and that a true path of heart is never an easy path, because it will force you to master the patterns of karma and step beyond into dharma. A path of heart will show us that what we see as our dark side, our shadow, really hides our shining and our beauty, and it is through the adversity of the journey to that discovery that we build strength of character. This is the most essential part of controlling the dream and assuming authority.

Lobo taught me that once we know who the natural self is, and we are outside our need for approval, acceptance, recognition, and security, then we can assume authority. And if we can't get beyond this need, we can never effectively go back through the Five Movements of the Book of Life at a higher evolutionary level.

This was a difficult lesson at age thirteen. Lobo taught me how to move easily from the need to be loved or liked by my peer group, friends, and schoolmates. Much more difficult for me to accept was to let go of that need in relation to my Elders, people with real knowledge and power I wanted to learn from. He said, "Don't give your authority over to someone else, no matter how much that person knows." I realized I would always be walking alone the way he did. He taught me the teachers of loneliness, feelings, testing and challenge, and love.

Then he showed me that it's not wise to look into the reflection of all human beings, only certain ones. For those who can mirror more knowledge and greater power to you, look deeply into their reflections. Those of similar power and maturity with you, teach and share with. Never look into those reflections that are less than yours, but instead reflect back to them who you are. If you look into their reflection, it will distract you from your true purpose and will only give you illusions of your shadow instead of the light of your undiscovered self in the shadow. A popular mythology today is that everyone is a legitimate mirror for us to look into and learn from, and that, in fact, we should do just that. Remember, your soul sent your spirit personality here for one thing—to evolve and master the physical. Attention is power. Where you choose to focus your attention will either help you refine your character and evolve your soul or distract you into entertainment and mediocrity. Life is a choice, and Lobo clearly demonstrated this to me.

When I returned home from the vision quest, I had developed a maturity, a physical stance, and a magnetic character, a charismatic presence that attracted roles of leadership to me. Lobo had helped me to traverse that first spiral through the Five Movements of my Book of Life and to know who I was. This was a major turning point in my life.

Section Five

What Is the Human Flowering Tree?

The Human as a Luminous Egg or Cocoon

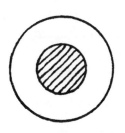

About Section Five

Humans are magnificent luminous light beings that carry the potential for enlightenment and resurrection, oneness with the Everything. We are electromagnetic, psychic-kinetic forms of vibrating energy, a luminosity (also called the *aura*) that looks like a *luminous egg* or *cocoon*. This energy body contains our physical presence as well as our immortality, and it is through this energy body that we are interconnected, interdependent, and interreliable with all other things in the Universe.

The human is referred to by many magickal traditions as the *Tree of Life,* and the Twisted Hairs call it the *Human Flowering Tree.* This section describes the components of the human luminous egg or cocoon and, finally takes us full circle as it shows what happens when we die and our spirit personality leaves the physical form and journeys back along its stream of intending into the fifth dimension of spirit.

17

The Suns and Comets in Our Luminosity: Entrances Into Other Realities

Several *solar bodies* in the microcosmic universe of our luminosity bear examination. They are invisible, energetic mirrors of our visible behavior patterns, and they are instrumental to our perceptions of reality and to our maturity into evolved spiritual beings. They are the three Assemblage Points: the *Stationary Assemblage Point* (SAP), the *Moving Assemblage Point* (MAP), and the *Great Light Assemblage Point* (GLAP).* These Assemblage Points have also been described in the work of Carlos Castaneda.

The Moving Assemblage Point (MAP)

When a child is first born, all three Assemblage Points, the MAP, the GLAP, and the SAP, are localized in the navel, and the child is in harmony and alignment with the Universe, completely knowing its oneness with the Everything. Immediately after a child is born, the MAP explodes from this *sun,* leaves the navel, and begins to

---

*The material in this chapter is edited and updated material taken from two sources: *Shamanic Wheels and Keys,* Vol. 1, by H. S. Reagan (Los Angeles: DTMMS, 1980, rev. 1994), pp. 149-51; and *The Mirror of Self-Reflection: The Inner Mirror Masks of the Mask of Self-Pity,* by H. S. Reagan (Los Angeles: DTMMS, 1988), pp. 21-38. Edited and reprinted by permission.

circulate throughout the meridians of the body like a comet. It is synonymous to the *chi* or *ki*, which flows through the meridians in a repeating twenty-four-hour cycle, and it holds the physical body together. The MAP establishes the normal cyclical ebbs and flows of biorhythms in all five aspects of our beings: the emotional, mental, physical, spiritual, and sexual. It is, therefore, responsible for creating our natural daily, monthly, and yearly energy cycles called the *naturals*.

The MAP holds our RNA, which carries our genetic coding and our memory of specificity within the human species, such as eye and skin color, height, and so on. It is the male energy of the body.

The Great Light Assemblage Point (GLAP)

The GLAP is our *inner sun* and remains situated in the navel throughout our life. It is the point from which we perceive the reality of the Universe. The *soul vine*, which is really two fibers of light within the luminous egg or cocoon, are sent out from the GLAP into the Universe to maintain our alignment with the Everything. Seen another way, the GLAP is the point from which the Great Spirit assembles us, as parts of its innumerable points of perception. In a sense, it could be said that the GLAP is the transmission line between human beings and the "Source of the Force," that is, the Source of the Everything. It is how we have the potential to perceive all realities within all the worlds and all the universes within the Everything. The GLAP is the female energy of the body, and it carries our ETA (Evolutionary Transformational Agents), our ability to evolve towards perfection of form within our species.

The Stationary Assemblage Point (SAP)

The SAP is a focal point of energy within the luminosity whose function is to govern how we perceive our reality. In a sense, it is like the aperture in a camera which regulates the amount of light coming in; its position in our luminosity determines how we "construct" the world. The SAP works in concert with the *octagonal mirror,* which is located in your left chest area (see Fig. 17-a).

Fig. 17-a   Our Octagonal Mirror and
Stationary Assemblage Point (SAP)

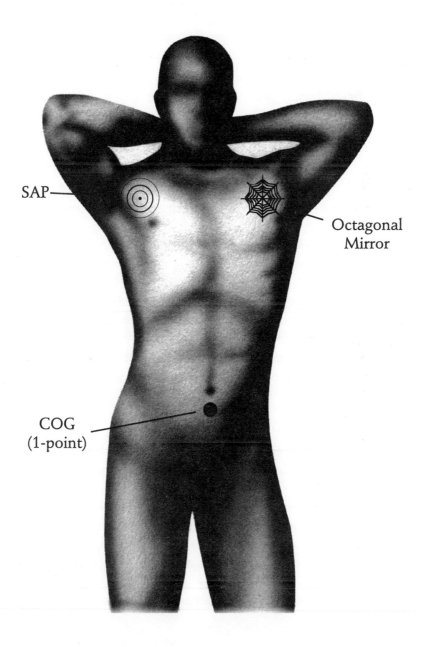

SAP

Octagonal
Mirror

COG
(1-point)

The octagonal mirror has eight faces or camera filters called *cognitive modes,* which determine how you will receive the light coming in through the SAP. This determines your patterns of behavior.

Suppose an attraction presents itself, and you focus your attention on that attraction. To see that attraction, you must *perceive* it through the octagonal mirror. Each of the eight lenses of the octagonal mirror receive stimulus input through our five senses (sight, hearing, taste, smell, touch), ten chakras, five shields, seven dancers, eight eyes, and three ears, which are energy sensors at various points in our bodies in addition to our two physical eyes and ears.

When a child is born, the SAP is situated in the navel. Over the course of the next three years, it begins to move up the chakra line and becomes situated in a predetermined position somewhere in the right chest area (again refer to Fig. 17-a). This position is determined by each of us before our birth to enable us to perceive reality in the way best suited for the specific growth experiences we need from this lifetime.

Once stationed in the right chest area, the SAP is essentially in a fixed position called the *circle of influence.* However, this position can be shifted back down towards the navel. When it is positioned in the right chest area, our perception is fairly narrow and separate. When it is situated in the central chakra line, we can begin to develop our *O'larien,* or psychic gifts, and move into balance and alignment.

There is a gradual, long-term movement of the SAP's resting position towards the center body line and then down during our lifetime as a result of spiritual growth and increasing orende energy levels. The more balanced and enlightened we become, the more the SAP moves towards the center chakra line and then down towards the navel again. If a one-inch or more shift is maintained for at least a year, then this will become the new resting position of the SAP. If this shift is maintained for at least three years, the SAP will never go back up over this point.

When we become fully enlightened as a result of our spiritual growth, the SAP becomes positioned in the navel along with the GLAP. Now our perception of reality and the Great Spirit's perception become one. At this point we can truly see through the eyes of the Great Spirit, perceiving all time, space, dimensions, and realities. Our intent becomes one with the intent of the Great Spirit.

We Access Bands of Awareness

Perception is determined by the location of the SAP. This location is called its *resonant station*. Compare this to a television. Each number on the dial is a channel that receives a specific frequency, a particular array of programming that, you might say, are "realities" unique to that channel. Each resonant station of the Assemblage Point is capable of illuminating or opening up forty-eight *bands of awareness,* out of which the average human can assimilate and tune in clearly to only six to eight, which is considered our range of "normal awareness." *To be aware* means "to be connected to internal and external potentialities, to be cognizant of and informed by." There are forty-eight ways for us to connect our inner realities with outer attractions at each resonant station.

We are able to perceive externally only those bands of awareness that match the ones illuminated internally, and these are a function of our molding, sculpting, and armoring, our perceptions through our five senses, and the influence of our image makers. Our internal Southwest concepts of self, and the worldview we carry with us internally through our life experiences, are assembled in this way, helping to create the box of limitations and circumscribing our ability to perceive outside the box.

Agitation of the SAP

In situations where we are having a "bad day" and getting our buttons pushed, the Assemblage Point begins to agitate or jiggle within the circle of influence. Emotionality, or being adversely affected by other people and events, destabilizes and agitates our Assemblage Point and results in a loss of energy. The position of the Assemblage Point of our parents and primary image makers creates the *collective circle of influence* for us as children. Once the child leaves the womb and its umbilical cord is severed, the SAP moves up and into that circle of influence called the *karma mirror*. When the Assemblage Point is agitating within this circle of influence, we are, in essence, seeking the *teaching,* or *dharma light,* in the *karma mirror*. This is what we have called a *pain game*.

To stop this agitation of the Assemblage Point and prevent the loss of energy, certain stabilizing disciplines can be employed. Through these disciplines, we can stop the feeling of having a bad day from actually becoming a bad day. Stabilizing provides clarity and brings an opportunity for choosing correct action that we were not capable of previously.

Shifting the SAP

We can temporarily shift the SAP from within our luminous egg or cocoon by correct breathing, proper alignment with the worlds of Grandmother Earth, increased orende surges brought about through intense energy exchanges, high-level orgastic experiences, chanting, singing songs of power, meditation, and proper alchemical ceremony, to name a few. All these experiences can be said to be more or less of a positive nature; they always induce a proper and powerful shifting of the SAP.

The Red Road

There are three basic *movement paths* the Assemblage Point can take according to what the energy impetus is, and each path has *resonant points* that are a definitive part of its characteristic experience.

The *Human Shift,* or movement along the *Red Road,* contains eleven primary resonant stations. As the SAP shifts progressively from one station to the next, we become more perceptually awake, aware, and alert. As we become more illuminated internally, we are capable of *seeing* more externally. The Elders call this *heightened awareness*.

Within the perceptual experience of each resonant point, we

perceive more and more accurately. Each resonant point has a very distinct and precise visual-auditory sense of reality. The subjective field of each of these resonant points is very different, and each gives the feedback of viewing or participating in a different reality, movie, or TV program. Some resonant points create entirely separate realities that can even appear like totally different universes, totally different dimensions, or totally different worlds. Also very important is the fact that at some of these resonant points our perceptions are enhanced to the extreme, so we experience a tremendous surge of orende as well as advanced *larien,* or psychic abilities.

Most people are not able to assemble the bands of awareness and perceive realities beyond their normal awareness. When Carlos Castaneda wrote about assembling other realities, he was talking about the ability to focus the SAP and assemble "other realities" by accessing all these bands of awareness.

The Blue Road

The *Animal Shift,* also called the *Blue Road,* is an unnatural and improper shift straight down the right side of the body. Extreme fear, anger, stress, guilt, shame, anxiety, jealousy, extreme shock, shattering of a symbol, exposure to tyrants, and hysteria will all move the SAP improperly along this path. In addition, any foods that are not in resonance with your orende can cause this shift. The longer you hold onto the energy emotion, the further down your Assemblage Point moves. This straight down shift causes a distorted view of reality. People whose perceptions are extremely distorted in all the senses may experience hallucinations.

The fourth point is halfway between the navel and the heart chakra and sometimes level with the navel. If the SAP moves here, the individual may sometimes experience catatonic schizophrenia. If the SAP moves down past the navel, death will occur. Common reactions to this shift by the three core personalities are: Space Cadets go into catatonia; Farts go into psychosis and rage; and Do-Gooders go into neurosis.

The Yellow Road

The *Plant Shift,* also called the *Yellow Road,* is a diagonal movement down and to the left of the body and has thirteen resonant points. It is considered to be a neutral shift and utilizes the boost of the sacred teacher plants, which are the catalysts in the plant kingdom. If used in proper alchemical ceremony, the SAP will move properly. If the teacher plants are used just to get high, then it will move improperly.

The use of these plants with music, chanting, drumming, and a proper ceremonial context insures the shift moves to the left and down. The teacher plants dislodge the SAP onto the neutral axis, but the drumming, singing, chanting, and ceremonial context shift it to the left and down, which is a proper movement. Ceremonies were always done in shamanic traditions to cause the shifting of the Assemblage Point. It takes more energy to dislodge the point and get it to move than it does to redirect its movement once it is in progress. Therefore, these plants were always used as the catalysts for the initial *breaking loose* of the SAP, and once freed, it was directed into the heart space through clear intent and proper alchemical ceremony.

Following the Red Road

It is the warrior's intent to follow the proper Red "Human" Road movement (see Fig. 17-b). With forty-eight bands of awareness at each resonant point, there are a total of 1,344 possible bands a human can assemble inside the luminous egg or cocoon by shifting the SAP. At each resonant point, therefore, we can assemble the bands of awareness into a unique and entirely different reality from the others. We can expand our awareness by increasing our sobriety, by seeking knowledge, by feeding our hungers, by stretching our potential to master the physical, and so forth. When we do, the SAP moves out of the circle of influence of its station. It can move from point 1 to point 2, for example. A *shift* means it skips resonant points.

Fig. 17-b   The Red "Human" Road

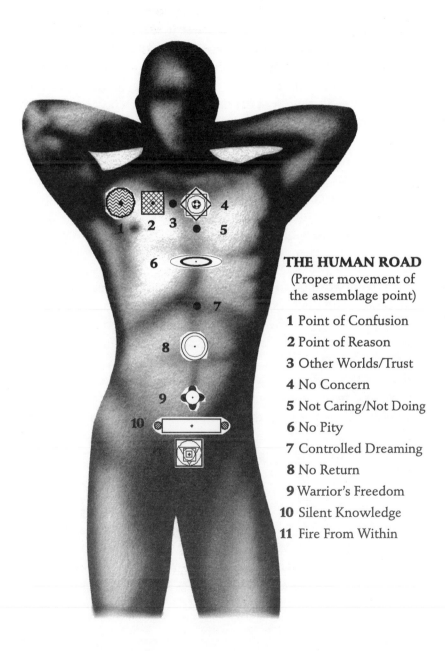

THE HUMAN ROAD
(Proper movement of
the assemblage point)

1 Point of Confusion
2 Point of Reason
3 Other Worlds/Trust
4 No Concern
5 Not Caring/Not Doing
6 No Pity
7 Controlled Dreaming
8 No Return
9 Warrior's Freedom
10 Silent Knowledge
11 Fire From Within

Point 1: The Stationary Assemblage Point

This is the static or fixed position of the SAP; it moves within a three-inch circle of influence in the right chest area. The Elders also call this the *Point of Confusion,* the seat of our perception of reality. It is the TV channel we are tuned to, and thus receive the programming determined by the collective circle of influence of our image makers, and it is a function of our molding, sculpting, and armoring. The sigils represent the nature of the perceptual awareness at each station. At point 1, the dot is the focus of the SAP itself. The round aspect is the octagonal mirror with test pattern waves. This is also the primary sigil for water, as this point of confusion is in heavy emotion. Therefore, when the SAP is in this station, our perception of reality is heavily influenced by emotion and emotionality. The light or picture which is admitted into the octagonal mirror and its lenses is very often out of focus and distorted.

Point 2: The Point of Reason

Our reality can be so drastically affected at this second station as to cause a full distortion of reality and put us into fantasy or illusion. The energy of this particular place is such that our reason becomes extremely dogmatic and persistent, insisting that our reality is the *only* true reality. This limitation causes us to rationalize and define the world in very absolute terms. This place is highly addictive, and people often get stuck in self-righteousness here, insisting that how they see the world from this place is absolutely correct. It is easy to stay stuck here, also, because this perceptual view allows us to feel secure; it keeps our view of reality predictable, and it helps to create our comfort zone.

Historically, this resonant point has been considered the major contributor to the movement away from individual, autonomous freedom and into religious conviction and belief systems. We cannot see our patterns when we are in this place; we are wearing blinders. Anyone stuck in reason sees through only one perspective and cannot access other viewing points. The spectrum of forty-eight bands of awareness is not accessed. A new set of forty-eight bands called *reason* is* active. If we are stuck in this point of reason, we are trapped in our box of limitations, and clarity becomes our number one enemy. This point has led to the creation of organized religion, industrialization, and technology out of balance. It continues to destroy Grandmother Earth and all her children in many ways. The Twisted Hairs Elders say that too many people today are caught in this resonant station, holding on to the familiar and the comfortable, preferring to be entertained, willing to give up individual freedom and autonomy in exchange for security provided by external entities. Ethnic genocide and religious conflict are the extreme of this point of reason.

On the light side, we can learn a certain spectrum of knowledge at this point. It is a good place to gather information, but very dangerous if we linger too long.

Point 3: The Point of Other Worlds

This is a transition point where we develop many different points of view beyond the sticky quagmire of our emotions and the rigidity of our belief systems. We are on our way to heightened awareness, awakening to our natural self and accessing our higher self, our hokkshideh.

Point 4: The Point of No Concern

When your Assemblage Point moves into this resonant station, you begin to know things without knowing how you know, and you increase your ability to hold many different points of view at one time. Although dualities and paradox never disappear, as they are inherent in the matrix of this Planet of the Children, you are now able to resolve the paradoxes for yourself and deal with the dualities, so that they are no longer dams across your stream of livingness. At this point, you exercise impeccable timing, and you have spun your spirit shields in front of you, thus accessing their power.

This is the first resonant station where you enter heightened awareness, and it provides the edge for the jump into the unknown. If you can get your Assemblage Point into this place, you conquer the enemy of fear, you become fearless and bold, you push your edge, expand your boundaries, and move beyond your limitations. You engage with the unknown, for you know that here is where you can make quantum leaps in your soul's evolution. Consequently, you can do things that defy description in normal reality.

Point 5: The Point of Not Caring

When your Assemblage Point reaches this resonant station, you are able once and for all to remove the masks of self-pity and self-importance. Not caring here does not mean you don't love anything or have compassion. Rather, it means that you care deeply, and that you love unconditionally without attachments, dependencies, or comparisons. Your caring doesn't come with a price that you exact from others. You are free, and you care for all things, unabashedly as a natural give-away of who you are. You feel more than ever your interconnectedness.

Point 6: The Point of No Pity

You must hold an extremely high orende level to maintain the Assemblage Point in this station. Dropping the mask of self-pity, you see the tremendous amount of energy you have expended to maintain the mask and the pretender self. You also see clearly and accurately your mirror of self-reflection and what it reflects back to you. It teaches the mood of ruthlessness. This is the ideal place for patients, healers, and all those involved in a healing circle during any ceremonial healing. Now in heightened awareness and recognizing the power and beauty of your true nature, you feel tremendous self-love and sobriety, and the energy surge is awesome. This is generally known as the sorcerer's or warrior's point of focus. With it, you can easily double (be in two places at once). Your Assemblage Point moves to this place in the dreamscape all the time, and it is the major working place of the nagual.

Point 7: The Point of Controlled Dreaming

At this point you have developed the art of controlled dreaming to such an extent that you control your asleep dreams and can bring these experiences back to your awake dream with total memory recall. Moreover, you overlap the asleep dream of the fifth dimension with the awake dream of the third dimension and make your world fourth-dimensionally determinate. This is similar to déjà vu. You are in a moment where you are so present that you are totally aware of what will happen, who will say what, and so forth, for a moment or several minutes at a time. This is stopping the world, wherein your higher self and dream guide body of the fifth dimension have temporarily reached down and grabbed your consciousness in third dimension and elevated it into the power and reality of the fifth dimension.

Thunder Strikes: *For example, as I become more and more illumined, 40 to 60 percent of my day is constant déjà vu experience.*

Point 8: The Point of No Return

If one's physical body can hold an extremely high orende for three years, the Assemblage Point will stabilize in this resonant station. Here you are able to transcend the limitations of time and space and move your Assemblage Point so that you can physically disappear from this dimension at will and have total recollection of all the times in heightened awareness in both fifth and third dimensions, including past and future lifetimes. This is where you finally finish your destiny pattern and achieve what you came here to do—step outside the cycles of reincarnation, resurrect, and become formless. You become an enlightened human being.

The Great Spirit's free will and intent are what guide you here, through your eyes and breathing, so your eyes change and begin to shine with your inner light. This is called the *shining*. You develop the *Gaze of Power,* the *Voice of Power,* and the *Touch of Power.* In this place, all four stalking moods are developed equally. You are impeccable, having let go of your personality and dropped the illusion of being a person. Therefore, you are formless in the sense that you have complete control over your physical form and your nagual or spirit essence and can choose whichever form from past or future lifetimes to manifest in. Upon his resurrection, the Christ Jesus appeared to Simon Peter and said, "I am as you knew me." He resurrected in the physical body of Jesus of Nazareth, even though he could have chosen any physical incarnation of any of his spirit personalities. This is enlightenment—complete control over your tonal physical form and nagual or spirit essence.

Point 9: The Point of Warrior's Freedom

You master chaos here and are formless.

Point 10: The Point of Silent Knowledge

You have instant recollection of a minimum of forty-five lifetimes collected in this body. Carlos Castaneda referred to this as the *power of silence.*

Point 11: The Point of Instant Memory/Fire From Within

This the place of total enlightenment. Most important here is to realize that we are all capable of this enlightened transformation and resurrection into formlessness. It is not reserved for the revered few. Christ, Buddha, Grandfather Two Bears, and many others have gone before us to show us the *Way* and the *Light.* The journey of our soul as it seeks its perfection is our *Way,* and it seeks the *Light* of that initial explosion out from the Source, to be one with the Everything. The Elders say that when a human being achieves this transcendence, the Universe vibrates with ecstasy.

18

The Microcosmic Universe
of the Soul:
Our Shields and Dancers

The human luminosity, or aura, is shaped like an egg with the
small rounded end at our head. The luminosity of a healthy
person extends out to about the tips of the fingers when the arms
are fully extended out from the side.

This luminous egg or cocoon contains twelve *planets,* or bodies
of light energy—*five shields* and *seven dancers*—which are psychic-
kinetic and electromagnetic force fields of energy. The five shields
keep our physical body present in this third-dimensional world and
carry the one spirit personality of our soul in this lifetime. Each has
an identity, an actual part of our personality, a definite aspect of
who we are as human beings. They are the temporary houses for
our physical body.

Our seven dancers, on the other hand, are immortal and carry
the spirit personality in its cycles of reincarnation from one lifetime
to another. As our infinite connection to the Great Spirit, they hold
our soul's memory; their primary function is to get us to wake up,
access that memory and remember who we are, step out of the cycles of reincarnation, resurrect, and become enlightened. The seven
dancers are the carriers of the soul in its spirit personalities as it
makes its Great SunDance Journey.

Our immortal soul dances all seven dimensions of reality with these force fields of energy, each with a consciousness of itself. Together the shields and dancers formulate the Magnetic Attracting Thought (MAT) space within which our soul resides as a spirit personality, and they define the real touchable reality of a MAT space of our soul. The shields are simply a leased space that allows tonal presence of consciousness in a brief learning experience of how to master the physical body in the physical world. While the shields have to be left behind at the moment of physical death, we move out of that house and into another. We are actually climbing up the real estate ladder into a bigger house. As it is written in the Bible "There are many mansions in my Father's kingdom." What many do not understand is that this is a metaphor for each dancer as a mansion, and the seven together resurrect into the Great Spirit's mansion, the castle of ultimate creation.

We Look Like a Wheel

The five shields and seven dancers resemble balls of light approximately one to three feet in diameter (see Fig. 18-a). The artist's rendering in the figure shows the relative positions of both the shields and the dancers in our luminosity. It illustrates the arrangement of the five shields (as well as the seven dancers) to show their directional orientation. These shields and dancers are attached at our navel by luminous fibers of light energy. These fibers are like tentacles about one to eight feet long that telescope in and out, connecting to the shields and dancers and holding them in place within the luminosity. In this respect, we look like a wheel. The greater our inner balance and the higher our orende, the more the shields expand in size.

Two other primary fibers at our navel, called the *soul vine*, connect our dancers back to the Great Spirit along our stream of intending. In addition, we have two fibers, each with twelve feeler filaments; through them, we connect with and communicate energetically with everything around us.

Our Five Shields

Our five shields are called the *Child Substance Shield,* the *Adult*

Fig. 18-a   The Twelve Planets of Our Microcosmic Universe:
The Five Shields and Seven Dancers in Our Luminosity

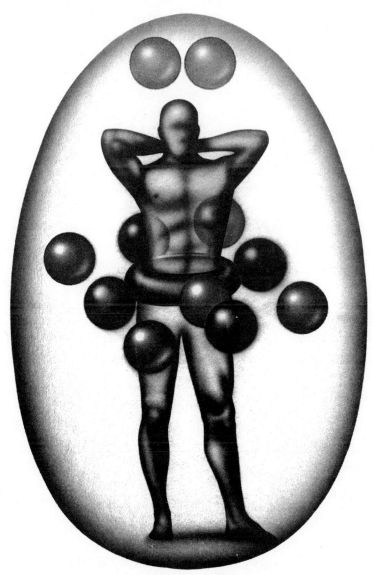

Note: The shields (darker balls) and dancers (lighter balls) are shown
much smaller than their actual size to depict their relative positions.

Substance Shield, the *Adult Spirit Shield,* the *Child Spirit Shield,* and the *Elder Shield* (see Fig. 18-b, which shows the directional orientation of these five shields). Within each of our shields are five elements or aspects (water, earth, wind, fire, void), and each is guided or influenced by one of the *chakras* in our luminosity. Chakras, called *energy wheels* by the Twisted Hairs, are spinning vortices of energy that look like wheels of light energy moving in and out of the body through the layers of the luminosity, which, in contrast to other traditions, the Twisted Hairs consider to be a chakra as well. In deference to the popular understanding of these energy wheels, they will be referred to here as chakras.

Each shield has a male and a female side as suggested by the yin-yang depiction in the figure. The male side is always guided by odd-numbered chakras, and the female side, by even-numbered chakras. Energy flows through the chakras either clockwise or counterclockwise, and it is opposite in men and women, thus greatly influencing our energetic expression. In women, odd-numbered chakras rotate counterclockwise and even-numbered chakras rotate clockwise. In men, they rotate in the opposite direction. That is why the two genders were designed to mesh together like gears in a machine. Proper flow of energy helps to maintain health and vigor not only in the physical body but also balances our emotional, mental, spiritual, and sexual aspects.

What Do Our Shields Look Like?

The physical appearance of the Child Substance Shield is that of a round glass globe of light filled with water. The Adult Substance Shield appears as a similar ball filled with swirling smoke. The Adult Spirit Shield is a crystal ball with spikes, channels, and grids lit up inside it. The Child Spirit Shield is an empty glass ball of light with a big fire in the middle and many little fires continually igniting, moving, spinning, and vibrating inside. The Elder Shield is seen not so much as a physical entity, but more as a quality of demeanor and carriage. When it is fully awake, people look older and wiser, but strong and powerful at the same

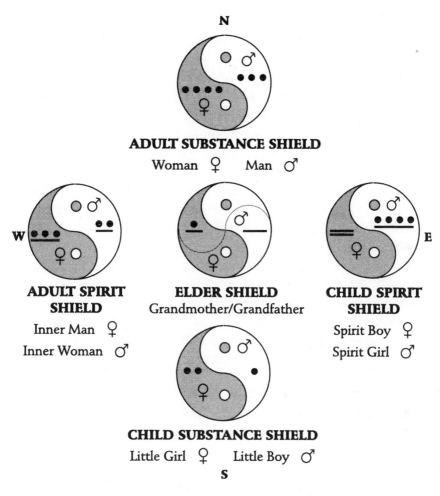

Fig. 18-6 The Five Shields

time. You can see it in their eyes and facial expressions.

The five shields are mortal or temporary, meaning that at the moment of physical death the four shields implode through your navel into your Elder Shield. Then they explode and disintegrate, merging with and becoming part of everything around you—the furniture, pets, people, and trees. So death occurs within the "One to the Many and the Many Back to the One" law.

Thunder Strikes: *When I was a little kid, I used to spend a lot of time out on the land, observing Nature, watching and learning from the animals, the insects, and the plants, always guided by my clan uncle, John Two Crows, and my grandmother, Spotted Fawn. I would tease the animals and insects sometimes in order to observe them and learn their behavior. For example, I would sometimes chew bubble gum, then tie it to a string and drop it down a tarantula hole, hoping the tarantula's hairy body would stick to the chewing gum. Then I would pull it out of its hole and play with it.*

On one particular day, I caught a tarantula this way and played with it, pulling it and making it jump over and over again. Pretty soon I got bored with this, so I pulled the tarantula onto an anthill, and war broke out. My grandmother came up behind me and scolded me, saying I was letting the spider be killed. I said I just wanted to see what would happen. She got very angry and said, "Then you will stay and get a teaching." She slapped me on the back of my neck, shifting me into a heightened state of awareness and forcing me into an act of seeing.

I saw the ants attack. They were formed in regimented divisions and came in waves like an organized army. Little by little, they took bites and nips out of the tarantula. In their natural state, the ant aura is pinkish green, and the tarantula's aura is violet or amethyst. The moment the tarantula died, I saw every ant light up with a bright violet hue. The tarantula's shields went into everything around it. My grandmother explained that I was seeing the transference of energy that demonstrated one of the Cosmic Laws: "Death Gives Life." That was my last act of cruelty.

By looking at a person's aura, we can see what is going to happen in that person's body three to nine months before it is encoded or manifested in the physical body. This is caused in part by the movement of the shields in the third and fourth rings of the aura. If the shields move, the energy is programmed into the body and the body is affected by it.

Our Shields Are Always Moving

Substance shields rotate vertically; spirit shields rotate horizontally (see Fig. 18-c). When a child is born, its Child Substance Shield

Fig. 18-c   The Movement of the Shields

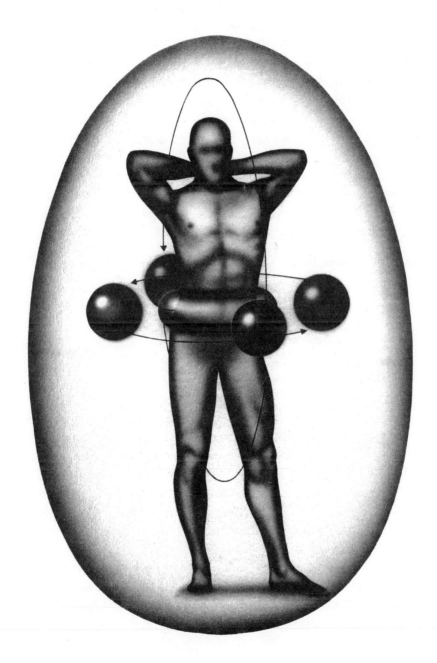

is situated in front of its body until it goes through puberty. When the young boy begins to ejaculate semen and the young girl begins her moon cycle (menstrual cycle), this shield moves behind in the luminosity, and the Adult Substance Shield swings out in front. In the child who is maturing properly after puberty and in any mature, healthy adult, this shield should remain behind and the Adult Substance Shield should be in front, with the Child Spirit Shield to the left and the Adult Spirit Shield to the right when you are sitting up or standing. Your Elder Shield stays in the center always.

The substance shields are susceptible to the dark side, to duality and paradox, to negativity and our own immaturity and destructive patterns. The spirit shields work to help rectify or find solution to our shadow, as they are the light within the dark. The Elder Shield is always guiding you towards the Light.

Being in a Shield

When we are *in a shield,* we are experiencing reality from the energy of that shield. When a shield moves in front of us in our luminosity, it will influence our personality and determine our perception of reality. When one of the substance shields is in front, we tend to be stuck in our patterns, and our shideh and karmic pretender ego get the upper hand. When one of the spirit shields is in front, our arenas of experience broaden, our basal metabolic rate increases, and we move into a space of multiple attention and fast thought. Our male and female aspects are in balance, and we act more mature. All of the behavior patterns we have talked about influence the balance of your shields. They are *you.*

We get so attached to everything that goes on in the shields that the mask dance of the shields keeps us at the effect of the image makers and our own destructive patterns. The Elders say we reincarnate time after time because we won't let go of our attachment to the physical body. The greatest fear of the unknown is the fear of death and what that experience is like, and the substance shields are afraid of death. Because they view growing up as a form of death, they will try to dominate and keep the spirit shields away from the front.

The Child Substance Shield

Subjectively, the *Child Substance Shield* is primarily an emotional shield as it holds the place of the South, the place of water and the emotions. When this shield is balanced and healthy, it is playful. It wants to have fun and explore the world with childlike energy, trust, and innocence. This shield also moves in front if we are happily playing with children or reminiscing about happy times. When dysfunctional or in the dark side, it has a childish, domineering, manipulative, and vampire-like quality.

The gender of your Child Substance Shield is the same as the gender of your physical body. For women, the Child Substance Shield is called your *Little Girl Shield,* and for men the Child Substance Shield is called your *Little Boy Shield.* One of the most important teachings in this path, which the Twisted Hairs stress over and over, is the importance of the balance of male and female energies. Both the Little Girl and the Little Boy have a female side and a male side, but the average two-legged has a tendency to stay in the same side of the same shield. Men tend to stay in their male side, and women tend to stay in their female side, which creates imbalance and immaturity.

The Child Substance Shield is usually the shield that is most at the effect of the image makers and the tyrants of life. It is the part of you that experiences the greatest amount of molding, or being cast into a part it doesn't want; sculpting, or being designed to be something it isn't; and armoring, or protecting the self from the pain. It is the part of you that loses itself, becomes the pussycat, and forgets it is really the jaguar. For example, if something happens and you get stuck in emotionality or lose your center, you will act like a needy, wounded, abandoned little girl or little boy. Your entire personality changes because that shield swings in front of you. When it does, you may even experience a voice change and a change in body language; you take on a definite childish attitude in the way you talk and act, completely different from a mature man or woman. As an adult, have you ever experienced conflict with your parents and found yourself reverting back to childhood patterns of body movement and voice when you tried to interact with them? Your Child Substance Shield moved in front of you, and you were operating from the dark, imbalanced side of that shield.

When Elders become senile, their Child Substance Shield moves back to the front of the luminosity. If they haven't reconciled all their emotional wounding, they'll revert back to the child because they are getting close to journeying back into the Great Round. When this happens, the Adult Substance Shield will rotate to the back.

The first chakra guides the Little Boy (the male side), and its influence is sexual arousal, lust, and orgasticness. If a man is in his Little Boy, male side, he is first chakra oriented—aggressive and sexual. When a man gets hurt or wounded, his Little Boy Shield comes out in front; he tends to sulk and pout, get aggressive, and manipulate to get his way. He usually does this through sexuality or through bravado and showing off. Men don't want to cuddle. That is why when you ask little boys, "Come and give me a hug," they will often respond, "Ugh!"

The second chakra guides the Little Girl (the female side), and its influence is a nurturing focus of career, family, and spiritual path. If a woman is in her Little Girl, female side, she is second chakra-oriented, that is, nurturing. When a woman gets hurt and is in her needy, wounded, abandoned child with her Little Girl Shield in front, she wants hugging, holding, nurturing, and caring. Right away, you see one of the basic innate differences between men and women which creates conflict.

To demonstrate how the first and second chakra orientations differ, consider this example of a man and woman in relationship. The woman is in her Little Girl Shield, female side, second chakra focus. The man's interaction with her is from his Little Boy Shield, male side, first chakra focus. He comes home from a hard day of work, and she wants to talk about her day. She has a soft look in her eyes, and her body is pulling, saying she wants to be held and talked to. The man wants to meet her needs, but being influenced by his first chakra orientation, the only way he can give her what she needs, he thinks, is to fuck her. (*Note:* The word *fuck* is used here not to shock or to offend, but rather to indicate the nature of the energy that men experience.) The woman is offended by what she perceives to be his focus on sex and his lack of sensitivity. Her partner is confused because it is his way of showing he cares because that is what he would want.

When you are in this shield, it is natural to play this "war between the sexes" game. Is there a solution to this conflict? Yes, and caring is the key to this shield. We must begin to communicate with sensitivity to these basic differences between a man and a woman. If you understand that these differences are innate, you can begin to develop the ability to step into the opposite side of your shields and step out of codependency and neediness. You no longer need to be rescued. The positive side of the male side of the Child Substance Shield is an explosive and creative actualizing energy that wants to explore, seeks adventure, and needs to know.

You heal your needy, wounded, abandoned child by going to the opposite side of your Child Substance Shield to heal it. A man works with the female side of his Little Boy Shield and a woman goes to the male side of her Little Girl Shield and works with that. This strengthens the weaker side in each and develops balance of the male and female energies in both. Balance comes because you are able to switch the sides of the shield and communicate openly. Your actions are clear, and you co-empower each other. This dynamic is about being a balanced human, not about being a man or woman.

The Adult Substance Shield

The *Adult Substance Shield* anchors in the elemental wind energy and the expression of the mind. Inwardly and subjectively, it holds the place of the North. This shield has a future orientation and a career focus as it gives meaning and purpose to our life. Our body is inside our mind: We are a consciousness that follows cyclical behavior in the process of mastering both the body and the mind.

We need to balance our male and female energies the most in

the South and North shields, in our heart and our mind. Like the Child Substance Shield, this is a same-gender shield. For a man, this is his Man Shield, and for a woman, this is her Woman Shield, each with a male and a female side. The male side is guided by the third chakra, so this prompts a man's desire for change, variety, intrigue, adventure, accomplishment, success, and conquering the world. The female side of the shield is guided by the fourth chakra, the heart. Therefore, women want stability, balance, security, solidity, and harmony. Again, a man can be in the female side and a woman in the male side.

The dark side of the Adult Substance Shield is called the angry, vengeful, manipulative adult. Keep in mind that we are in the dark side of this shield only if a man is always in his male side and a woman is always in her female side, unbalanced. This causes the second war between the sexes. When a man is in his Adult Substance Shield, he seeks change and wants to go out and conquer the world. For example, he comes home, to the same home he and his wife have lived in for fifteen years, and says, "I've been offered a promotion in Hawaii, and I want to accept it." The woman comes unglued and says, "Not so fast! We have lived here all this time. We have a secure life here and friends and neighbors we are close to. The children have attended school here, and you want to tear us up from all this?" To the husband, the move is nothing; he is ready. The wife, on the other hand, wants stable, predictable security. Now, that doesn't mean that we can't do the opposite. Many of us do. All we have to do is go to the opposite side of our shield. If you stay in your gender side of the shield, it gets more and more imbalanced. You are "rescuing" the needy, wounded, abandoned child or the angry, vengeful, manipulative adult instead of helping that part of you to grow up.

If you are out of balance in this shield, man or woman, you will constantly sabotage your world. You will exhibit a lack of self-worth, a lack of self-esteem, and an unwillingness to stick to something to completion. Very often such a person cannot hold a job and resents having to be mature and responsible. The negative side of the fourth chakra is the need to dominate, manipulate, and control to force your will on someone else. It is the need to have it your way. If a man is in his male dark side and the woman is in her female dark side, a typical scenario would be: The man will stay stuck, and the woman will constantly put him down. Parents will often neglect their responsibilities to their children when they are in the dark side of this shield. This is a major contributor to the modern dysfunctional family.

In the light side of the third chakra, there is a willingness to accept change and an appreciation of the sacredness of life, and you assume responsibility for your actions. In the light side of the fourth chakra, there is a respect for one's lineage, your Elders and inherited family responsibilities. More than anything, you respect the fact that others have walked farther than you have and that they have more knowledge.

All of this comes back to the balance of the male and female within ourselves. Male and female will continue to misunderstand and war with each other as long as there is imbalance. Here is another example of this imbalance: Early in the Women's Liberation Movement, many women swung to the male side of their Woman Shield, started wearing men's clothes, took on many of the macho male mannerisms, and talked about the power of women. They imitated the very thing they were warring with. That is not the power of woman. They created imbalance in the opposite extreme by turning their backs on their female side and immersing themselves wholly in their male side. They created greater conflict and turmoil with men as a result.

Female power is soft power—the balance of the feminine, receptive-creative, intuitive energy with the masculine, active-conceptive, aggressive energy. This is a woman who is soft and sensual but strong at the same time. Moving to the opposite side of the shield is an energetic move. It does not mean that a person becomes more masculine, or "butch," or more feminine, or "effeminate," in the popular conception of what that looks like. It is the ability to utilize the essence of the energies to develop caring and sensitivity to the differences. Within that balance lies our power and the key to our true humanness.

It is just as difficult for a man to get out of his anger, his stress, his vengeful, manipulative aspect, and into balance, stability, solidity, strength, and alignment as it is for a woman to embrace change. When women react to stress, what heals their stress is stability. Moving, or going into action, heals a man's stress. That is why men tend to be impulsive. A man goes from his head to his heart; he figures something out with his mind first, then his heart can accept it. A woman examines something with her heart first, and if her heart accepts it, then she goes to her head. If she is awake and wise, she goes to her womb, her real root of power. Our natural disposition or tendency is to stay in our same gender side of our Substance Shields, so we have to break our patterns and do just the opposite of what we usually do. That is not easy, but it is a necessary part of growing up.

Whatever shield needs expression appears in the front of a person's luminosity. As in billiards, when one shield moves, they all have to shift to different positions. Expressions such as "I lost my center" are unconscious expressions of what is actually happening. The shields can move in any number of combinations. How that combination happens is directly attributable to how much energy we hold. The movements of the shields are also affected by the battle between our shideh and hokkshideh, our karmic pretender ego and dharmic commander ego. The shields shift as a function of our karmic patterns, our balance and imbalance in the expression of our elemental energies, and so forth.

As you work with the wheels that have been presented thus far, correlate all you have learned about your behavior patterns with what is presented here. As you begin to alter your patterns, rewrite your story as a story in the light, and so forth, you will balance your shields and keep them in their proper alignment.

Spirit Shields

The *spirit shields* are the light within the dark. They carry no darkness and they do not engage in any pretense pain games. Both male and female energies in these shields are balanced at the same time, and each is your opposite gender. They are not easily accessed because most people have not attained enough maturity in their substance shields.

The Adult Spirit Shield

The *Adult Spirit Shield,* an earth-oriented and physically oriented shield, is positioned to the right of you in your luminosity, but inwardly and subjectively it is a West Shield. It is a woman's *Man Shield,* her male Warrior with a male and female side. It is a man's *Woman Shield,* his female Warrior with a male and a female side. The male side of the shield is guided by the seventh chakra—touching life and others with Beauty, sharing Beauty, and creativity. The female side is guided by the eighth chakra—reflecting pattern, timing, and balance.

Once your Adult Spirit Shield has moved in front of your luminosity, you are out of the pain games and no longer at the effect of the image makers. It is here that you process your symbols, thoughts, ideas, and images through your conscious, subconscious, and unconscious minds. This is where you dream and process your experience of life. This is where your bodily knowing, which is unity of mind/body/spirit, resides. This is your soul force physically manifested. All martial arts focus on this shield. This shield sees what needs to be seen and does what needs to be done. It works with your Adult Substance Shield and offers a marriage so that there can be balance.

Your Adult Spirit Shield is the part of you that is walking with death as an ally. It understands death and change, sees death as inevitable, and knows death gives life, so it is not afraid to die. It is your magickal alchemical transformer.

Being out in Nature and doing proper alchemical ceremony will always put you in this shield. This shield pushes people to share with and care for one another. It longs for balance in its dream and beauty in its process, so it helps you break patterns and actualize your dream. If you are going to meet change, to create new movement in your life, to go in a new direction, or to correct your own self-development in a positive way, the impetus comes from your Adult Spirit Shield. These are all West energies.

This shield is the most physical aspect of yourself. The key to mastery of the physical world, the key to being able to actualize and have economic success, the key to understanding the body as a limited autonomous thing, lies in the ability to learn from the Female Warrior (for men) and from the Male Warrior (for women). You get into this shield if you engage in any physical activity that you are really good at or that really turns you on. When you let go, you experience joy in being physical, and you are extremely conscious of your presence through movement. When you hit that place, time stops.

This shield is always a warrior and moves to the front of the luminosity if there is a threat or if you must engage in physical action with clarity and no hesitation. It also comes in front during intense passion and lust. In addition, this shield helps you to get in touch with your inner Elder.

The Adult Spirit Shield, both male and female sides, is called the *Attention Shield* because it keeps your attention focused in the moment and keeps you present. As long as you are in the substance shields, you deny your power of attraction, thereby distracting or diffusing your attention. Attraction means you know yourself so well that you do not give your power away. You are independent, responsible, and walking your talk. You need no one's perception of yourself to know who you are and your measure of self-worth, so people are drawn to you. One of the primary functions of this shield is to interact as a sexual attraction energy with members of the opposite sex. This West Shield is rooted in sexuality as a physical act of transformation, as the spirit shields have no issue with sexuality. You look into the reflecting mirrors with others through this shield.

Conflict with the opposite sex retards your evolutionary journey. You cut off your enlightenment the minute you cut off your mirrors, and your most important mirrors are those of the opposite sex. Your West Shield draws you to someone in a love affair. Every person of the opposite sex you have ever made love with was a mirror for your entire opposite side, and that reflection was necessary to balance your inner female and male.

The shields go through a balancing process, which is the maturation of the Child Substance Shield and the Adult Substance Shield. As this happens, the Adult Spirit Shield becomes larger and more encompassing and takes on a greater energy. When a man is in this shield, he is much more intuitive, and he can go more deeply into a state of controlled introspection. This shield holds that part of you that has experienced other lifetimes in other body forms, and thus it understands the genetic identity of the opposite sex. The more you refuse to grow up and take responsibility for your world, the less this shield will come in front.

Your Adult Spirit Shield has a time reference that stands outside of time. You have no concern with time and can truly function in the Now without past reference or future concern. It stays in pure action and does not accept anything less than major resolution or full solution to a problem. The Elders say you are sitting in the gateway of continuous illuminations in this shield. It sparks moments of inspiration, helps you to better choreograph your world, and is essential for self-actualization. What you learn in the fifth-dimension dreamtime is carried down into the third dimension and encoded within this shield.

All artistic or creative endeavors are an expression of this and the East Child Spirit Shield. This shield gives you discipline, commitment, and follow-through. It is like a platform or launching pad for your artistic originality, which fully expresses itself with power and Beauty in the Child Spirit Shield.

A man who is able to attract and make an impact with very powerful women without competition has a strong Woman Shield. A woman who can work with men and be powerful and sensual at the same time, while holding her space with authority, has a powerful Man Shield. The Adult Spirit Shield and the Child Spirit Shield are the most unused parts of your luminosity. They are the parts of you that are the most connected to your soul force, your higher self.

The Child Spirit Shield

The *Child Spirit Shield* is a fire/spirit shield and subjectively and inwardly holds the place of the East. It sits to the left of you in your luminosity. It is your opposite gender, so for men this is your Little Girl guided by the ninth chakra. For women this is your Little Boy guided by the tenth chakra.

The Elders call this the *Freedom Shield* because its primary energy is humor and the total absence of fear. It has an omnipotent trust and a benevolent innocence. It does not know "cannot, should not, don't know," and it encourages you to explore the edges and welcome challenges.

This shield is the part of you that enjoys your interdependence with the minerals, plants, animals, spirit world, and other two-leggeds. The spirit child has a deep-rooted and passionate inquisitiveness. It is the jumper that takes you into the nagual, the spirit realms. To some people, this aspect of themselves is terrifying. It drives you into the very thing you are most afraid of because it knows that is where you will learn the most. To do this, it plays the heyoehkah, the trickster, which may trick you into jumping into your shadow to embrace your brilliance. At the same time, this shield never puts you in danger. In addition, no one ever succumbs to an addictive personality paradigm if this shield is awake and in front in your luminosity. It will not allow that to happen.

The other side of this shield is the part of you that gets excited with anything new, especially if it gives you knowledge that works. It has an insatiable curiosity about life and the world, it must stretch and grow, and it wants more than anything to become enlightened. It is that part of you that loves mystery and knows who you really are. When you have this shield in front of you, you experience contentment and a serious devotion to yourself without seriousness. It does not get its buttons pushed and does not allow itself to be at the effect of the molding, sculpting, and armoring process.

This shield has a totally unlimited imagination, and because it is the light within the Light, it knows no *closed symbols* or *dark mirrors*. "You must become as a child before you can enter the kingdom of heaven" refers to stepping into this shield as a balanced enlightened human.

This is the part of you that creates art, music, and poetry with power and beauty. It talks to all the other shields, but is the direct voice to the dancers, as is the Elder Shield.

The Elder Shield

The *Elder Shield* in the center is a perfect balance of the male and female and is about the size of the circumference of a person's waist at the navel. This shield provides your direct connection to the spirit world, as it is never separated from spirit. It is omnipotent, wise, benevolent, powerful, the "old wise one at the inner river of self." It knows what you have written in your Book of Life and says, "Go for broke. Be the star in your movie." When you pray or go into deep introspection, the Elder Shield brings the answer. When you go into this shield, you go in balanced, and you can utilize your larien or psychic gifts. When you dream, this shield is always present. This and the Mirror Dancer leave the body in dreamtime and during astral projection.

The Elders say that this shield is really two shields within one: not a male/female divided shield but rather the wise Grandmother and Grandfather married within, two energies merged as one. It is your maturity as a man or a woman. The more mature you are, the more access you have to this shield.

The male side is guided by the fifth chakra, which facilitates openhearted communication. It is your Grandfather and speaks the unspeakable with wisdom and truth. It carries your inner justice. The female side is your Grandmother and is guided by the sixth chakra, which carries your internal attitude and approach to life, your self-concepts of beauty and power. It carries your ancestor lineage (the power of the knowledge that has come down from all your families Since Always).

The Elder Shield is the part of you that always gains resolution and solution to any problem. The intent of this center shield is the perfection of the Great Spirit inside you. Hearing the voice of the Everything, it brings that voice inside you as your own voice. It is also the part of you that feels a spiritual, sexual connection to everything around it, and you access it when you go into introspection and deep meditation. It feels centered and at home and has the answers if you are willing to look. Let your inner guide talk to that wise Elder inside.

When you connect strongly with the Elder Shield—which you can do only by having one of the spirit shields in front first—all the others are incorporated, creating a prominent luminosity. If your other shields are balanced, they should be about three feet in diameter and touch the Elder Shield. If you are in your substance shields, it is too far a stretch to go into the Elder Shield. The movement goes something like this: The opposite-side gender of the Adult Substance Shield is the gateway into the Adult Spirit Shield. If you are in your Adult Substance Shield as a mature male adult, you will then move into the female side of that shield. You soften and move more fully into your opposite side, and the Adult Spirit Shield comes forward. From there, you will see the spirit child of your Child Spirit Shield and say, "Ah, that's not too big of a jump." From there, you can enter the place of the Elder. A woman would do the same thing from her opposite side.

The Elder Shield is a comforter and nurturer, and prompts the healing of the wounded child. "You are okay. You can do it. Make your choices, and take responsibility for them," it tells us. It is how the child can take care of itself without relying on others. A child who is traumatically affected by a father or mother screaming in anger is not listening to the Elder Shield. Often we see examples of brothers and sisters who have grown up in the same family, subjected to the same family dynamics, but one grows up unaffected by the family dysfunction while the other child is traumatized and grows up with abused victim stories. One is listening to the voice of their wise inner Elder; the other is not.

The Movement of the SAP Moves the Shields

The movement in your shields is determined by the position of your Stationary Assemblage Point (SAP). The location of that point determines your entire view of reality. When the SAP shifts, the shields move. When something happens, you are influenced by the SAP position first. When it shifts, your shields spin, or shift positions in your luminosity. Whatever shield comes in front, therefore, determines your personality expression, your way of perceiving, your reactions, actions, movement, energy—everything at that time.

The SAP can shift and pick up eleven different stations or TV channels. Most people on this planet today are running around with their television sets off! When they do turn them on, they haven't the foggiest idea what station or channel they are watching. This lack of knowing what station you are on, that lack of clear perception, is called a lack of sobriety by the Elders. In other words, many people are not awake, aware, and alert.

If your SAP is in the *Circle of Influence* or the *Point of Confusion,* you are in the context of your lower self, your shideh, which activates the dark side of your substance shields, and they are out of balance. What we see on Grandmother Earth today are many two-leggeds either in their needy, wounded, abandoned child or their angry, vengeful, manipulative adult.

Our Shields Influence Our Attraction and Empowerment

How does the movement of our shields influence our power of attraction and our empowerment? Obviously we are in the greatest state of empowerment when our shields are balanced. The more balanced our shields, the greater our level of attraction and the more significant our impact.

Women have an important role to play in taking the initiative to heal and bridge the gap between the sexes. A woman with balanced shields possesses an understanding of proper energy choreography in how she puts her world together, in her priorities, choices, and decisions (her own Northeast), and in the way she processes, experiences, and lives her dream (her Southwest). By virtue of the fact that she is a living embodiment of Grandmother Earth in a two-legged form, she becomes the birther and the creatress symbolizing the need or necessity of destruction for the sake of creation. When she engages with a man with her shields balanced, she accepts him totally as he is. Her acceptance and her ability to reflect to him his worth, and her tolerance of the differences between them draw him into a clearer concept of himself. This is about caring—the careful consideration of the differences.

A woman with balanced shields is more receptive to the kinds of creativity, spontaneity, fluidity, flexibility that are necessary to create communication. This is her natural way, whereas it is not the natural way of a man. Therefore, it is important for her to be the initiator, the receptacle, and the teacher. A woman caught in the victim syndrome pulls negative energy to herself and can easily fall into a victim attitude. But a woman with balanced shields is alert to this and can receive energy without becoming a victim or being negatively affected by the energy. She can receive it and do with it what she wants.

On the other hand, a man's responsibility is to open himself up to his receptive side so that he can learn to receive and therefore balance the responsibility for clear communication and harmony. A woman's responsibility is to initiate the action, pushing out towards the man, which she can do much more easily than the man can initiate a receptive pulling of her energy towards him. Why? Men do not have a womb that tells them how to do this. And if they have no mirrors showing them how to do it, they certainly won't.

Our five shields interact with our seven dancers, or energy mind bodies. The dancers constantly work with our shields to balance them and to guide us into awakening, enlightenment, and, ultimately, resurrection.

19

Our Immortal Dancers

The seven dancers in our luminosity are called the *Immortal Energy Mind Bodies*, or *Dreamers and Dancers of Energy* (see Fig. 19-a). When conception occurs, the embryo has substance form, but the spirit dancers are not present. During the fourth and one-half month, the dancers, or spirit, enter the womb, and the embryo at that point transforms from protoplasm to an entity with life-force energy and consciousness. The embryo takes on the features of a human, whereas before that it was going through phases similar to those of other animals.

At the moment of physical death, the dancers implode into the Elder Shield, then explode out the *soul vine* and go back to the fifth dimension, the Great Round, where they will come back once again into another physical body. They carry no darkness or negativity whatsoever.

The dancers are the guides and the carriers of the spirit personality. They are your inner voice, and a child talks to them like imaginary friends. While your spirit shields work to pull you into the light and to balance your substance shields, the dancers work to guide all your shields into awakening. When your shields move out of the cardinal directions (as a literal shield to reality), they become mirrors which reflect reality. Furthermore, the dancers are trying to push your shields into the noncardinal directions in order to free your Elder Shield and your Mirror Dancer into a literal ascension up into the halo, at which point you become totally enlightened. (The cardinal positions hold and stabilize. The Elder Shield and Mirror

Fig. 19-*a*   Our Seven Immortal Dancers

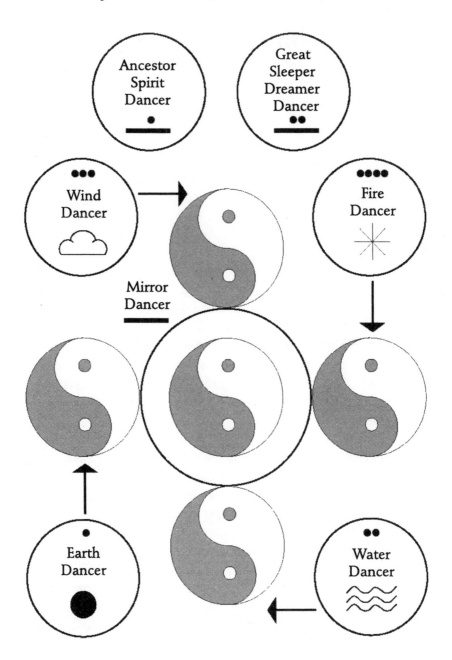

Dancer cannot move unless the shields shift into the noncardinals to allow movement in the entire luminosity.)

The Appearance of the Dancers

The dancers are round, mirrored spheres or balls like Christmas tree ornaments, about one to three feet in diameter (again refer to Fig. 18-a in the previous chapter). They have distinct consciousness, and only at the moment of enlightenment do they become pure light. Whereas your shields are transparent or translucent balls, the dancers are mirrors. The Water Dancer is a very intense orange ball which appears to be sweating or to have condensation on the outside. The Wind Dancer is a mirrored ball with steam swirling and blending in and out and around it. It is a very beautiful violet to blue purple or indigo. The Earth Dancer appears as a glass ball painted on the inside in shades of blue. Sometimes it looks like a window. The Shadow Fire Dancer contains an intense fire that appears as a green light then flashes yellow like an atomic flash. The Mirror Dancer in an immature person looks like a faceted glass ball you see hanging in a ballroom or disco. The Mirror Dancer in someone spiritually evolved is smoothed out to look like a solid mirror ball. The Ancestor Spirit Dancer and the Great Sleeper Dreamer Dancer in your halo merge into a golden ellipse with slight tinges of pink rose. The light dominates so strongly that it is hard to see the pink amethyst mirrors. Sometimes they appear in a more rounded shape.

At all times the dancers are slowly revolving around each of your shields: The Water Dancer is with your Child Substance Shield; the Wind Dancer is with your Adult Substance Shield; the Earth Dancer is with your Adult Spirit Shield; the Shadow Fire Dancer is with your Child Spirit Shield; the Mirror Dancer is with your Elder Shield. The dancers are moving around, above, below, and through your shields, presenting an infinite number of reflections and mirrorings for each shield. The purpose of this movement is to get you to stop identifying yourself as a person and realize that you are truly a mysterious character, meaning that you are all seven of these brilliant shining mirrors of self-reflection. They are saying, "Hey, look here. See yourself in the mirror. See who you really are." Periodically, in a moment of sobriety, you drop the mask of self-pity and look directly into the mirror of self-reflection to get a look at who you truly are. These temporary moments of waking up are called illuminations, when one of your shields has frozen the turning ball of the dancer and gotten a pure mirror of self-reflection, which reveals your character. The moment you acknowledge and accept this, your body changes metamorphically and encodes the new image.

Jan: This is what happened to me after the shamanic drama described in Chapter 8; after my mirrors shattered, my body began to change to encode the new image.

The dancers are working overtime to try to awaken your shields. When the dancers push the shields into the noncardinal directions (refer again to Fig. 19-a, which illustrates which dancer influences which shield), the movement creates the Wheel of Life (see Fig. 19-b). This is where the familiar symbol comes from. You see it in many Native American drawings and petroglyphs. The Wheel of Life has arrows to show which dancer influences and moves which shield. The movement is clockwise. Your Water Dancer sits in the right rear corner of your luminosity. When you can balance your Child Substance Shield and your Adult Substance Shield, as in billiards, the Water Dancer pushes your Child Substance Shield out from behind you and actually shifts it to the left rear corner of your luminosity, and the dancer takes its place.

If you turn the wheel to the noncardinals and make it go counterclockwise, you produce evil in its purest form. When the wheel is reversed and turned into the noncardinal position, it stops the dancers from having contact with the shields. That creates in the shields absolute dependency, fanatical personality, and, consequently, slavery. The Nazi swastika is an example of such dark-side energy manipulation.

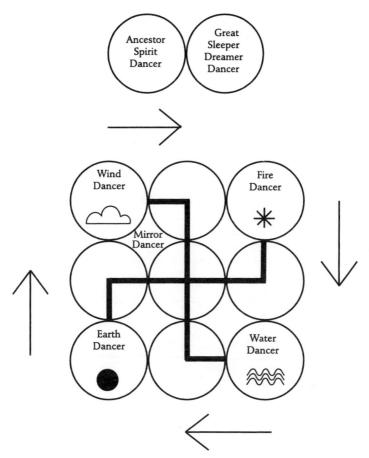

The dancers push the shields in a clockwise movement.

Fig. 19-b   The Wheel of Life

The Water Dancer

The *Water Dancer* is the *Great Giver* of energy that guides your Child Substance Shield. Its primary function is to heal the wounding in your little child, help it to rewrite its pain game story, erase personal history, and get the child to grow up healthy and mature. It tries to get your attention to focus properly and work with what attracts you. "Wouldn't you really like to do this? Come on, focus your attention over here. You can say no to drugs or stealing that car. This is not the attraction you need to look at." The peer group and your need to be loved and liked are often much stronger than the Water Dancer.

The Water Dancer is the part that has true compassion and caring in trust, truth, and innocence. It conquers the enemy of fear.

The Water Dancer communicates from the past. It causes you to get away by yourself, talk to imaginary friends, go inward, and do whatever you need to do to get back in balance after that core of you has been hurt or punished. This dancer sees the *little people*, the *tolilahqui*, and is interested in magick and wants to know. It works with your worldview, and if your Child Substance Shield listens to the Water Dancer, your self-concept will improve markedly. Many people have negative or poor self-concepts because they listened to parents and other image makers instead of to the internal voice of their Water Dancer.

The Wind Dancer

The *Wind Dancer* is your mental energy mind body and is the *Great Receiver*. Its focus is on your Adult Substance Shield, trying to get you to stop the world, quit worrying about the past. The Elders call it the *Attention Dancer* because it tries to get you to wake up and pay attention, to extend your boundaries and limitations, to understand more clearly your place in the world, and to answer the question "What am I here for?" Your Wind Dancer is your photographic memory, recording all stimuli in the environment in fast thought, and provides you with access to all that data. Your Wind Dancer knows how to do something you never learned in this lifetime because it transcends time and has memory of every time you have been in a physical body. This is the part of you that dreams and records your dreams. After you dream, the Mirror Dancer and the Wind Dancer get together, talk it over, and work together to wake you up to your dreams. This dancer has vision.

The Wind Dancer gets you to meet death as an ally, advisor, and companion. It holds your Book of Life spiritually, and encourages your Adult Substance Shield to accept and confront the karma, thus quickly getting the dharma teaching. You cannot do this if you do not meet death, the greatest of all teachers. This does not necessarily mean you have to physically die to get the teaching, but the Wind Dancer shows you how you can choose your death as an act of power. In this there is freedom.

The Body Is in the Mind

The body is in the mind, and our sacred mind is a combination of these seven parts or seven energy mind bodies. However, as in all things, the mind is greater than the sum of its parts. The sacred mind is not to be confused with the brain, which is a physiological receiving and transmitting station that takes direction from the mind. The dance of the shields and dancers in our luminosity has been the process of our evolution from the unbalanced two-leggeds in the center of the animal world into our own human world. It is how we evolve into human beings, our humanity embodying humans in unity. This is not about an evolution of the physical form so much as it is an evolution of consciousness. Since the body is in the mind, once the consciousness has shifted to the level of a balanced human, then the physical form changes automatically.

The Earth Dancer

The primary influence of the *Earth Dancer* is as the sculptor of the physical body, starting in the womb through age twelve. It sculpts your body character and structure and gets you in touch with the power of your body feelings in the present. It works with your Adult Spirit Shield as your death advisor, called the *Great Holder/Transformer*. It focuses on your health, longevity, and physical mastery to insure survival adaptability with evolutionary excellence. The Earth Dancer and your Adult Spirit Shield transcend all physical limitations, fighting to keep you alive but doing it in a way that you enjoy the process of living. This means not only surviving but embracing the challenge of anything physical. In situations where you are under a lot of stress and the odds are over-whelmingly against you, but you know you are going to make it and you gain energy and power in the process, you are listening to the voice of the Earth Dancer. This dancer enables people to per-form miraculous feats of strength and power far beyond their nor-mal capabilities in emergencies and crisis situations.

The Earth Dancer uses willpower to guide you into discipline, commitment, and follow-through, serving as that part of you that is willing to die to change and grow. The most important aspect of willpower is perseverence and determination to hang in there and make something happen. It encompasses dharma and success and light.

The Earth Dancer is the part of you that knows when you are going to die.

The Shadow Fire Dancer

The *Shadow Fire Dancer,* an electromagnetic energy mind body, is called your *Great Determiner,* and works with your Child Spirit Shield. It is the part of you in the nagual that is the *Great Jumper.* It contacts your ancestor spirit beings and communicates to the spirit world. Where your Child Spirit Shield looks to the unknown, this dancer gets glimpses of the unknowable, occasionally seeing the face of the Great Spirit or God. When you have a vision, this is your Shadow Fire Dancer connection showing you what you are here to accomplish in this lifetime. It helps you go into the shadows to see your brilliance there.

The Shadow Fire Dancer draws you to a wise teacher and onto a path of heart. It draws you magnetically to your destiny or fate, in some cases pushing you as you dig in your heels. But it is also the key to all attractions for you—what foods you like, and all your preferences that are in the light. It is the great attractor, acting like a giant magnet.

As the light within the darkness, the Shadow Fire Dancer is the part of you that battles evil and confronts the dark side. It recog-nizes justice and truth and knows that there is no sense of fairness in the world. It leads you to the light, and the light itself is justice.

Artists who create works of great beauty, power, and vision access this dancer. It also works with humor and encourages you to lighten up and not take yourself so seriously.

The Mirror Dancer

The *Mirror Dancer* is the dream energy mind body that works with your Elder Shield. In addition, it works as an interpreter and translator between your other shields and the Elder Shield. It contains the memory of all of its spirit personalities and combines the energetic characteristics of the other dancers. It enables you to demonstrate your larien, or your psychic gifts. The Mirror Dancer carries the essence of the process of the experience of the dream and travels out of your luminosity every time you dream and do astral projection.

When you sleep and dream, this dancer projects out through the octagonal mirror (described in Chapter 17) and enters the fifth-dimension dreamscape. Your Elder Shield accompanies the Mirror Dancer when you engage in controlled dreaming, that is, you know you are dreaming, and can control the action in your dream. When this happens, you double—you create a second, ethereal body.

This dancer's focus is to make you realize that this dimension is the world of illusion and maya and that the fifth-dimension dream world is the world of power. It gets you to dream awake in the third dimension and bring perfect memory recall of the fifth dimension into the third dimension at the same time. It knows exactly when you are asleep (not in sobriety), and exactly what it has to do to get you awake. It is often called your voice of conscience.

The Ancestor Spirit Dancer

The *Ancestor Spirit Dancer* sits on your right-hand side above your head as part of the halo in your tenth chakra. Its primary function is as your screenplay writer. It wrote your Book of Life for this lifetime. It is the part that allows you to change the script and redirect your focus because it sees past, present, and future. It is your inner way, your light, and your inner vision. It is the part of you that is in contact with the upper powers, the Great Enlightened Ones from all paths. It holds your Book of Life and will read it to you if you get in touch with it. It has the ability to affect major change and focus in your life, and it works to get you to wake up to who you really are. If you have awakened to this dancer, it will, in concert with your Mirror Dancer and your Elder Shield, wage war against evil in the fifth-dimension dreamscape and spirit realms as your Night Warrior.

The Great Sleeper Dreamer Dancer

The *Great Sleeper Dreamer Dancer* is the producer and director of your life movie and sits on your left in the halo of the tenth chakra. It is a totally integrated energy mind body that integrates this and all your other lifetimes. It is your original soul that was first born out of the Great Goddess WahKahn, and it has been dreaming itself awake through all your lifetimes. Its focus is to get you to take responsibility for your journey as an enlightened soul. It guides your shields as they present themselves in a physical body and pick up a core personality with moods of stalking. The Great Sleeper Dreamer sends a message down to your Mirror Dancer, which communicates to your Elder Shield, saying, "We had better make this kid be a ruthless Fart so he can make it out there." In the last three months in the womb and the nine to twelve months after birth, your core personality is established in your Child Substance Shield. Young children can hear this inner dialogue between the Great Sleeper Dreamer and their Child Substance Shield. Premature babies are often startled by the Great Sleeper Dreamer's communication of what they have to be and do in the physical, and they come out too soon.

The Dancers Are the Award Winners

If you recall a moment when you have demonstrated true excellence, did that excellence stem from an immediate knowing in the present? If so, it was your Earth Dancer that was receiving the

Academy Award. Did it come from your seeing the potential of what you could do in the future and then making a major change to actualize it? If so, that was your Wind Dancer in action. Did your knowing come from something you had done in the past and all of a sudden you recognized it and released it? If so, it came from the Water Dancer. In all these cases, it is the actualization, the breaking of a pattern, and the action that are critical, not just the recognition of the pattern.

The screenplay contains the image of ourselves that all the dancers are trying to get us to grow into and be. That is what we wrote before we came down from the Great Round. We are re-editing the script here to try to get back to the original intent—to be the jaguar instead of the pussycat. All of these dancers, these energy mind bodies, are working overtime to get us to connect and wake up.

The dancers function as major actors and actresses who are all giving Academy Award performances. Your shields are minor characters who are looking up to the Academy Award performance of the dancers so they can someday become stars. At the moment of enlightenment, your shields move into that place of power and receive the Academy Award that has been held out as a reflection by the dancers for your entire lifetime.

Movement of the Dancers and the Shields

Now, let us look more closely at the movement and interaction of the dancers as they attempt to spin the shields and push them out of their cardinal positions into the noncardinals. It is important to recognize here that the shields and dancers are *you*, and when we say, "The shield chose to rewrite its story," that means *you* chose to rewrite *your* story.

1. Your Child Substance Shield sits in the past with pain and wounding and wants to get in front to get attention. At some point, it freezes the motion of the Water Dancer, stops time, and sees its clear reflection in the mirror, looks inside and sees who it really is—no wounding, no pain, no guilt, no blame, no shame. It has

nothing to hide.' Your Little Girl/Little Boy now is absolutely vulnerable and protected.

2. Choosing to get out of the mythology over into its dream, your Child Substance Shield inwardly starts to see its dream; it wakes up and faces the light. At this point, it comes back into balance, having done its healing. The shield is a mirror.

3. The Wind Dancer pushes your Adult Substance Shield out of its belief systems into perfect choreography of energy and male/female balance. The shield looks up and makes a choice to become enlightened, bounces back, and becomes a mirror.

4. The Earth Dancer moves your Adult Spirit Shield out of holding onto power and moves it into understanding its enlightenment. The shield flips there in the Northwest, becomes balanced, and bounces back.

5. When the Shadow Fire Dancer pushes your Child Spirit Shield into the Southeast, this shield flips and bounces back in the light of its enlightenment.

6. At this point, the Mirror Dancer ascends to join the Ancestor Spirit Dancer and the Great Sleeper Dreamer Dancer in the halo. Thus, the human transforms into an enlightened being and transcends the reincarnation cycles. In this state, the human can choose resurrection and formlessness, which means the ability to choose any physical form from past or future or present lifetimes.

What Happens When We Die?

Death is an energy entity that abides on your left and stays with you all your life. At the moment of your physical death, it moves from your left to your right, and you can see it out of the corner of your eyes. Only *Benevolent Death* will appear there. Benevolent Death will advance down your soul vine, right through your Adult Substance Shield, and be embraced by your Earth Dancer. Accept it. Death will walk you through the tunnel of darkness to the veil of lights. To do this, your shields flip out and assess what you have done in this lifetime, what you have accomplished, and determine if it is time to meet Death. Benevolent Death steps back and asks,

"Are you ready?" If it is not time, you will experience an out-of-body, or a near-death, experience, and your shields will come back in.

On the other hand, if you are ready, your shields will implode into your Elder Shield and explode out into all matter. The dancers will implode, flip, and travel back out along the soul vine to the Great Round of the fifth-dimensional world of spirit. If you have gained enough power and orende, the Mirror Dancer and your Elder Shield will stay together and then come back with the same spirit personality in a different body. If not, your Elder Shield explodes also and goes into all matter. You step into the abyss towards the brightest light with no fear and with great empowerment. Thus, the cycle of reincarnation continues.

Stalking Death, on the other hand, is evil. It is the personification of our collective fears, attracted by our own personal fear. If you are facing your physical death and you are afraid, or you are in your dark side, Stalking Death will come for you, appearing directly in front or behind you. It is an energy vampire and will try to possess you, consuming your shields, which feed it. It will also try to get the dancers before they go to the Great Round. Smelling of sulfurous oxide, it is a black moving shadow with gray edges. It cannot take you if you are willing to face it, look directly at it, and say, "No!" You can banish it. You give it entrance only if you fear death.

The human luminous egg or cocoon, and particularly our shields and dancers, make up the essence of the human being. Gaining the knowledge and understanding of this magnificent miracle breaks the stranglehold of religion, thus removing the fear of death from human consciousness. This is how the higher psyche finds its identity as an immortal instead of a helpless human afraid of death and life and, therefore, living without meaning and purpose. The author and wise teacher Hyemeyohsts Storm once said that this gives us hope. It gives us the gift of the conscious embrace of immortal existence by giving us hope in this one mortal existence.

Epilogue

Thus ends the *Song of the Deer,* a song of sacred knowledge. The magick medicine of the deer calls to you now to renew your dedication to your journey of self-discovery and the refinement of your character. Find your inner truth, and recreate yourself in your own sacred image. And throughout your journey, offer your beauty and your empowerment as gifts to your family, your community, your country, and always, to Grandmother Earth.

Thunder Strikes: *Speaking with the voices of the Elders and for all my ancestors, Tungashilah, I leave you with these words:*

Once you have awakened and begun the journey to discover the true temple of your soul, realize it must be a hero's journey. While you may aspire to goals and be inspired by others, it is your responsibility to find your own internal motivation and determination to succeed, no matter how difficult the journey may become, no matter the degree of adversity, strife, stress, or failures. Most important, remember the small things in life do matter, and one of the smallest things to pay attention to is actually the largest: Self-discovery is found in the little things along and within the path, never at the end. It is not the goal that gives attainment; it is how you interact at each footstep along the way.

Being fully conscious in every moment as though this were the last moment of your existence is to face each moment looking clearly into the crystal matrix of your own mirror of self-reflection. If you are willing to look deeply enough, you will always look into the eyes of Beauty. It is this Beauty that is a blessing. Now it is up to you to make it your way. Let your path with heart become a Blessed Beauty Way: your soul's journey of self-discovery.

I have spoken! Awanestika!

Stella Many Names, Elder Matriarch of the Twisted Hairs Council of Elders, speaks of the Great SunDance Journey of Our Souls.

In the beginning, there was the desire for many, many souls to dance across the veils of time and come from the other eleven worlds with human life here to the Planet of the Children, here to Eheytomah, to Grandmother Earth. The ancestor spirit beings that we call the Sskwanasie, the Star Nation Beings, came here eons ago in order to guide this planet back into the gathering together circle of the twelve planets with human life.

This dance of long ago was the first of all SunDances. For they came here bringing with them the gifts of the sacred shields, the shields of each planet with human life, in order that this knowledge not be lost. In order that this knowledge be preserved until such time as in the beginning cycles of reincarnation began here on this planet they have continued on the other planets with human life in this but one Universe of the Great Spirit's being.

Many of us are of that nature. You are of the ones born who came from Sirius and Osiricanwiyah, and many of you are those that were born of Pleiheitakah in the constellation of the Pleiades, and many of you were Earth beings and have been here from the lower world since the beginning. However, one thing is of certainty: At this moment in time and space and for all the lifetimes that you have reincarnated one after the other in the continuous circle of SunDances, the reincarnation of souls is the Great SunDance, where the spirits of all beings that possess a spirit personality as a soul SunDance back and forth between the world of spirit in the fifth dimension and the Earth in the third dimension. Then they SunDance as a child in the womb, and finally the child emerges to take its first breath where it meets Earth Mother, Quetzal, the Daughter of the First Breath, and stands in the radiant spirit of the wind and of Earth Father, Coatl, and once again is united back into the physical temple of life.

It is within this physical temple that the spirit is drawn into the teachings it has chosen. Some of those teachings go far, far into the dark side of the soul, into the deepest depths of the shadow. Others go into the greatest light of the persona and into the absolute brilliance of total enlightenment, illumination, and resurrection. And there are most who dance somewhere between these two extremes. This SunDance from the Great Round into the small round of the womb and then into the life round—all are symbolically represented when you step into a SunDance Lodge. In this lodge there are star trees, a sun tree, and earth trees, one for each of the twelve planets with human life.

Standing at the center, the SunDance tree itself represents the gateway through which the souls journey to the third dimension here on Grandmother Earth, Eheytomah, and back out to Grandfather Sun, Sohotomah, through the LawBelt, to the planet Jupiter, and there to dance with one's own 18 in the Great Round SunDance.

Appendix A:
Recapitulation Exercise and Stepping Into the Silence

Practiced as a spiritual discipline, *recapitulation* is a powerful tool for transformation. Recapitulation accomplishes several things. It separates and clearly distinguishes *reality* from what we think "really" happened or what we considered to be "real." This practice shows you how to recall your past accurately and forces you to pay attention to the small things that do and did matter. It shows you where your attention was distracted and where you didn't get the lessons the Universe presented to you. Your resistance to getting the lesson took on the form of an obstruction or dam across your stream of livingness; consequently, the lessons became harder, the stress increased, and armoring resulted.

Recapitulation allows you to unwind the process, gain the learning from these past experiences, give away the pain and pretense, remove the dam, and open up your stream of livingness. This frees your energy and brings it forward to the Now, the only thing that matters. Recapitulating your whole life will take months, maybe several years, depending on how old you are and how disciplined you are in practicing this technique. Nonetheless, it is very powerful. How much of an investment are you willing to make to evolve your soul and empower your life?

Discipline means consistency, and recapitulation works best when you set aside time each day to do it. Several times a week is better than not at all. You may wish to record your recapitulations by writing them down or recording them on audiotape or videotape.

Recapitulation has four forms or phases:

Phase 1: Simply recall your life backwards in reverse order from the Now, step-by-step, day by day, through your past history, *objectively*. Continue doing this until you get good at it and no longer miss blocks of time. Carlos Castaneda called this *Clearing the Island*. If you do not see your life backwards, you will not catch how you were distracted. You will catch the reality you didn't see in living your life forward. You will see the power moments of minimal chance you missed and, sometimes, the ones you caught, and you will begin to observe recurring patterns.

Phase 2: Go backwards through your life in reverse sequence again, but this time recapitulate it as you experienced it inwardly and *subjectively*, full of the emotional content you experienced. Then rewind and play one sequence at a time forward to see where you were in pretense and projected perception. When you come forward, open the gates and let the energy come back in as a stream of livingness.

Phase 3: Repeat going backwards step-by-step in detail, but this time switch your perceptual frame of reference from yourself as the viewer to the perspective of those who interacted with you. See how they saw you in the interactions. Seen through someone else's eyes, can you say, "I was attractive and irresistible"? You are no longer a victim. See the reality! This phase allows you to see who you are in your power.

Phase 4: Go backward and forward randomly from all frames of reference.

Clearing: After a recapitulation session, it is essential to do a clearing. Do anything that helps you reground and clear away whatever came up for you during the session. Otherwise, you will carry it around and rehash it and lose energy over it, especially if you remembered something unpleasant or painful. Whatever you do, it should be physical so that you can release all stress. Sometimes a little nap after your activity helps. Part of clearing, also, is to recap every day; a little bit of something is better than nothing.

Stepping Into the Silence

To prepare yourself before each recapitulation session, practice the following *Stepping Into the Silence* technique to relax, empty your mind, and align with the Twenty Powers. Record the process on audiotape so that your own voice becomes your guide.

Preparation: Create a space for yourself that is comfortable and relaxing and where you won't be disturbed. Burn some incense or smudge to cleanse the space and purify your energy.

Step 1: Relax. Lie down in a comfortable position. Breathe deeply and slowly several times to help you relax. Let the tension drain out of your body and begin to breathe naturally. The intent is to relax every part of your body, starting at your feet and ascending. It is important not to move inwardly or outwardly during this procedure.

Bring your awareness first to your feet. Tense the muscles, and then relax them completely. Feel that part of you become warm and heavy, sinking into the floor. Continue throughout your body in this way. Don't rush.

Step 2: Eye Drop Signal. With your eyes closed, roll them up and back. Hold them for a count of three, then relax them and drop. 1-2-3-Drop! (This opens your dream eye located at the crown of your head and drops you into a deeper level of consciousness.)

Step 3: The Count from 10 to 1. Begin to count yourself down into even deeper levels of consciousness by counting the powers of the Twenty Count descending from 10. For example, at 10, say the following: "10. You are at 10. You are the potential of many possibilities. You carry the light arrows of self-acceptance and self-love. You are 10." This voice is your hokkshideh, your higher self, talking to you. Continue next to 9, then 8, and so on to 1. At each number, speak about everything you know about that power and your experience of it, *in the light.*

Step 4: Repeat the Eye Drop Signal.
Step 5: Begin your Recapitulation.

Step 6: The Count From 1 to 7. When you feel complete with your recapitulation session (don't try to do too much the first few times), begin to count yourself back to full consciousness—awake, aware, and alert. Again, "speak" these numbers of the Twenty as powers of empowerment for you. At 7, snap your fingers and come fully awake.

Step 7: Dance Your Dream Awake. Lie still for several minutes to reestablish yourself in the space. Then, while your memory recall is strongest, begin to record your experience, describing what you saw and what you learned.

Step 8: Clearing. Perform a *clearing* by doing something physical.

Appendix B:
Sun Astrology Sitting Place Wheel

Note: There are two sitting places in each noncardinal direction.

See *The Medicine Wheel* by Sun Bear (New York: Prentice Hall, 1986).

To find your birth totem animal, locate your birth date on this wheel.

Appendix C:
Ceremonial Connection
With Your Totem Animals

On this path apprentices do a particular personal ceremony to awaken the presence and power of their totem animals inside them, and thenceforth these totem animals are internal teachers that speak to them through their inner knowing and introspection.

You can do a modified version of the ceremony to awaken your totem animals in you. Start with your birth totem animal (see Appendix B); then one by one you can add the others. You can do this for animals you feel a close affinity to as well.

1. Lie down, breathe deeply, and relax, allowing your brain chatter to subside.

2. When you are calm and centered, envision yourself entering a cave or tunnel or huge hollow tree—some kind of opening that will take you deep into the Earth and into the underworld. See yourself emerging from that dark passage into a landscape. Accept the landscape that presents itself, whatever it may be.

3. Call for your totem animal to appear in three different forms. For example, if your totem is the elk, it may appear as an adult elk, or a newly born fawn, or an elk with flowers in its horns, or a magickal glowing elk, and so forth. Whatever form it takes is a message and a teaching for you. Continue to call it until it has appeared three times. Then thank it, ask it to come with you as your guide and teacher, and slowly bring yourself back up to the surface and fully awake.

4. Next, mime and mimic the characteristics of the animal: its sound, its movements, and any other characteristics you have learned from gathering information about it. *Feel* it and *hear* it in your body, and align with its spirit.

5. Then face each of the four directions in turn and declare the animal as your own. It is only through imagination that we do any magickal work. If your imagination and imaging of the animal are strong and vivid, the animal will be present and make its attributes accessible to you. It becomes your guide and ally.

Call on the animal when you need to, and it will communicate. You don't have to figure how to dialogue with the animal; just open up and give it the space to come in and work with you.

Index

References to Wheels and Figures are in **bold type.**

About the Authors

Thunder Strikes is a Twisted Hairs Elder and Naqual leader within the Sweet Medicine SunDance Path. As a teacher, shamanic counselor, and healer, he inspires and enriches the lives of many apprentices and students worldwide.

A descendant of Cherokee and Irish parents, Thunder Strikes was guided from a very young age by his grandmother, Spotted Fawn, a Cherokee medicine woman. His early training motivated him to seek excellence in many arenas. Accomplished in the martial arts, he was inducted into the Martial Arts World Hall of Fame in 1994. He has pursued extensive studies in psychology, philosophy, religion, and ancient mystery school traditions. He served in Vietnam in the First Marine Division, First Force Reconnaissance Battalion.

Jan Orsi is an educator, editor, and writer. An apprentice of the Sweet Medicine SunDance Path for many years, she integrates the wisdom of the ancient knowledge and the ceremonial experiences into her spiritual growth and her daily life.

The publisher invites your comments and inquiries.

A companion workbook to *Song of the Deer,*
which will guide you in working with the Medicine Wheels,
will be available soon.

To find out more about
the Sweet Medicine SunDance tradition and teachings,
or to contact the authors,
or if you wish to be added to our mailing list,
please write or e-mail us at the addresses below:

Jaguar Books, Inc.
23852 Pacific Coast Hwy., Ste. 756
Malibu, CA 90265
jagpub@aol.com

**JAGUAR
BOOKS**ᴵᴺᶜ